**Evening Standard**

The London
Restaurant Guide
2000

Evening Standard

The London Restaurant Guide 2000

NICK FOULKES

SIMON & SCHUSTER

A VIACOM COMPANY

First published in Great Britain by Simon & Schuster UK Ltd, 1999
A Viacom Company

1 3 5 7 9 10 8 6 4 2

Simon & Schuster UK Ltd
Africa House
64–78 Kingsway
London WC2B 6AH

Text design: Rachel Hardman Carter
Typeset by: Stylize Digital Artwork
Printed and bound in Italy

A CIP catalogue record for this book is available from the British Library

ISBN 0 671 03334 4

Also published in this series:
The London Pub & Bar Guide
Children's London
Where to Live in London
Where to Get the Look

CONTENTS

Acknowledgements   6

Foreword   7

Taking the Waters   8

Introduction   11

Maps
  Key Map of London   12
  North East   14
  North West   16
  South West   18
  South East   20
  EC1   22
  WC2   24
  W1   26
  SW1   28
  W2–W11   30

London Restaurants A–Z   32

ACKNOWLEDGEMENTS

Considerable thanks are due to Christian Konig, who assisted me ably in the coordination of restaurant visits, in spite of his cartographical ineptitude. Without Christian's enthusiasm, palate and company this guide would have been even more difficult and considerably less amusing to write. I would also like to thank those restaurant PR people who were able to arrange visits to restaurants that would have otherwise been beyond the budget allocated to this book. Among those who have been most helpful are Elizabeth Crompton-Batt, Pam Carter at the Savoy, Maureen Mills, Anouschka Menzies, Maeve Murphy, Alix Robson, Jori White, Rochelle Cohen and Ros Choate. I would also like to thank the many people who have agreed to act as 'companions' on these visits or, even better, have actually taken me out to lunch or dinner. At the risk of sounding like an entry in Jennifer's diary these include Clare Milfordhaven, Count Franz Larosee (and his charming Countess), David Linley, Mr and Mrs Christopher Gilmour, Andrea Riva, Capt. Garfio, Jean Pierre Martel, Yann Debelle de Monthby, Mr and Mrs Edward Sahakian, Mr and Mrs Clive Aslet, Mr and Mrs Robert Calcraft, Mr and Mrs James Hanning, Terry O'Neil, Simon Mills, David Jenkins, Peter Harrison, Naomi Hancock, Sophie Laybourne, Anne Marie Colban, and Jenny Halpern. I would like to thank Breitling watches for supplying the chronograph with which I was able to time our restaurant visits and Terry '25 years on the Row' Haste for making my clothes and for ensuring that Christian began to look respectable. I have also been extremely fortunate in the mature guidance and accomodating attitude of Janet Copleston of Martin Books. Without Luigi Bonomi, perhaps the most cunning literary agent ever, who manages to combine high-pressure sales techniques with almost infinite wisdom, tolerance and wit, I would never have been able to afford to take this project on. However without my wife, Alexandra, I would probably be dead or at best sleeping rough and enjoying the invigorating properties and stimulating bouquet of methylated spirits. At the risk of overpowering sentimentality I must thank her for exerting an incredibly benign influence on my life and the lives of those lucky enough to meet her.

FOREWORD

Abbey Well has always been a great supporter of restaurants in the UK. When Abbey Well Natural Mineral Water was introduced in the mid 1980s, it was specifically designed to complement the best food, fine wines and table settings of the best British restaurants and hotels.

Today Abbey Well Natural Mineral Water is an established part of the London restaurant scene. Its distinctive label incorporating the picture of David Hockney by Peter Blake is as recognisable and contemporary as the artists themselves.

Interestingly, some forward-thinking restaurants are now offering their customers a selection of waters with their own bottled water list alongside the wine list.

Abbey Well is delighted to be supporting *The Evening Standard London Restaurant Guide 2000* and we are confident you will find within these pages a true reflection of the cosmopolitan treats now available on the London scene.

Tony Robson

Managing Director
Abbey Well Natural Mineral Water

TAKING THE WATERS

The European preference for bottled drinking water is gradually being adopted in Britain. Over the course of the past decade our consumption has increased more than tenfold.

But what exactly is it that we are drinking? The term 'bottled water' refers to the vast range of different carbonated and still varieties of water described variously as 'spring water', 'filtered water', 'table water' and 'natural mineral water', all very different in source and composition. Of all these, the most popular and fastest growing is natural mineral water. It is a fact that almost three quarters of all bottled waters sold are natural mineral water.

Here is the reason why. The term 'natural mineral water' may only be applied to waters that satisfy the stringent procedures and regulations laid down by the European and British bottled water regulations. These ensure that a natural mineral water is natural and wholesome without treatment. These waters are the only waters which are guaranteed to be free from pollution, free from additives (except in some cases where carbon dioxide is added to make them sparkle) and consistent every time.

The regulations require natural mineral waters to conform to a whole range of compositional, bottling and labelling conditions, for example:

- the only treatment permitted is filtration to remove unstable constituents
- the water must contain naturally-occurring minerals
- the water must contain no pathogenic bacteria
- the typical mineral analysis and source must be officially recognised by the EC
- in addition to the standard legislation, labels must state that it is a natural mineral water and the source
- the mineral analysis must be shown on the label or be available to the public on request
- bottles must have tamper-proof seals which must be intact upon purchase
- the water must be bottled at source
- the water must comply with EC Directive 777
- the water must first undergo a two year analysis period proving its consistency

It is these requirements that make Natural Mineral Water, as a category, unique.

The different characteristics of natural mineral waters depend upon the type of rock strata they travel through, with different journeys yielding different minerals. Abbey Well Natural Mineral Water for instance comes from deep in the Northumberland hillside where, far away from the atmosphere and pollution, it filters slowly through 315 million year old water-bearing white sandstone.

All waters are not created equal. Only if the label bears the entire description Natural Mineral Water are you guaranteed the reassurance that you are getting the consistency and quality that you expect. It is a very different story for many other bottled waters such as spring, natural, purified or table waters. These may be drawn from any source including underground or surface waters or even tap water and the source does not have to be recognised or protected. The water may be artificially purified and chemically treated to destroy both pathogenic and benign bacteria. Other processing may include blending, UV treatment, filtration and pasteurisation or ozonization. Such waters are regulated by the Water in Container Regulations 1992 and are bottled in accordance with EC Directive 778.

A recent phenomenon is the use by restaurateurs of back-of-house filtration units from which tap water is then bottled and sold in attractive containers.

Whilst filtration can remove some of the chemicals from the tap water, it will still contain a residue of some of the chemicals that are present in mains water as part of the cleansing operation.

The regulations referred to above are correct in the UK at the time of writing but the British regulations affecting bottled water are currently under review. Whilst all waters sold in the UK for drinking are safe, some of these may have been treated with chemicals which many people prefer to avoid.

Abbey Well Natural Mineral Water was discovered by Thomas Robson in 1910 and is named after his favourite Northumbrian landmark, a 12th Century Cistercian Abbey.

Abbey Well is still drawn from the original underground source and is recognised as a natural mineral water under the Natural Mineral Waters Regulations (1985). The company remains a British-owned family concern and is today run by Tony and Michael Robson, Thomas Robson's grandsons.

Both still and sparkling natural mineral waters are available from Abbey Well, in returnable and recyclable glass and recyclable plastic bottles in a range of sizes to suit most occasions.

INTRODUCTION

Ten years, a decade, a tenth of a century have passed since I first got seriously involved with writing about restaurants. In 1990 I joined the Evening Standard as editor of what was then called the *London Life* section. Among my responsibilities were Fay Maschler's restaurant pages, and it is to Fay that I and, I think it is fair to say every other restaurant critic working today, are indebted for introducing me to restaurants in London.

As editor of *London Life* and then Associate Editor of *ES Magazine*, I was also able to bring on writers such as Andrew Jefford and Charles Campion, both of whom have since won Glenfiddich awards for their work. When I retired from *ES Magazine* at the end of 1994, I was fortunate enough to be encouraged by both Adam Edwards and his successor as editor of ES, Louise Chunn, to write the magazine's restaurant column.

However nothing in my experience had prepared me for the assault on the physical system, and the senses that writing this guide would be. Had Hercules been alive today he might have been given something like the *Evening Standard Restaurant Guide* to write as one of his Labours. Rather like tidying the Augean Stables, writing a guide to London restaurants at a time when the London restaurant scene changes and mutates every week is a daunting undertaking. Quite how daunting, I did not realise ... until I started to write it. This guide is far from perfect, it does not even pretend to be definitive. It is at times extremely subjective, but I hope that I have sign-posted my own likes and dislikes, prejudices and irrational phobias, sufficiently clearly to allow people to be able to disagree violently with them ... or even to go to a restaurant to find out for themselves. It would also be interesting to think of this book as a sort of social history, documenting and defining an interesting moment in the social life of the capital.

Above all I hope that this guide entertains. Restaurants should be amusing. Too often these days a restaurant visit has all the allure of the morning chapel services I seem to remember enduring at school: serious, sepulchral and best avoided. I like restaurants. To me they are the perfect entertainment. What surprises me, is that after writing this book I have grown to like them even more.

KEY MAP

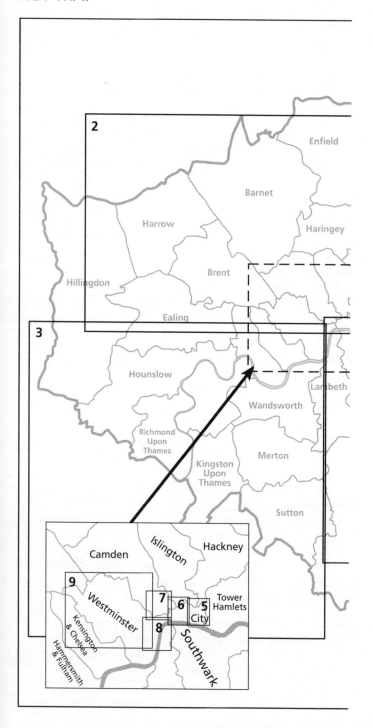

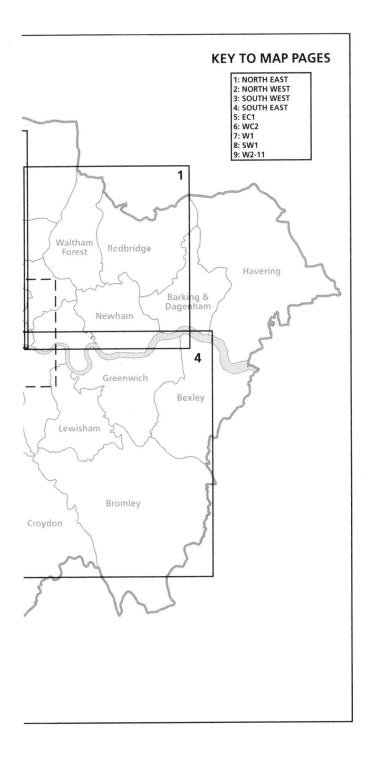

KEY TO MAP PAGES

1: NORTH EAST
2: NORTH WEST
3: SOUTH WEST
4: SOUTH EAST
5: EC1
6: WC2
7: W1
8: SW1
9: W2-11

NORTH EAST

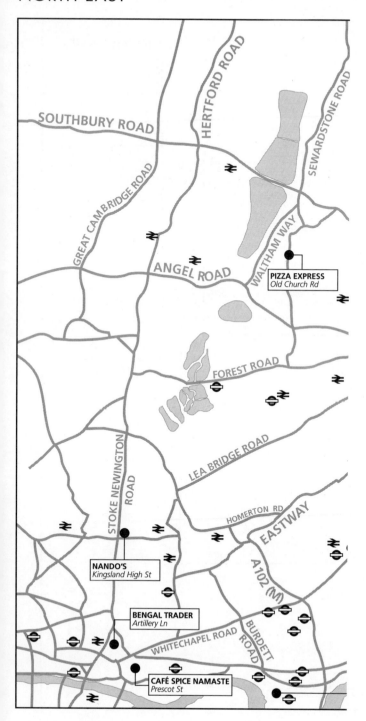

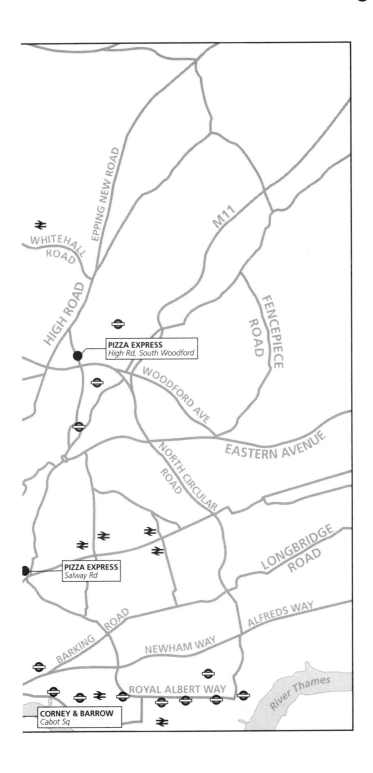

NORTH WEST

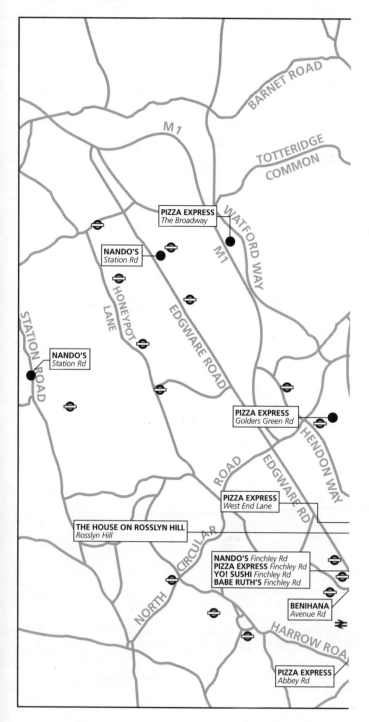

PIZZA EXPRESS
The Broadway

NANDO'S
Station Rd

NANDO'S
Station Rd

PIZZA EXPRESS
Golders Green Rd

PIZZA EXPRESS
West End Lane

THE HOUSE ON ROSSLYN HILL
Rosslyn Hill

NANDO'S *Finchley Rd*
PIZZA EXPRESS *Finchley Rd*
YO! SUSHI *Finchley Rd*
BABE RUTH'S *Finchley Rd*

BENIHANA
Avenue Rd

PIZZA EXPRESS
Abbey Rd

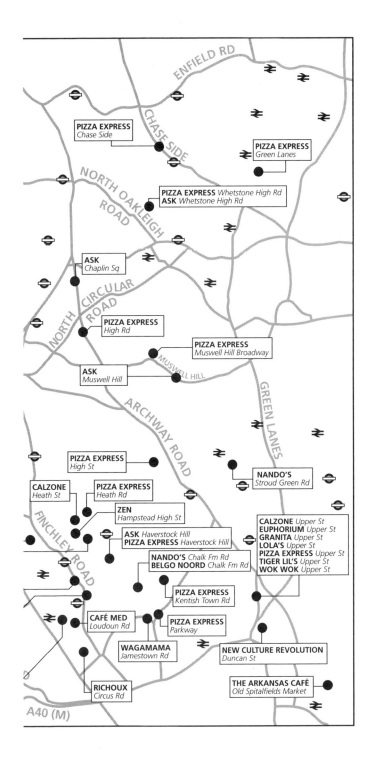

SOUTH WEST

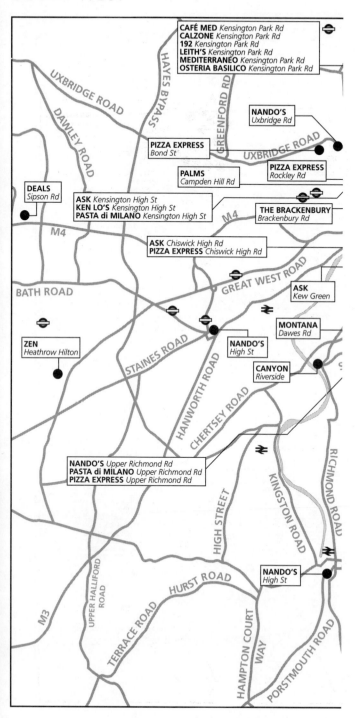

CAFÉ MED *Kensington Park Rd*
CALZONE *Kensington Park Rd*
192 *Kensington Park Rd*
LEITH'S *Kensington Park Rd*
MEDITERRANEO *Kensington Park Rd*
OSTERIA BASILICO *Kensington Park Rd*

NANDO'S
Uxbridge Rd

PIZZA EXPRESS
Bond St

PIZZA EXPRESS
Rockley Rd

PALMS
Campden Hill Rd

DEALS
Sipson Rd

ASK *Kensington High St*
KEN LO'S *Kensington High St*
PASTA di MILANO *Kensington High St*

THE BRACKENBURY
Brackenbury Rd

ASK *Chiswick High Rd*
PIZZA EXPRESS *Chiswick High Rd*

ASK
Kew Green

BATH ROAD

MONTANA
Dawes Rd

ZEN
Heathrow Hilton

NANDO'S
High St

CANYON
Riverside

NANDO'S *Upper Richmond Rd*
PASTA di MILANO *Upper Richmond Rd*
PIZZA EXPRESS *Upper Richmond Rd*

NANDO'S
High St

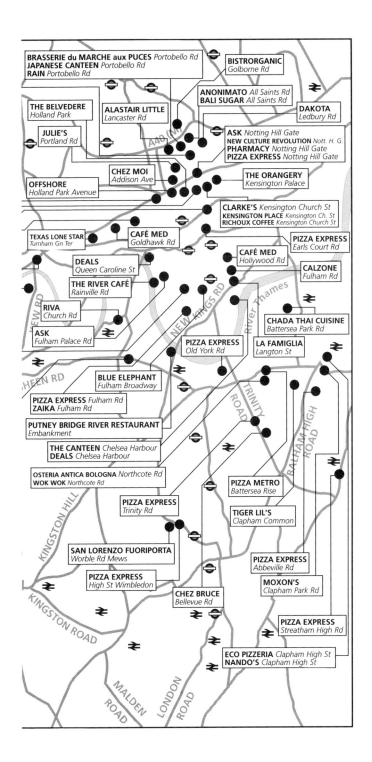

BRASSERIE du MARCHE aux PUCES Portobello Rd
JAPANESE CANTEEN Portobello Rd
RAIN Portobello Rd

BISTRORGANIC Golborne Rd

THE BELVEDERE Holland Park

ALASTAIR LITTLE Lancaster Rd

ANONIMATO All Saints Rd
BALI SUGAR All Saints Rd

DAKOTA Ledbury Rd

JULIE'S Portland Rd

ASK Notting Hill Gate
NEW CULTURE REVOLUTION Nott. H. G.
PHARMACY Notting Hill Gate
PIZZA EXPRESS Notting Hill Gate

CHEZ MOI Addison Ave

THE ORANGERY Kensington Palace

OFFSHORE Holland Park Avenue

CLARKE'S Kensington Church St
KENSINGTON PLACE Kensington Ch. St
RICHOUX COFFEE Kensington Church St

TEXAS LONE STAR Turnham Gn Ter

CAFÉ MED Goldhawk Rd

PIZZA EXPRESS Earls Court Rd

CAFÉ MED Hollywood Rd

DEALS Queen Caroline St

CALZONE Fulham Rd

THE RIVER CAFÉ Rainville Rd

RIVA Church Rd

CHADA THAI CUISINE Battersea Park Rd

ASK Fulham Palace Rd

PIZZA EXPRESS Old York Rd

LA FAMIGLIA Langton St

BLUE ELEPHANT Fulham Broadway

PIZZA EXPRESS Fulham Rd
ZAIKA Fulham Rd

PUTNEY BRIDGE RIVER RESTAURANT Embankment

THE CANTEEN Chelsea Harbour
DEALS Chelsea Harbour

OSTERIA ANTICA BOLOGNA Northcote Rd
WOK WOK Northcote Rd

PIZZA METRO Battersea Rise

PIZZA EXPRESS Trinity Rd

TIGER LIL'S Clapham Common

SAN LORENZO FUORIPORTA Worble Rd Mews

PIZZA EXPRESS Abbeville Rd

MOXON'S Clapham Park Rd

PIZZA EXPRESS High St Wimbledon

CHEZ BRUCE Bellevue Rd

PIZZA EXPRESS Streatham High Rd

ECO PIZZERIA Clapham High St
NANDO'S Clapham High St

SOUTH EAST

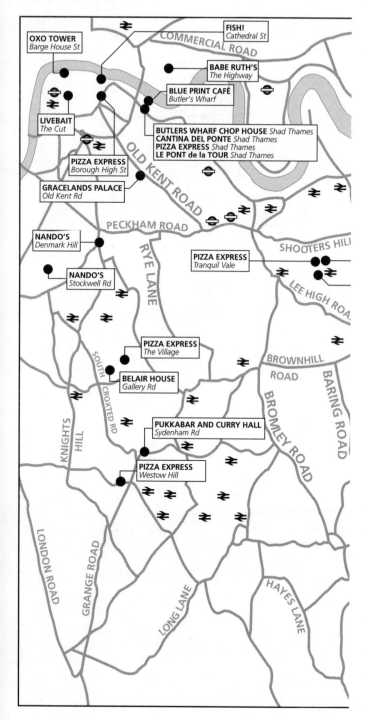

OXO TOWER
Barge House St

FISH!
Cathedral St

BABE RUTH'S
The Highway

BLUE PRINT CAFÉ
Butler's Wharf

LIVEBAIT
The Cut

BUTLERS WHARF CHOP HOUSE *Shad Thames*
CANTINA DEL PONTE *Shad Thames*
PIZZA EXPRESS *Shad Thames*
LE PONT de la TOUR *Shad Thames*

PIZZA EXPRESS
Borough High St

GRACELANDS PALACE
Old Kent Rd

NANDO'S
Denmark Hill

PIZZA EXPRESS
Tranquil Vale

NANDO'S
Stockwell Rd

PIZZA EXPRESS
The Village

BELAIR HOUSE
Gallery Rd

PUKKABAR AND CURRY HALL
Sydenham Rd

PIZZA EXPRESS
Westow Hill

COMMERCIAL ROAD
OLD KENT ROAD
PECKHAM ROAD
RYE LANE
SHOOTERS HILL
LEE HIGH ROAD
SOUTH CROXTED RD
BROWNHILL ROAD
BARING ROAD
KNIGHTS HILL
BROMLEY ROAD
LONDON ROAD
GRANGE ROAD
LONG LANE
HAYES LANE

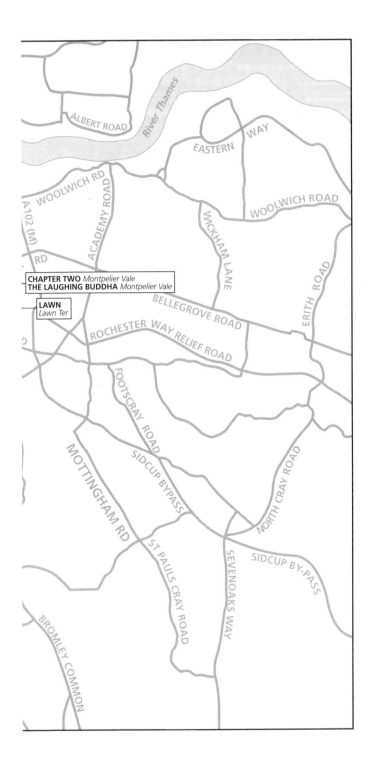

ALBERT ROAD

River Thames

EASTERN WAY

WOOLWICH RD

A102 (M)

ACADEMY ROAD

WOOLWICH ROAD

WICKHAM LANE

ERITH ROAD

RD

CHAPTER TWO *Montpelier Vale*
THE LAUGHING BUDDHA *Montpelier Vale*

BELLEGROVE ROAD

LAWN
Lawn Ter

ROCHESTER WAY RELIEF ROAD

FOOTSCRAY ROAD

SIDCUP BYPASS

MOTTINGHAM RD

NORTH CRAY ROAD

SIDCUP BY-PASS

ST PAULS CRAY ROAD

SEVENOAKS WAY

BROMLEY COMMON

EC1

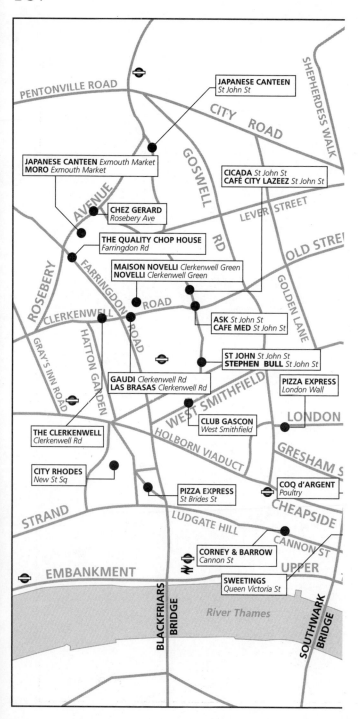

JAPANESE CANTEEN *St John St*

JAPANESE CANTEEN *Exmouth Market*
MORO *Exmouth Market*

CICADA *St John St*
CAFÉ CITY LAZEEZ *St John St*

CHEZ GERARD *Rosebery Ave*

THE QUALITY CHOP HOUSE *Farringdon Rd*

MAISON NOVELLI *Clerkenwell Green*
NOVELLI *Clerkenwell Green*

ASK *St John St*
CAFE MED *St John St*

ST JOHN *St John St*
STEPHEN BULL *St John St*

PIZZA EXPRESS *London Wall*

GAUDI *Clerkenwell Rd*
LAS BRASAS *Clerkenwell Rd*

CLUB GASCON *West Smithfield*

THE CLERKENWELL *Clerkenwell Rd*

CITY RHODES *New St Sq*

COQ d'ARGENT *Poultry*

PIZZA EXPRESS *St Brides St*

CORNEY & BARROW *Cannon St*

SWEETINGS *Queen Victoria St*

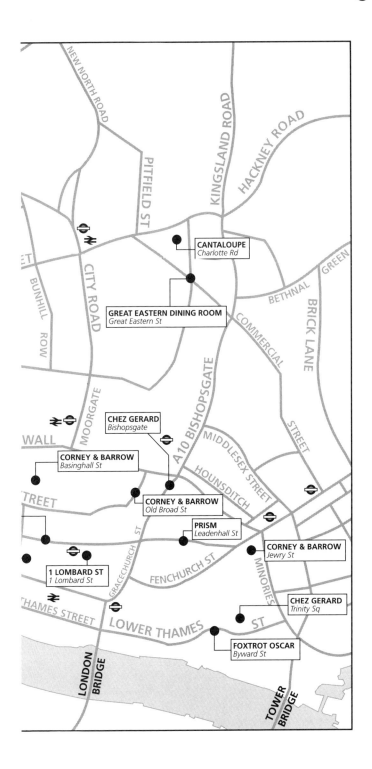

WC2

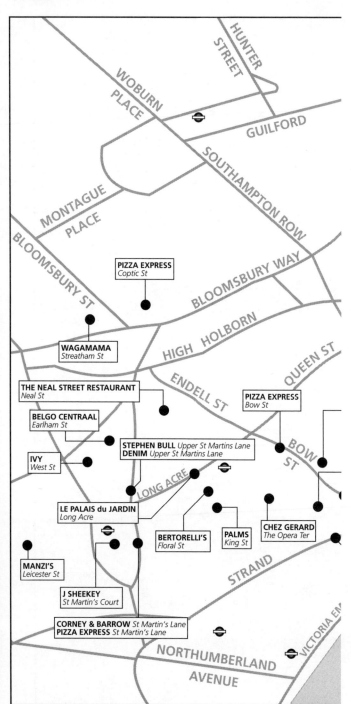

PIZZA EXPRESS
Coptic St

WAGAMAMA
Streatham St

THE NEAL STREET RESTAURANT
Neal St

PIZZA EXPRESS
Bow St

BELGO CENTRAAL
Earlham St

STEPHEN BULL *Upper St Martins Lane*
DENIM *Upper St Martins Lane*

IVY
West St

LE PALAIS du JARDIN
Long Acre

BERTORELLI'S
Floral St

PALMS
King St

CHEZ GERARD
The Opera Ter

MANZI'S
Leicester St

J SHEEKEY
St Martin's Court

CORNEY & BARROW *St Martin's Lane*
PIZZA EXPRESS *St Martin's Lane*

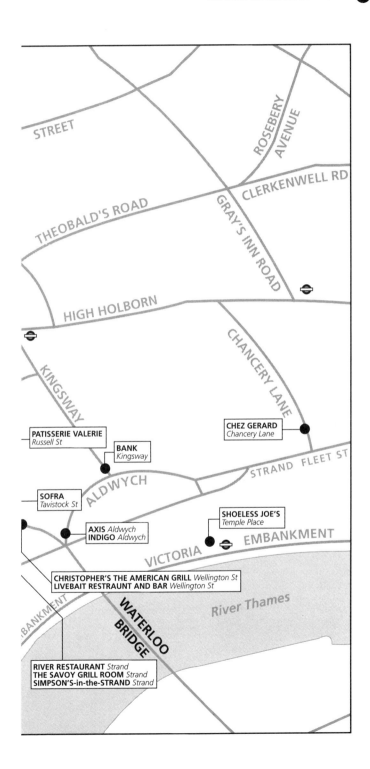

STREET

ROSEBERY AVENUE

CLERKENWELL RD

GRAY'S INN ROAD

THEOBALD'S ROAD

HIGH HOLBORN

CHANCERY LANE

KINGSWAY

PATISSERIE VALERIE
Russell St

BANK
Kingsway

CHEZ GERARD
Chancery Lane

STRAND FLEET ST

SOFRA
Tavistock St

ALDWYCH

SHOELESS JOE'S
Temple Place

AXIS *Aldwych*
INDIGO *Aldwych*

EMBANKMENT

VICTORIA

CHRISTOPHER'S THE AMERICAN GRILL *Wellington St*
LIVEBAIT RESTRAUNT AND BAR *Wellington St*

River Thames

BANKMENT

WATERLOO BRIDGE

RIVER RESTAURANT *Strand*
THE SAVOY GRILL ROOM *Strand*
SIMPSON'S-in-the-STRAND *Strand*

W1

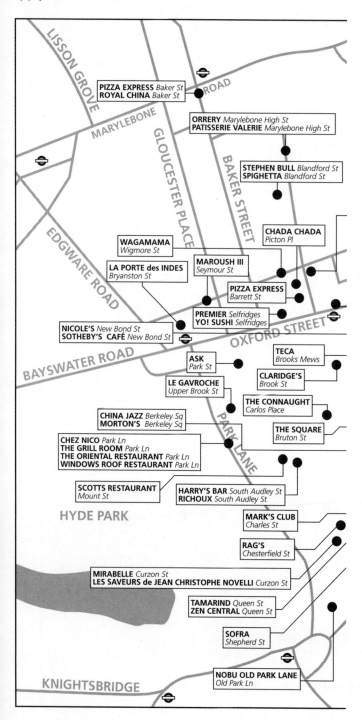

LISSON GROVE

MARYLEBONE

GLOUCESTER PLACE

BAKER STREET

EDGWARE ROAD

PIZZA EXPRESS *Baker St*
ROYAL CHINA *Baker St*

ORRERY *Marylebone High St*
PATISSERIE VALERIE *Marylebone High St*

STEPHEN BULL *Blandford St*
SPIGHETTA *Blandford St*

CHADA CHADA
Picton Pl

WAGAMAMA
Wigmore St

MAROUSH III
Seymour St

LA PORTE des INDES
Bryanston St

PIZZA EXPRESS
Barrett St

PREMIER *Selfridges*
YO! SUSHI *Selfridges*

NICOLE'S *New Bond St*
SOTHEBY'S CAFÉ *New Bond St*

OXFORD STREET

BAYSWATER ROAD

ASK
Park St

TECA
Brooks Mews

CLARIDGE'S
Brook St

LE GAVROCHE
Upper Brook St

THE CONNAUGHT
Carlos Place

CHINA JAZZ *Berkeley Sq*
MORTON'S *Berkeley Sq*

THE SQUARE
Bruton St

PARK LANE

CHEZ NICO *Park Ln*
THE GRILL ROOM *Park Ln*
THE ORIENTAL RESTAURANT *Park Ln*
WINDOWS ROOF RESTAURANT *Park Ln*

SCOTTS RESTAURANT
Mount St

HARRY'S BAR *South Audley St*
RICHOUX *South Audley St*

HYDE PARK

MARK'S CLUB
Charles St

RAG'S
Chesterfield St

MIRABELLE *Curzon St*
LES SAVEURS de JEAN CHRISTOPHE NOVELLI *Curzon St*

TAMARIND *Queen St*
ZEN CENTRAL *Queen St*

SOFRA
Shepherd St

NOBU OLD PARK LANE
Old Park Ln

KNIGHTSBRIDGE

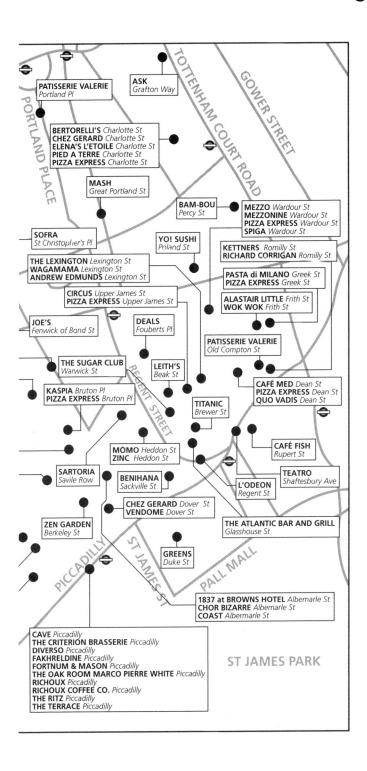

PATISSERIE VALERIE *Portland Pl*

ASK *Grafton Way*

TOTTENHAM COURT ROAD

GOWER STREET

PORTLAND PLACE

BERTORELLI'S *Charlotte St*
CHEZ GERARD *Charlotte St*
ELENA'S L'ETOILE *Charlotte St*
PIED A TERRE *Charlotte St*
PIZZA EXPRESS *Charlotte St*

MASH *Great Portland St*

BAM-BOU *Percy St*

MEZZO *Wardour St*
MEZZONINE *Wardour St*
PIZZA EXPRESS *Wardour St*
SPIGA *Wardour St*

SOFRA *St Christopher's Pl*

YO! SUSHI *Poland St*

KETTNERS *Romilly St*
RICHARD CORRIGAN *Romilly St*

THE LEXINGTON *Lexington St*
WAGAMAMA *Lexington St*
ANDREW EDMUNDS *Lexington St*

PASTA di MILANO *Greek St*
PIZZA EXPRESS *Greek St*

CIRCUS *Upper James St*
PIZZA EXPRESS *Upper James St*

ALASTAIR LITTLE *Frith St*
WOK WOK *Frith St*

JOE'S *Fenwick of Bond St*

DEALS *Fouberts Pl*

PATISSERIE VALERIE *Old Compton St*

THE SUGAR CLUB *Warwick St*

LEITH'S *Beak St*

REGENT STREET

KASPIA *Bruton Pl*
PIZZA EXPRESS *Bruton Pl*

TITANIC *Brewer St*

CAFÉ MED *Dean St*
PIZZA EXPRESS *Dean St*
QUO VADIS *Dean St*

MOMO *Heddon St*
ZINC *Heddon St*

CAFÉ FISH *Rupert St*

SARTORIA *Savile Row*

BENIHANA *Sackville St*

TEATRO *Shaftesbury Ave*

L'ODEON *Regent St*

CHEZ GERARD *Dover St*
VENDOME *Dover St*

ZEN GARDEN *Berkeley St*

THE ATLANTIC BAR AND GRILL *Glasshouse St*

PICCADILLY

ST JAMES ST

GREENS *Duke St*

PALL MALL

1837 at BROWNS HOTEL *Albemarle St*
CHOR BIZARRE *Albemarle St*
COAST *Albermarle St*

CAVE *Piccadilly*
THE CRITERION BRASSERIE *Piccadilly*
DIVERSO *Piccadilly*
FAKHRELDINE *Piccadilly*
FORTNUM & MASON *Piccadilly*
THE OAK ROOM MARCO PIERRE WHITE *Piccadilly*
RICHOUX *Piccadilly*
RICHOUX COFFEE CO. *Piccadilly*
THE RITZ *Piccadilly*
THE TERRACE *Piccadilly*

ST JAMES PARK

SW1

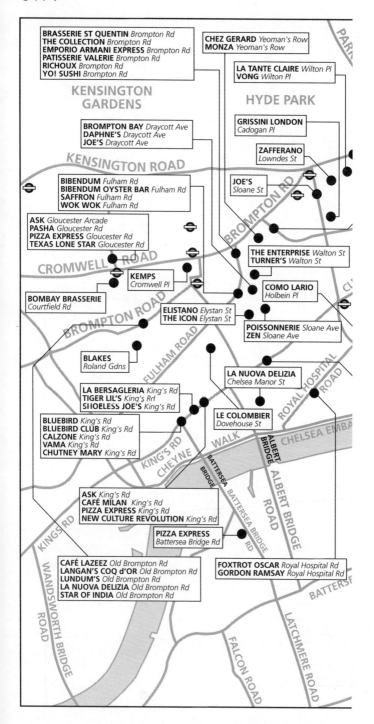

BRASSERIE ST QUENTIN *Brompton Rd*
THE COLLECTION *Brompton Rd*
EMPORIO ARMANI EXPRESS *Brompton Rd*
PATISSERIE VALERIE *Brompton Rd*
RICHOUX *Brompton Rd*
YO! SUSHI *Brompton Rd*

CHEZ GERARD *Yeoman's Row*
MONZA *Yeoman's Row*

KENSINGTON
GARDENS

HYDE PARK

LA TANTE CLAIRE *Wilton Pl*
VONG *Wilton Pl*

BROMPTON BAY *Draycott Ave*
DAPHNE'S *Draycott Ave*
JOE'S *Draycott Ave*

GRISSINI LONDON
Cadogan Pl

KENSINGTON ROAD

ZAFFERANO
Lowndes St

BIBENDUM *Fulham Rd*
BIBENDUM OYSTER BAR *Fulham Rd*
SAFFRON *Fulham Rd*
WOK WOK *Fulham Rd*

JOE'S
Sloane St

BROMPTON ROAD

ASK *Gloucester Arcade*
PASHA *Gloucester Rd*
PIZZA EXPRESS *Gloucester Rd*
TEXAS LONE STAR *Gloucester Rd*

THE ENTERPRISE *Walton St*
TURNER'S *Walton St*

CROMWELL ROAD

KEMPS
Cromwell Pl

COMO LARIO
Holbein Pl

BOMBAY BRASSERIE
Courtfield Rd

BROMPTON ROAD

ELISTANO *Elystan St*
THE ICON *Elystan St*

POISSONNERIE *Sloane Ave*
ZEN *Sloane Ave*

BLAKES
Roland Gdns

FULHAM ROAD

LA NUOVA DELIZIA
Chelsea Manor St

LA BERSAGLERIA *King's Rd*
TIGER LIL'S *King's Rd*
SHOELESS JOE'S *King's Rd*

LE COLOMBIER
Dovehouse St

ROYAL HOSPITAL ROAD

BLUEBIRD *King's Rd*
BLUEBIRD CLUB *King's Rd*
CALZONE *King's Rd*
VAMA *King's Rd*
CHUTNEY MARY *King's Rd*

KING'S RD

CHEYNE WALK

BATTERSEA BRIDGE

ALBERT BRIDGE

CHELSEA EMBA

ALBERT BRIDGE ROAD

ASK *King's Rd*
CAFÉ MILAN *King's Rd*
PIZZA EXPRESS *King's Rd*
NEW CULTURE REVOLUTION *King's Rd*

PIZZA EXPRESS
Battersea Bridge Rd

KINGS RD

WANDSWORTH BRIDGE ROAD

CAFÉ LAZEEZ *Old Brompton Rd*
LANGAN'S COQ d'OR *Old Brompton Rd*
LUNDUM'S *Old Brompton Rd*
LA NUOVA DELIZIA *Old Brompton Rd*
STAR OF INDIA *Old Brompton Rd*

FOXTROT OSCAR *Royal Hospital Rd*
GORDON RAMSAY *Royal Hospital Rd*

BATTERSE

FALCON ROAD

LATCHMERE ROAD

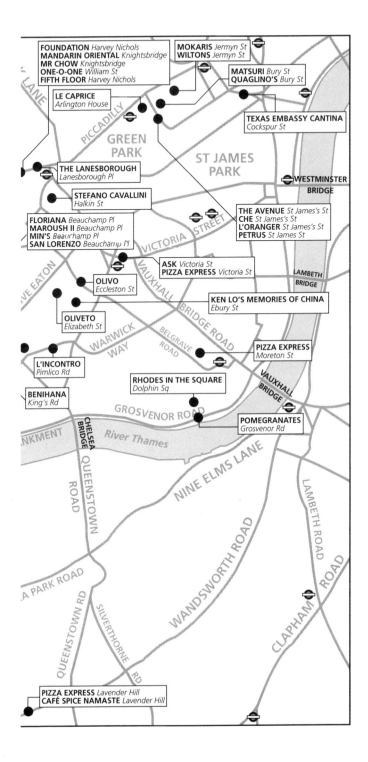

FOUNDATION *Harvey Nichols*
MANDARIN ORIENTAL *Knightsbridge*
MR CHOW *Knightsbridge*
ONE-O-ONE *William St*
FIFTH FLOOR *Harvey Nichols*

MOKARIS *Jermyn St*
WILTONS *Jermyn St*

MATSURI *Bury St*
QUAGLINO'S *Bury St*

LE CAPRICE
Arlington House

TEXAS EMBASSY CANTINA
Cockspur St

PICCADILLY

GREEN
PARK

ST JAMES
PARK

THE LANESBOROUGH
Lanesborough Pl

WESTMINSTER
BRIDGE

STEFANO CAVALLINI
Halkin St

THE AVENUE *St James's St*
CHE *St James's St*
L'ORANGER *St James's St*
PETRUS *St James St*

FLORIANA *Beauchamp Pl*
MAROUSH II *Beauchamp Pl*
MIN'S *Beauchamp Pl*
SAN LORENZO *Beauchamp Pl*

VICTORIA STREET

LAMBETH
BRIDGE

ASK *Victoria St*
PIZZA EXPRESS *Victoria St*

OLIVO
Eccleston St

KEN LO'S MEMORIES OF CHINA
Ebury St

VAUXHALL BRIDGE ROAD

OLIVETO
Elizabeth St

WARWICK
WAY

BELGRAVE
ROAD

GRAVE EATON

PIZZA EXPRESS
Moreton St

L'INCONTRO
Pimlico Rd

VAUXHALL
BRIDGE

BENIHANA
King's Rd

RHODES IN THE SQUARE
Dolphin Sq

GROSVENOR ROAD

POMEGRANATES
Grosvenor Rd

NKMENT

CHELSEA
BRIDGE

River Thames

River Thames

QUEENSTOWN
ROAD

NINE ELMS LANE

LAMBETH ROAD

A PARK ROAD

QUEENSTOWN RD

SILVERTHORNE RD

WANDSWORTH ROAD

CLAPHAM ROAD

PIZZA EXPRESS *Lavender Hill*
CAFÉ SPICE NAMASTE *Lavender Hill*

W2–11

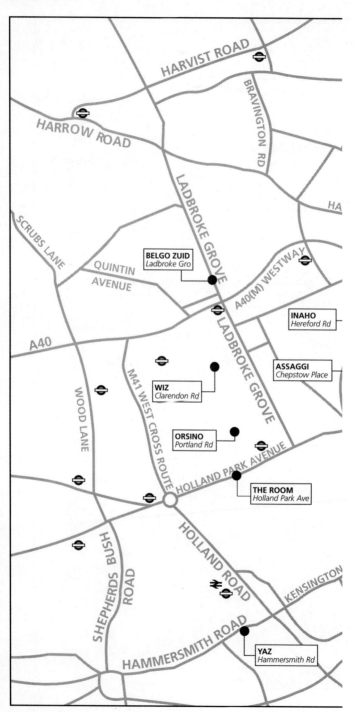

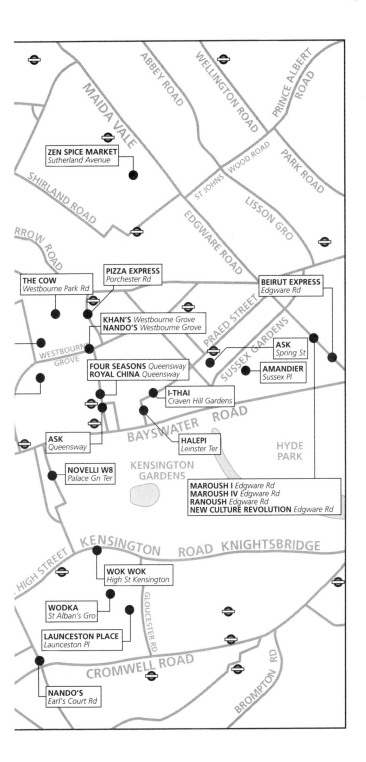

ZEN SPICE MARKET
Sutherland Avenue

THE COW
Westbourne Park Rd

PIZZA EXPRESS
Porchester Rd

BEIRUT EXPRESS
Edgware Rd

KHAN'S *Westbourne Grove*
NANDO'S *Westbourne Grove*

ASK
Spring St

FOUR SEASONS *Queensway*
ROYAL CHINA *Queensway*

AMANDIER
Sussex Pl

I-THAI
Craven Hill Gardens

ASK
Queensway

HALEPI
Leinster Ter

HYDE
PARK

NOVELLI W8
Palace Gn Ter

KENSINGTON
GARDENS

MAROUSH I *Edgware Rd*
MAROUSH IV *Edgware Rd*
RANOUSH *Edgware Rd*
NEW CULTURE REVOLUTION *Edgware Rd*

WOK WOK
High St Kensington

WODKA
St Alban's Gro

LAUNCESTON PLACE
Launceston Pl

NANDO'S
Earl's Court Rd

192

192 Kensington Park Road, London W11
☎ 0171 229 0482

This vaguely casual bar and restaurant is a sort of Rovers Return
for the affluent, if increasingly Jurassic, bohemians of Notting Hill.
Owned by the Groucho Club and designed by Tchaik Chassay,
this vintage piece of eighties restaurant culture is as much of a
London institution as Simpsons on the Strand (qv). In its time,
192 has employed numerous now-famous chefs and restaurant
managers, including Alastair Little (qv). At the end of 1998, a
new chef was installed and the menu has been refreshed and
includes such dishes as seared scallops with samphire and lemon
beurre blanc; tagliatelle with tuna bottarga; Morrocan lamb
shank with couscous and harissa sauce; grilled brill with roasted
fennel and lemon butter. The exemplary and intriguing wines
are supplied by John Armit, who runs an upmarket off-licence
next door.

- **DRESS** *Ageing trustafarian*
- **TUBE** *Notting Hill Gate*
- **HOURS** *Lunch Mon–Fri 12.30–15.00; Sat–Sun 12.30–15.30
        Dinner Mon–Sat 18.30– 23.30; Sun 19.00–23.00*
- **AVERAGE PRICE** *Lunch/Dinner £20*
- **CREDIT CARDS** *All major cards*
- **MOBILES** *Allowed*
- **CIGARS** *Allowed in the bar*

1837 AT BROWNS HOTEL

Albemarle Street, London W1
☎ 0171 493 6020

In these times of exploratory cuisine, where every other restaurant
one visits seems to feel under an obligation to challenge the
palate with a pan global array of flavours, ingredients and
methods, it is wonderful to find a restaurant that wants to do
classic French cooking. 1837, the restaurant at Browns is such a
place. The menu degustation gives a clear idea of what one can
expect: vichyssoise; pointes d'asperges à la vinaigrette de truffes;
foie gras chaud roti à l'orange; loup de mer au fenouil cuit en
papillotte; soufflé a l'emmental et sa salade au noix; sorbet de
saison; parfait glacé à la vanille et ses cerises confits and café et
petits fours. Something about all those possessives, 'sa salade'
and 'ses cerises', inspires confidence. The food is generally good
with a few outstanding moments and given the enthusiasm of the

brigade and the excellence of the sommelier, who has a phalanx of individually temperature-controlled cupboards to suit wine regions – there is nothing worse than claret served too warm – things look like improving further. The staid, comfortable and faintly provincial surroundings are also a welcome break from the self-consciously over, or under, designed interiors that characterise so many contemporary restaurants. 1837 deserves to build a large and loyal following.

- **DRESS** *Smart*
- **TUBE** *Green Park*
- **HOURS** *Lunch Mon–Fri 12.30–14.00; (closed Sat–Sun)*
  Dinner Mon–Fri 19.00–22.30; Sat 19.00–22.30;
  (closed Sun)
- **AVERAGE PRICE** *Lunch £25; Dinner £55*
- **CREDIT CARDS** *All major cards*
- **MOBILES** *Not allowed*
- **CIGARS** *Humidor*

ALASTAIR LITTLE
136a Lancaster Road, London W11
☎ 0171 243 2220

I have always found Alastair Little a pleasant man. Like many chefs these days, he also manages to find work as a journalist, in this case writing about food for Country Life. Unlike many chefs, he is also reasonably qualified to work as a commentator on matters rural and gastronomic as he is a countryman, having been brought up in Derbyshire. Happily, Little is keener on the hills of Italy than the peaks of Derbyshire – he also finds time to run a brace of cookery schools, one in Umbria, the other in Tuscany. His food is a mixture of Italian with British elements, for example a menu that lists pappardelle with a braised rabbit sauce and parmesan; bufalo mozzarella with rocket, red onions and balsamic; vino santo with cantuccini, might also boast duck and chicken liver terrine with medlar jelly and toast; oxtail and mash and Colston Bassett Stilton with cranberry chutney and oatcakes. There is a simple professionalism about Little's cooking that is refreshing at a time when some others seem to clutch at every flitting culinary neologism. He also understands simple dishes like marinated sardines, which have a haunting sweet flavour. Service, too, is simple and understated but pleasant. However, it is only fair to say that even simple understated things are not always cheap.

- **DRESS** *Modern minimalist meets Notting Hill hobo*
- **TUBE** *Ladbroke Grove*
- **HOURS** *Lunch Mon–Fri 12.30–14.30; Sat 12.30–15.00; (closed Sun)*
  Dinner Mon–Sat 19.00–23.00; (closed Sun)
- **AVERAGE PRICE** *Lunch £20; Dinner £28*
- **CREDIT CARDS** *No Diners Club*
- **MOBILES** *With discretion*
- **CIGARS** *Allowed*

ALSO AT
Frith Street, London W1;
  0171 734 5183 TUBES Tottenham Court Road; Oxford Circus;
  Leicester Square

AMANDIER

26 Sussex Place, London W2
☎ 0171 723 8395

This is a conventionally smartish, seriousish French restaurant in
an area of town not overburdened with fine dining opportunities.
The room is done up with soft shades and, a touch I thought
had gone out fashion, framed posters of important works of art.
Amandier offers good Provençal-influenced food. Sea bass, as
in tranche of sea bass with creamy mashed potatoes and pistou
oil, is handled well and pan-fried red mullet 'à la Niçoise' is a
pleasantly summery dish. If ravioli appears on the menu, expect
it to be a smart French interpretation i.e. the filling (for example,
a huge chunk of goats' cheese) draped with diaphanous sheets
of pasta. The downstairs Bistrot Daniel offers heartier food for
less money.

- **DRESS** *Blazerish*
- **TUBES** *Lancaster Gate; Paddington*
- **HOURS** *Lunch Mon–Fri 12.00–14.15; (closed Sat–Sun)*
  Dinner Mon–Sun 19.00–22.45
- **AVERAGE PRICE** *Lunch £25; Dinner £45*
- **CREDIT CARDS** *No Diners Club*
- **MOBILES** *Not allowed*
- **CIGARS** *Prohibited*

ANDREW EDMUNDS

46 Lexington Street, London W1
☎ 0171 437 5708

What Momo (qv) is to young people, Andrew Edmunds is to literary bohemian types. This dark, candle-lit den is a Soho classic. The food is good and hearty enough to soak up the heroic quantities of booze that get consumed here; for example, marinated herring fillets with new potatoes, apple, crème fraîche and chives; penne with tomatoes, courgettes, pousse, gorgonzola, garlic and chilli oil; smoked haddock and cod fish cake, creamed spinach and tomato sauce; cassoulet and either something like lemon tart or Neal's Yard cheeses with pears (the last a perfectly good excuse to order another bottle of red wine). As well as the restaurant, there is a splendid first floor club called the Academy. This is presided over by the remarkable Mandana Farrell. Mandana is a woman with whom I have travelled in Cuba; I have seen her smoke a dozen cigars in one day and emerge from the bar of the Nacional Hotel in Havana still clad in her evening clothes at a time when everyone else was gathering for a late breakfast. Next door is the Andrew Edmunds print shop, above which is located Auberon Waugh's Literary Review.

- **DRESS** *Bohemian ad man*
- **TUBES** *Oxford Circus; Piccadilly Circus*
- **HOURS** *Lunch Mon–Fri 12.30–15.00; Sat–Sun 13.00–15.00 Dinner Mon–Fri 18.00–22.45; Sat 18.00–22.45; Sun 18.00–22.30*
- **AVERAGE PRICE** *Lunch £25; Dinner: £25*
- **CREDIT CARDS** *No Diners Club*
- **MOBILES** *None, on principal*
- **CIGARS** *Prohibited*

ANONIMATO

12 All Saints Road, London W11
☎ 0171 243 2808

I am not a particular fan of Notting Hill, yet from time to time there are powerful reasons for visiting it. One such reason is Anonimato. On the site of a trustafarian eatery once known as All Saints, Anonimato mercifully bears few similarities to its former incarnation. Its walls are a sort of bleached umber, the food is Japanese/Brazilian/British/Italian and it is a genuinely pleasant place to go and spend an evening. At a time when so many restaurants are slickly-run clones, it is genuinely nice – yes nice –

to come across a proper family-run restaurant. Mrs Aregis (personal trainer to the stars) runs the front of house and Nilton Campos Aregis (who knows, perhaps a man destined to become Argentina's first superchef) cooks. The result is a delight. Some dishes like the Szechwan seared kangaroo are attention-grabbing talking points. Others, notably the Devon hen with pinto beans are generously proportioned and understatedly delicious. Wines are almost as eclectic as the cooking – try the Argentinian Andean Cabernet Sauvignon. The customers tend towards Notting Hill folk heroes and contemporary pop stars, but do not let that put you off.

- **DRESS** *Notting Hill casual*
- **TUBES** *Westbourne Park; Ladbroke Grove*
- **HOURS** *Dinner Mon–Sat 19.00–23.00; (closed Sun)*
- **AVERAGE PRICE** *Dinner £25-30*
- **CREDIT CARDS** *All major cards*
- **MOBILES** *Allowed*
- **CIGARS** *Not allowed*

THE ARKANSAS CAFÉ
Old Spitalfields Market, London E1
☎ 0171 377 6999

This is not one of those minimalist-style eateries where a seven-figure sum has been thrown at the décor and a famous architect has been engaged with a view to winning an award for the design. Arkansas Café is little more than a shed inside the vast aircraft hangar-like space of Old Spitalfields Market. It has the sort of appearance that would have most architects reaching for the bulldozer. This is a genuine rib shack. The proprietor enters into the backwoods spirit by calling himself Bubba (his real name is Kier Holm Helberg) and wearing silly hats. Happily, he is also an accomplished barbecue chef. His skill with the South African lump charcoal has made him a revered figure in carnivorous circles. Do not expect too much finesse – one of the mirrors inside bears the legend 'Nice Girls Don't Spit' – but do expect moderately priced, generous portions of chargrilled rib eye steak (either Irish or US), free-range pork rib, corn-fed chicken etc. Puddings are an opportunity for patriotism: New Orleans pecan pie, New York-style cheesecake, and chocolate Alabama fudge cake. Drinks include Mexican wines, American beers and French ciders.

- **DRESS** *After-hours City boy*
- **TUBE** *Liverpool Street*

- **HOURS** *Lunch Mon–Fri 12.00–14.30; Sun 12.00–16.00;*
  (closed Sat)
  Dinner (closed)
- **AVERAGE PRICE** *£10–12*
- **CREDIT CARDS** *No Diners Club or American Express*
- **MOBILES** *Allowed*
- **CIGARS** *Allowed*

ASK

145 Notting Hill Gate, London W11
☎ 0171 792 9942

This chain of pizza and pasta restaurants is the only credible rival
to Pizza Express (qv). As at Pizza Express, the typical pizza at Ask
is a mid-sized affair that does not benefit from the thin and crispy
crust that is the hallmark of the increasingly numerous band of
pizzerias with wood-fired ovens. That Ask would seem to be in
direct competition with Pizza Express is something borne out by
the informal but efficient approach, the location of the outlets and
the price. Indeed some of the pizzas, for instance Reine (ham,
mushrooms, olives, mozzarella, tomato) and Fiorentina (spinach, egg,
parmesan, olives, mozzarella and tomato) sound disconcertingly
similar. I am probably more fond of, or perhaps used to, Pizza
Express. However there are some interesting ideas at Ask, such as
the pizza Genovese, where the tomato sauce is replaced by pesto
sauce, toppped with sautéed courgettes, roasted aubergine, olives
and mozzarella. Also use is made of such ingredients as sun-dried
tomatoes and goats' cheese in pizza toppings, which, while hardly
le dernier cri, is interesting in a high street chain. Pasta dishes
are plentiful and include classics like spaghetti Bolognese and
Carbonara. Starters (anti pasti on the menu) are an uneasy mix of
the vaguely contemporary; for example, bruschetta and crostini,
with more old-fashioned ideas along the lines of baked avocado.
A friend who is old enough to know such things identified baked
avocado as a staple of old-style Forte and British Rail hotel catering
(a culinary school which also apparently gave us baked grapefruit).
The drinks list is best described as concise.

- **DRESS** *Casual*
- **TUBE** *Notting Hill Gate*
- **HOURS** *Mon–Sun 12.00–23.00*
- **AVERAGE PRICE** *£15*
- **CREDIT CARDS** *All major cards*
- **MOBILES** *Allowed*
- **CIGARS** *Not allowed*

ALSO AT

103 St John Street, London EC1;
0171 253 0323 TUBE Farringdon
121–125 Park Street, London W1;
0171 495 7760 TUBE Marble Arch
48 Grafton Way, London W1;
0171 388 8108 TUBE Great Portland Street
Whiteley's Shopping Centre, 151 Queensway, London W2;
0171 792 1977 TUBE Bayswater
41–42 Spring Street, London W2;
0171 706 0707 TUBE Paddington
219–221 Chiswick High Road, London W4;
0181 742 1323 TUBE Turnham Green
222 Kensington High Street, London W8;
0171 937 5540 TUBE Kensington
160–162 Victoria Street, London SW1;
0171 630 8228 TUBE Victoria
300 King's Road, London SW3;
0171 349 9123 TUBE Sloane Square
345 Fulham Palace Road, London SW6;
0171 371 0392 TUBE Putney Bridge
23–24 Gloucester Arcade, London SW7;
0171 835 0840 TUBE Gloucester Road
43 The Broadway, London N10;
0181 365 2833 TUBE Highgate
Great North Leisure Park, Chaplin Square, London N12;
0181 446 0970 TUBE East Finchley, then bus 263
1257 High Road, London N20;
0181 492 0033 TUBE Totteridge & Whetstone
216 Haverstock Hill, London NW3;
0171 433 3896 TUBE Belsize Park
85 Kew Green, Richmond, Surrey, London TW9;
0181 940 3766 TUBE Kew Gardens

ASSAGGI

39 Chepstow Place, London W2
☎ 0171 792 5501

This unadorned first floor room above a pub was little short of a
sensation when it first opened, with critics' voices united in praise
of the Italian food served here. It continues to be well booked and
it can be difficult to get a table. I remember being particularly
impressed by the carta di musica bread. Dishes are simply but
well done, for example, monkfish tail with pancetta; calves liver;

red mullet and artichoke salad; bottarga and baby fennel and, the sort of thing I could eat lots of, tagliolini with bottarga.

- **DRESS** *To match casually modern surroundings*
- **TUBE** *Notting Hill Gate*
- **HOURS** *Lunch Mon–Fri 12.30–14.30; Sat 13.00–14.30; (closed Sun)*
  Dinner Mon–Sat 19.30–23.00; (closed Sun)
- **AVERAGE PRICE** *Lunch/Dinner £30–35*
- **CREDIT CARDS** *All major cards*
- **MOBILES** *Not encouraged*
- **CIGARS** *Allowed*

THE ATLANTIC BAR AND GRILL
20 Glasshouse Street, London W1
☎ 0171 734 4888

The Atlantic Bar & Grill first came to prominence as a subterranean venue for early nineties hedonism. It is the creation of Oliver Peyton who restored the basement of the Regent Palace Hotel to its former early twentieth century grandeur with columns, mouldings, friezes, coffered ceilings and all. Its fame as a louche destination for the cocktail-swigging classes has rather tended to eclipse the excellent and imaginative cooking of Richard Sawyer, who is always finding clever and delicious ways of putting ingredients together. Typical of his imaginative approach is a summer dish of chilled gazpacho with herb-infused Cornish crab, crisp organic cucumber and sweet purple basil. The wine list, as at Peyton's other establishments, Mash (qv) and Coast (qv), is a joy and includes everything from cheap easy-drinking New World white to the deadly serious stuff like Cheval Blanc '82. For the teetotal, there is the thoughtful touch of a fruit cocktail list. There are two excellent reasons for eating lunch here. The first is that Sawyer experiments with new dishes, via the three course, competitively-priced lunch menu. The other is the absence of the tiresome, trying to be trendy, post-work drinking crowd.

- **DRESS** *With a nod to trendiness*
- **TUBE** *Piccadilly Circus*
- **HOURS** *Lunch Mon–Fri 12.00–14.45; (closed Sat–Sun)*
  Dinner: Mon–Fri 18.00–23.30; Sat 18.00–23.30;
  Sun 19.00–22.00
- **AVERAGE PRICE** *Lunch/Dinner £35*
- **CREDIT CARDS** *All major cards*
- **MOBILES** *Don't work underground*
- **CIGARS** *Humidor*

THE AVENUE

7–9 St James's Street, London SW1
☎ 0171 321 2111

Chris Bodker was a City boy who ate in quite a few restaurants and then decided that he wanted to become a restaurateur – much in the way that you or I, having written a few cheques, might have a go at opening a merchant bank. Bodker has however made more of being a restaurateur than I would have done with banking, he now also has Circus (qv). Avenue is a big open space down near Lock and Lobb; it strikes a defiantly modernist note in both its look and food. When I have eaten here, there has never been much on the menu that has had me leaping up and down with excitement yelling at the top of my voice. It has instead tended to be a case of ordering those things which least offend, which is a pity because when it arrives it all tends to be well enough prepared. It is perhaps that the combos are just a little too eccentric for my taste, take for example veal escalope with tapenade, monkfish with buttered vegetables and Tuscan salami or calf's liver with gnocchi and Parma ham. The star turn is the 'greeteress' they all love to love – 'Maid' Marian Scruton, a woman I love to tease because I only ever see her out and about on the London night. Mind you, she buys her cigarettes at Davidoff so she must be all right really.

- **DRESS** *Snappy*
- **TUBE** *Green Park*
- **HOURS** *Lunch Mon–Sun 12.00–15.00*
  Dinner Mon–Thurs 17.45–24.00; Fri–Sat 17.45–00.30;
  Sun 19.00–22.00
- **AVERAGE PRICE** *Lunch £25; Dinner: £35–40*
- **CREDIT CARDS** *All major cards*
- **MOBILES** *Not a great signal for mobiles, depending on table*
- **CIGARS** *Humidor*

AXIS

No 1 Aldwych, London WC2
☎ 0171 300 0300

This is the cavernous basement restaurant buried under Gordon Campbell-Gray's fashionable inner city hotel Number One Aldwych. The fascistic resonance of the name is echoed in the futurist mural splashed across the wall (shades of Pearl and Dean skyscrapers), which is rather evocative of 1930s Italy. Be sure to take a pre-prandial sharpener at the leather-floored gallery bar, which looks out over the teeming restaurant a little like a box at an opera house. Among the starters, rather tasty things like devilled king prawn cocktail, poached haddock and cheese soufflé tart are billed as Axis specialities. Risotto with Cornish crab, another Axis speciality, stands out among the pasta and rice dishes. Main courses of fish and meat are catholic ranging from the jugged hare 1922 recipe – served boneless with creamed celeriac, turnip and potato bake – through to large ravioli of fresh water prawn and crayfish with braised endive, baby spinach and lobster froth to Japanese grilled saikyo cod with udon noodles, ginger shoot, pumpkin and dashi. Steak and chips is most superior – a generous slab of grilled 'Glenbervie' rib eye. Puddings are most kindly described as eccentric, often served in overly fancy glasses and include 'an excellent trifle from 1880', warm English plum cake with a glass of homemade Love Potion Liqueur, and 19th century baked rice and apricot castle. The last is a dish that even Campbell-Gray describes as looking like a Scotch egg. I have eaten it and am unlikely to repeat the exercise; while not evil, it has a distinctly Victorian solidity about it.

- **DRESS** *If you have an iron cross, wear it*
- **TUBES** *Covent Garden; Charing Cross*
- **HOURS** *Lunch Mon–Fri 12.00–15.00; (closed Sat–Sun)*
  Dinner Mon–Fri 18.00–23.30; Sat 18.00–23.30;
  (closed Sun)
- **AVERAGE PRICE** *Lunch £30; Dinner £35–40*
- **CREDIT CARDS** *All major cards*
- **MOBILES** *Don't work*
- **CIGARS** *Humidor*

BABE RUTH'S RESTAURANT
172–176 The Highway, London E1 (near Tower Bridge)
☎ 0171 481 8181

George Herman Ruth (1895–1948) was an all-American baseball legend. He accumulated over 700 home-runs (whatever they might be) and the moniker 'Sultan of the Swat'. But these days sports stars can forget records and nicknames; posterity is themed restaurants and sports bars, of which this burgeoning chain offers superior examples. The original restaurant is a large art deco-style corner building on the fringes of the City/Docklands/East End. As well as video screens, an abundance of sporting memorabilia, a large glass-sided box containing a one-to-one basketball court, and a souvenir shop, there is suprisingly good food. All the usual ribs, burgers and Tex Mex dishes are in place so as not to disappoint those in search of the standard themed experience, but even these display some finesse. And the simple yellow fin tuna salad (grilled fresh tuna steak served over field greens with mango cucumbers, sweet peppers, cherry tomatoes, tossed with chipotle vinaigrette and topped with roasted corn salsa) would not be unwelcome in many much smarter restaurants. Caesar salads come in half size and full size, with blackened salmon steak or with grilled chicken. There are also entry-level oriental dishes: sushi, spring roll, hoisin chicken salad and Oriental salmon. The last dish seems to encompass most of the mysterious East on one plate: salmon steak served over Japanese noodles with Chinese greens, red onions, red and yellow peppers and cherry tomatoes tossed in a Thai plum sauce. Cheesecake and Pecan pie are exquisite in a vast, calorific fashion and Frozen Chocolate Turtle must be the most curiously named pudding east of Tower Bridge. Dom Perignon (no I am not kidding) is competitively priced and the cocktail list carries the reassuring words: 'All our cocktails contain at least 50ml of alcohol.'

- **DRESS** *Sporty casual*
- **TUBES** *Tower Hill; DLR Shadwell*
- **HOURS** *Mon–Thurs 12.00–23.00; Fri–Sat 12.00–24.00; Sun 12.00–22.30*
- **AVERAGE PRICE** *Lunch £10–15; Dinner £15–25*
- **CREDIT CARDS** *No Diners Club*
- **MOBILES** *Allowed*
- **CIGARS** *Allowed*

ALSO AT
255 Finchley Road, London NW3;
    0171 433 3388 TUBE Finchley Road

BALI SUGAR
33a All Saints Road, London W11
☎ 0171 221 4477

Located at the Notting Hill address formerly known as The Sugar Club (qv), Bali Sugar offers a similar fusion approach to dining, with a vaguely Hispanic Latin American twist given to Eastern dishes. For example, the Bali plate of mixed ceviche, oyster and Thai beef salad and roast corn-fed chicken breast with chorizo mash and chipotle pan juices. Particularly good was a dish of rare grilled tuna with rock shrimp salsa, purple potato and coriander mojo – one can never accuse it of looking dull on the plate but if the purple potatoes do not brighten up your plate sufficiently, order a portion of wasabi mash. Wines match the food for geographic diversity: it is good to see such bottles as Trimbach's Gewürztraminer cropping up on the list alongside Robert Mondavi's Chardonnay Reserve.

- **DRESS** *From suits to dreadlocks*
- **TUBES** *Ladbroke Grove; Westbourne Park*
- **HOURS** *Lunch Mon–Sun 12.30–15.00*
        Dinner Mon–Sun 18.30–23.00
- **AVERAGE PRICE** *Lunch £30; Dinner £38*
- **CREDIT CARDS** *All major cards*
- **MOBILES** *Allowed*
- **CIGARS** *Prohibited*

BAM-BOU

1 Percy Street, London W1
☎ 0171 323 9130

Mogen Tholstrup's fourth restaurant got off to a controversial start in the spring of 1999, when he wrote a note to the restaurant critic AA Gill, (the man thrown out of Gordon Ramsay's restaurant) asking him not to come to Bam-Bou. Presumably the Great Dane was trying to save both men the embarrassment of either throwing or being thrown out. Gill was outraged and launched a splenetic attack on Tholstrup in the Sunday Times, indeed the feud between these two men is shaping up to be one of the longest running sideshows the London restaurant scene has to offer. It would seem that the quickest way to achieve blanket coverage for your restaurant would be to write to AA Gill asking him not to visit or, if he does happen to turn up, sling him out. I happen to like both men although I do think AA can be a bit too cruel from time to time. But then I am probably jealous that AA gets to write the Le Caprice cookbook, even though Bam-Bou and Le Caprice are now part of the same restaurant conglomerate headed up by entrepreneur Luke Johnson – what a tangled web we weave! Anyway Bam-Bou itself is located on hallowed ground; No. 1 Percy Street was for years the location of The White Tower, a fabled restaurant. Then, after a brief stint as the No. 1 Cigar Club of London, it was made over by talented interior designer Andrew Norrey. Arranged over several floors, it evokes the French Colonial Vietnam that Graham Greene must have known when he wrote The Quiet American, with antiques, slightly kitsch art and black and white views of Hanoi in the old days. Food is good if not palate-twistingly excellent and such starters as grilled shrimp on sugarcane are intriguingly innovative and offer the contrasting textures of crunchy sugar cane and fleshy shrimp. Interest is maintained with main courses like caramelised ginger chicken and curried frogs' legs. Barbecued pork ribs with lemon grass recall, albeit in a more piquant and seasoned way, teenage trips to the Texas Lone Star (qv). A side order of aubergine, tomato and tofu is a satisfying dish in itself. And as regards puddings, the caramelised banana and coconut pudding is extremely popular; coconut ice-cream is tasty, however, banana fritters with honey, sesame and vanilla ice-cream, are too gritty – the fault of the sesame I fear. Service apart from one man who seemed to be doing everything is pretty near clueless, not that the Eurotrash customers with whom I shared my last visit seemed to mind. Also, the hard surfaces of the ground and second floor dining rooms makes it all very noisy. If you want to eat outside, there is a small terrace abutting the pavement.

- **DRESS** *Off-duty Eurotrash*
- **TUBES** *Goodge Street; Tottenham Court Road*
- **HOURS** *Lunch Mon–Sat 12.00–15.00; (closed Sun)*
        Dinner Mon–Sat 18.00–23.30; (closed Sun)
- **AVERAGE PRICE** *Lunch £25; Dinner £35*
- **CREDIT CARDS** *All major cards*
- **MOBILES** *Allowed*
- **CIGARS** *Humidor*

BANK
1 Kingsway, London WC2
☎ 0171 379 9797

Bank is one of those places that will be looked back on by social historians of the future and identified as the prototypical nineties dining experience. Located in a former Nat West Bank, Bank is designed by Julyan Wickham whose credits include Fifth Floor (qv) and Kensington Place (qv). It is big, quite brash and is dominated by a ceiling of stalactitic glass shards that are part of a 20 tonne chandelier/sculpture. The food is almost as modish as the surroundings. Adjectives like 'seared', 'caramelised', 'wok-fried', 'griddled' and 'blackened' abound on the menu. Food is competently prepared under the guidance of Christian Delteil, and the range is wide. Dishes run from the classic (for example, fish soup with rouille and croûtons) through to the rustic (for example, roast rabbit leg, sage butter, creamed polenta) to the modern (for example, griddled scallops, plum-tomato salad, sweetcorn and cucumber salsa). The whole thing is run with

charm and military precision by Eric Garnier, the man who was
the first manager of Terence Conran's Quaglino's (qv), and the
computerised bookings and reservations system is one of the
marvels of the modern restaurant world. Bank is a welcome
addition to an area hitherto not spectacularly well served by
good restaurants and has done well. It is also apparently popular
for breakfast in the bar. Although I have never got there in time
for this horrendously early meal, it is probably nice and quiet-ish.

- **DRESS** *Suits*
- **TUBE** *Holborn*
- **HOURS** *Breakfast Mon–Fri 07.00–11.30; (closed Sat–Sun)*
  Lunch Mon–Fri 12.00–15.00; Sat–Sun 11.30–15.30
  Dinner Mon–Sat 17.30–23.30; (closed Sun)
- **AVERAGE PRICE** *Lunch/Dinner £35*
- **CREDIT CARDS** *All major cards*
- **MOBILES** *Allowed*
- **CIGARS** *Humidor*

BEIRUT EXPRESS
See MAROUSH page 143

BELAIR HOUSE
Gallery Road, Dulwich Village, London SE21
☎ 0181 299 9788

Set back from the road and looking out over a park, this imposing
late eighteenth-century house must be a lovely place to lunch on
a sunny Sunday. I have only ever seen the place in the dark and
though I have tried, never been able to eat here. My last attempt
saw me arrive shortly after 11 pm on a Friday night, by which
time the place was completely empty and in the process of being
shut up for the night. This would indicate that habitués of Belair
House are not the liveliest, rockingest of individuals: a supposition
that would seem to be borne out by flyers in the lobby proselytising
'Wine and Dine Evenings', extravaganzas that are doubtless
pivotal social events in the leafy purlieus of SE21. Such evenings
kick off with a 'Champagne reception on arrival with wine
tasting' and finish on a high note with an 'after-dinner talk from
winemakers about wine and winemaking (rather than as one
might have expected, underground film-making, or the politics
of repression) followed by a question & answer session.' The
transformation of wine from instrument of pleasure into a bourgeois
hobby must be amongst the most regrettable by-products of our

increasingly gastronomically-aware society. I was disappointed to learn that while cigars, by the peerless firm Davidoff, are offered, 'Customers are asked to refrain from smoking cigars in the restaurant.' Dishes offered on an à la carte menu included: grilled tuna niçoise; scallop and crab millefeuille, tomato; pancetta-wrapped monkfish, spinach, beetroot polenta, butter sauce; roast rump of lamb, crushed Jerusalem artichoke, green beans; banana vol-au-vent, pistachio mousse and crème fraîche ice-cream; and scrambled duck egg on brioche with anchovy.

- **DRESS** *Bourgoise suburban*
- **RAIL** *West Dulwich*
- **HOURS** *Lunch Mon–Sun 12.00–14.30*
      Dinner Mon–Sat 19.00–22.30; Sun 19.00–22.00
- **AVERAGE PRICE** *Lunch £25; Dinner £45*
- **CREDIT CARDS** *All major cards*
- **MOBILES** *Allowed*
- **CIGARS** *Humidor; in bar only*

BELGO CENTRAAL
50 Earlham Street, London WC2
☎ 0171 813 2233

There is a sci-fi craziness about these three mussel and beer halls and their monastically attired attendants, that leads one to believe that the proprietors have a warped sense of Belgium. Sigourney Weaver and the Aliens III crowd would feel particularly at home in the Covent Garden branch with its wire cage elevator and sprawling subterranean eating halls. As one might suspect, with a list of 101 Belgian brews, slotted sticks holding up to 32 glasses of Schnapps and a youngish clientele – Belgo offers what might kindly be called a lively atmosphere. Mussels are served in pots (steamed in their shells) or platters (open-faced and grilled). Permutations range from uncomplicated 'marinières' through a reminder of Belgium's colonial past 'Congo' (coconut cream and lemon grass) to the bang-up-to-date moules 'pizza' (open-faced mussels topped with tomato cheese and herbs but without a base). If you are not mad on shellfish, try wild boar sausages with Belgian mash and forest fruits or rotisserie chicken (half a Belgian chicken served one of three ways). Whatever you order, it is difficult to avoid frites and/or mayo. Belgo bargains are well worth snapping up; for instance, on Blue Monday when for a limited time each menu item is £5.55 or less on a Monday lunch. Arrive between 5 and 6.30 pm and choose from three specials for which you pay 'the time you order' and this includes a beer as well!

- **DRESS** *Modern Belgium*
- **TUBE** *Covent Garden*
- **HOURS** *Non-reservation restaurant*
  Mon–Thurs 12.00–23.30; Fri–Sat 12.00-24.00;
  Sun 12.00–22.30
  Reservation Restaurant
  Lunch Mon–Sun 12.00–14.30; Dinner Mon–Thurs
  17.30–23.30; Fri–Sat 12.00–22.30; (closed Sun)
- **AVERAGE PRICE** *Lunch £14; Dinner £18*
- **CREDIT CARDS** *All major cards*
- **MOBILES** *Allowed*
- **CIGARS** *Allowed*

ALSO AT
BELGO ZUID, 124 Ladbroke Grove, London W10;
  0181 982 8400 TUBE Ladbroke Grove
BELGO NOORD, 72 Chalk Farm Road, London NW1;
  0171 267 0718 TUBE Chalk Farm

THE BELVEDERE
Holland Park, London W8 (off Abbotsbury Road)
☎ 0171 602 1238

Wednesday tends to see me having lunch in the almost sylvan
surroundings of the Belvedere with the great Johnny Gold. On
a gentle summer day, there are few better places in London than
the Belvedere's terrace and even when it rains the place has
its *rus in urbe* charm. Wednesday lunch is a ritual Johnny and
I have observed for four or five years, during which time I
have tried, without success, to persuade him to let me write his
biography. Gold is a hero of mine and for a man who has
spent a large proportion of the last three decades presiding
over a basement in Jermyn Street that is the world's most famous
nightclub, Tramp, he is remarkably normal. He bought the
Belvedere in the early nineties. Recently he has been joined
in the venture by some Scottish partners and they have spent
considerable sums tidying the place up. Where this injection of
cash is most noticeable is in the kitchen. The chef is a delightful
man called Mark Brown who used to work for Anton Edelmann.
He came here in August 1998 and since then the cooking has
moved up several gears. For example, Pacific fish marinated in
Asian spices and steamed in a bamboo basket is agreeably
simple and tenderly flavoursome, while char-grilled venison
steak served with a confit of red onions, pommes galette, ceps,
shallots persillade and balsamic jus caters to more robust tastes.
The seared tuna with a brandade of cod and haddock spiked

with peri peri is memorably good. Starters such as Scottish smoked salmon served with a confit of lemon and mesclun salad are listed for those who are not quite up to lasagne of scallops and langoustine served with a cappuccino of fresh garden peas and foie gras.

- **DRESS** *John Gold wears Doug Hayward suits*
- **TUBE** *Holland Park*
- **HOURS** *Lunch Mon–Sat 12.00–15.00; Sun 12.00–15.30*
  Dinner Mon–Sat 19.00–23.00; (closed Sun)
- **AVERAGE PRICE** *Lunch £30–35; Dinner £30–35*
- **CREDIT CARDS** *No Diners Club*
- **MOBILES** *Allowed*
- **CIGARS** *Allowed*

BENGAL TRADER
44 Artillery Lane, London E1
☎ 0171 375 0072

This is an adequate, inoffensively contemporary curry house which opened in 1998 and seems popular with local City folk. Its location, within easy staggering distance of Liverpool Street, can do it no harm either. Dishes range from the acceptable, for example, the unfortunately named Akni (spring lamb flavoured with aromatic spices and saffron and served with pilau rice and vegetable curry) to the good, for example, the Bengal-style aubergine dish, spicy begoon. For a vividly-coloured curry, ask for golda chingri massala, (Bay of Bengal prawns baked in the clay oven and then simmered in a bright red spicy sauce). Unfortunately most of the tables are in the basement, which although decorated in pale colours and cheered up with contemporary canvases is still, as basements have a habit of being, underground.

- **DRESS** *Off-duty City suits*
- **TUBE** *Liverpool Street*
- **HOURS** *Lunch: Mon–Fri 11.30–15.00; (closed Sat–Sun)*
  Dinner: Mon–Fri 18.00–24.00; (closed Sat–Sun)
- **AVERAGE PRICE** *Lunch/Dinner £15*
- **CREDIT CARDS** *All major cards*
- **MOBILES** *Allowed*
- **CIGARS** *Allowed*

BENIHANA

37 Sackville Street, London W1
☎ 0171 494 2525

This international teppanyaki chain is actually a bit of a laugh, provided you like interactive dining experiences and enjoy watching cooks at their work under your nose. The idea is that you sit at a counter in front of a teppan and let the knife-wielding chef dazzle you with his dexterity. American influence is obvious with the presence of steak in nearly all the Benihana specialities, for example the Surf 'n' Turf (Hibachi steak and calamari fillet) and the Benihana Royal (fresh lobster and filet mignon with mushrooms). Apart from eating straight from the teppan, the appeal of the place seems to lie in the 'experience' of eating the Benihana way, in seeing the chef handle his blade and juggle with his cooking implements. Advertisements for the place show a group of people, who look as though they have just walked off an American advertisement for low-tar cigarettes, howling with laughter and generally having a good informal time of it – catch a good chef and he probably will be amusing company. However, eating lunch at one of two occupied teppans in the otherwise abandoned hangar-like premises of the Kings Road branch is more of a solitary experience.

- DRESS *Casual*
- TUBE *Piccadilly Circus*
- HOURS *Lunch: Mon–Sun 12.00–15.00*
  Dinner Mon–Thurs, Fri–Sat 18.00–24.00;
  Sun 18.00–23.00
- AVERAGE PRICE *Lunch £15; Dinner £20–25*
- CREDIT CARDS *All major cards*
- MOBILES *Allowed*
- CIGARS *Prohibited*

ALSO AT
77 King's Road, London SW3;
   0171 376 7799 TUBE Sloane Square
100 Avenue Road, London NW3;
   0171 586 9508 TUBE Swiss Cottage

LA BERSAGLERIA
372 King's Road, London SW3
☎ 0171 352 5993

This is a pizzeria and pasta restaurant of the old school. It may not be particularly famous, it is certainly not smart, but in its way it has become a part of the furniture of the World's End stretch of the King's Road. It is a no-nonsense example of what neighbourhood Italian restaurants used to be like prior to the mania for char-grilling and olive oil drizzling. Pizzas are cheap, good and have thin crispy bases. At the top of the range are things like the Four Seasons (mushrooms, pepperoni, capers, anchovies, olives, tomato, mozzarella and ham) and the Capricciosa (ham, peppers, anchovies, eggs, capers, mozzarella and tomato). The house special is the Bersagliera (mozzarella, tomato, aubergine and parmesan). Fresh pastas of the day are displayed on a counter at the back of the restaurant. Other dishes include coppa di gamberetti (prawn cocktail) and pollo alla Kiev (chicken Kiev). House wine is cheap and the beers include the pizza house classic Peroni and the more esoteric Sardinian quaff, Ichnusa.

- **DRESS** *Informal*
- **TUBE** *Sloane Square*
- **HOURS** *Dinner Mon–Fri 17.30–24.00; Sat 12.00–24.00;*
  (closed Sun)
- **AVERAGE PRICE** *Lunch/Dinner £10*
- **CREDIT CARDS** *Visa; Mastercard*
- **MOBILES** *Allowed*
- **CIGARS** *Allowed*

BERTORELLI'S
19 Charlotte Street, London W1
☎ 0171 636 4174

During the early years of the century, the Bertorelli brothers came from northern Italy to Fitzrovia. Shortly before World War I they opened a restaurant with five tables. Business improved, the restaurant soon became a 100 seater and the brothers moved into the ice cream business and the wine trade. Now Bertorelli's is part of the ubiquitous Laurence Isaacson's Groupe Chez Gerard and has been given a modern makeover although the fascia of the old Bertorelli's has been set into a wall at the back of the ground floor. The ground floor houses a busy bar and café, which featured in *Sliding Doors* and has since been the venue of choice for Gwynneth Paltrow wannabes. The first floor is the

location of a smarter restaurant and two private dining rooms.
The café menu includes various pizzas, pasta dishes, salads and
sandwiches. Typical of them are: pizza with four salami, green
chilli, tomato, mozzarella and fresh roquette; and warm salad of
baby spinach with croûtons, avocado, mushrooms, crispy bacon
and pecorino shavings. Food in the upstairs restaurant is slightly
more elaborate with a good selection of fish dishes and the
predominantly Italian wine list is well chosen with whites from
Alois Lageder and Giovanni Puiatti. However, if you are after
challenging Italian food, there are other restaurants to visit.

- **DRESS** *Ad agency creative*
- **TUBE** *Covent Garden*
- **HOURS** *Lunch Mon–Fri 12.00–15.00; (closed Sat–Sun)*
       Dinner Mon–Sat 17.30–23.30; (closed Sun)
- **AVERAGE PRICE** *Lunch/Dinner £25–30*
- **CREDIT CARDS** *All major cards*
- **MOBILES** *Allowed*
- **CIGARS** *Prohibited*

ALSO AT
44a Floral Street, London WC2;
    0171 836 3969 TUBE Covent Garden

BIBENDUM
Michelin House, 81 Fulham Road, London SW3
☎ 0171 225 1222

This is where gourmands go if they are good and very, very rich.
Simon Hopkinson ceased working here ages ago, but you can
still buy his book, delicately displayed on a little easel. These
days Matthew Harris does the cooking and even though the
place is old enough to be something of a monument – it was the
destination restaurant of the late eighties. Sumptuous food and the
beautiful light and bright room still have tremendous following
and reclame. Several years after it opened, an invitation to dinner
at Bibendum still has the power to impress. This is not however
always a good choice for the squeamish – wild mushroom ravioli
might appear with bone marrow and brown butter, veal tails 'en
crepinette' (with risotto alla Milanese and gremolata) and ris de
veau can usually be found lurking somewhere. Otherwise things
are often kept simple: Spanish charcuterie with pickled chillies
and onion confit, Baltic herrings à la crème, and deep-fried
plaice with chips and tartare sauce. The wine list can keep
company with the best, and priciest, in town.

- **DRESS** *Smart*
- **TUBE** *South Kensington*
- **HOURS** *Lunch Mon–Fri 12.30–14.30; Sat–Sun 12.30–15.00*
  Dinner Mon–Sat 19.00–23.30; Sun 19.00–22.30
- **AVERAGE PRICE** *Lunch £45; Dinner £55*
- **CREDIT CARDS** *All major cards*
- **MOBILES** *Not encouraged*
- **CIGARS** *Humidor*

BIBENDUM OYSTER BAR

Michelin House, 81 Fulham Road, London SW3
☎ 0171 589 1480

The oyster bar is much more than a mere adjunct to the grand
restaurant above and in many ways I prefer its easy, café-like
informality. There is not really any hot food here, but there are
things like smoked eel with potato and chive salad and sauce
ravigote or potted salmon with cucumber and dill. Salads are
generous and even faintly luxurious, for example, the salad of
avocado and brown shrimps with truffle dressing. But the fruits
de mer are the obvious things to go for and the cute 'camionette'
at the front of the building flogs the same stuff but for consumption
at home. The wine list is surprisingly good, concentrating on
whites of course, with a good line in zingy Sauvignon Blanc.

- **DRESS** *Well-heeled Conran shopper*
- **TUBE** *South Kensington*
- **HOURS** *Mon–Sat 12.00–22.30; Sun 12.00–22.00*
- **AVERAGE PRICE** *Lunch/Dinner £18–25*
- **CREDIT CARDS** *All major cards*
- **MOBILES** *Allowed*
- **CIGARS** *Humidor*

BISTRORGANIC (FORMALLY WOZ)

46 Golborne Road, London W10
☎ 0181 968 2200

Lurking in the shadow of the Trellick Tower, this Golborne Road
branch of Worrall Thompson's west London empire enjoyed fame
when it was held up by Rolex robbers on its opening night …
so if you are planning on supper here leave the Bentley at home.
In fact the vaguely modern rustic décor and the five course set
menu dining is not likely to attract the Bentley-driving classes.
The food is the sort of thing that AWT does best: elegantly hearty,
if that is not too much of an oxymoron. Although I would suspect

that he is not in the kitchen all of the time, his influence is clear to see and taste. Book in for dinner and expect mixed hors d'oevures, Caesar salad, pot-roast poussin, Manchego cheese and pud. The wine list is commendably good and the staff, headed by a man whom I have dubbed Captain America and looks like he belongs in *Easy Rider*, are kind, intelligent and correctly judged. If Captain America is still working at Woz by the time this guide comes out, he should be given a huge bonus. Wozza is a talented chef who burned out a bit during the early nineties; he also appears a lot on telly. But people seem to forget his ground breaking Beauchamp Place eatery, Menage à Trois, and then there was the OTT rusticity of 190 Queen's Gate.

- **DRESS** *So as not to attract the attention of muggers*
- **TUBES** *Westbourne Park; Ladbroke Grove*
- **HOURS** *Lunch Tues–Sun 12.00–16.00; (closed Mon)*
          Dinner Mon–Sat 19.00–23.00; (closed Sun)
- **AVERAGE PRICE** *Lunch/Dinner £30*
- **CREDIT CARDS** *No Diners Club*
- **MOBILES** *Allowed*
- **CIGARS** *Allowed*

BLAKES
33 Roland Gardens, London SW7
☎ 0171 370 6701

Blakes is one of those places that tends to slip the mind when thinking of somewhere to go and eat in the gastronomic theme park that is brave new London, which is a pity. Blakes is one of the original and, to my mind, one of the best boutique hotels London has to offer. I have been going to Blakes on and off for well over a decade and there was a time at the end of the eighties that I considered moving into the basement bar. Blakes has always captivated me with its decadent grand-luxe, opium-den look. And in spite of all the brickbats, some warranted and some not, that its creator Anouska Hempel (Lady Weinberg to you and me) has had to suffer, Blakes is a work of genius. It is one of those environments that so thoroughly transports one from the banality of daily life, that one almost ceases to heed the exorbitant cost. Blakes could be accused of pioneering multi-cultural cuisine in the capital and it was certainly years ahead of the current trends. This shows with a sureness in the execution of such dishes as charred rare Ahi tuna on lotus crisps with wasabi aioli and soy mirin glaze; roast sea scallops with ginger and basil; wok-fried salt and peppered soft shell crabs; sugar-cured tuna with miso Dijon dressing and green tea noodles; chicken Fabergé filled with lobster and ginger, basil sauce; and Szechwan duck with roasted salt and pepper. Luxury too is one of the keynotes of the menu: truffles, foie gras, and great dollops of caviar crop up unannounced in various dishes. If the presentation is sometimes extravagant, as for example, even simple side dishes like parmigiano and endive salad with leaves served standing up, this is only in keeping with the surroundings.

- DRESS *Up*
- TUBE *South Kensington*
- HOURS *Lunch Mon–Sun 12.30–14.30*
        Dinner Mon–Sun 19.30–23.45
- AVERAGE PRICE *Lunch £40; Dinner £65*
- CREDIT CARDS *All major cards*
- MOBILES *Allowed*
- CIGARS *Humidor*

BLUE ELEPHANT
4–6 Fulham Broadway, London SW6
☎ 0171 385 6595

'To walk into our restaurants' runs a flyer for the Blue Elephant, 'is to enter temples of excellence.' That's as may be, but the most powerful sensation upon walking into the Blue Elephant is of strolling onto an elaborate set for something like *The King & I*. I have always enjoyed eating here – it might be slightly kitsch but I have a real fondness for the fountains, the little bridges, the ponds with fish, the courteous staff clad in some ornate form of Eastern court dress and so on. Sometimes menu descriptions are correspondingly ornate, for example, chuchi chong is described as 'a tropical storm of subtle (sic) flavours with king prawns and a lightning flash of dry red curry.' The food is consistently enjoyable, and the prawn curry, hot and yellow with coconut milk, is a personal favourite. And side dishes like Phad Thai and the sticky rice are done well – but then the Blue Elephant makes a thing about flying in the ingredients from Thailand. If you have the appetite, the Royal Thai Banquet Menu is the thing – it manages to offer what seem like the highlights of the menu: Thai fishcakes, 'paper prawns', massaman (a southern Thai lamb dish) and plenty else – if you have the appetite.

- DRESS *Fulham*
- TUBE *Fulham Broadway*

- **HOURS** *Lunch Mon–Sat 12.00–14.30; Sun 12.00–15.00 Dinner Mon–Fri 19.00–24.30; Sat 18.30–00.30; Sun 19.00–22.30*
- **AVERAGE PRICE** *£35–40*
- **CREDIT CARDS** *All major cards*
- **MOBILES** *Allowed*
- **CIGARS** *Humidor*

BLUEBIRD

350 King's Road, London SW3
☎ 0171 559 1000

Bluebird functions as a sort of Chelsea canteen, where it is possible to spot most of the social stereotypes that inhabit the Royal Borough. Noisy, big and bright – this is the place for big lunches where dysfunctional families can get together and not feel the need to talk, as there is quite enough of that going on elsewhere. John Torode was drafted in from Mezzo to help perk up this most westerly outpost of the Conran empire. Such dishes as soy-glazed reef fish with wakame and cucumber, or wood roast peppered kangaroo with sweet potato and yoghurt give a vaguely whacky global edge to the menu. Otherwise Conran signatures, such as the crustacea altar and the covetable ashtray, are where they should be and I have eaten some good pizzas here at the weekend. The café offers everything from bagel with smoked salmon and scrambled egg to Thai duck salad, green papaya, glass noodles and chilli dressing.

- **DRESS** *Informal chic*
- **TUBES** *Sloane Square; South Kensington*
- **HOURS** *Mon–Fri 10.00–22.00; Sat 9.00–21.00; Sun 12.00–18.00*
- **AVERAGE PRICE** *Lunch £20; Dinner £35*
- **CREDIT CARDS** *All major cards*
- **MOBILES** *Consideration requested*
- **CIGARS** *Humidor*

BLUEBIRD CLUB

350 King's Road, London SW3
☎ 0171 559 1129

Sir Terence Conran probably wishes that his smart club celebrating Sir Malcolm Campbell's record-breaking exploits were fuller. I relish the fact that at times, such as a recent lunch, only four tables were occupied. Great room, great food. The bar is a good place to hole up in winter with a Welsh rarebit and a glass of beer. Upstairs is for more serious eating. Food tends to be hearty, yet sophisticated, and I was impressed to see a pea and ham soup arrive with what looked like the better part of a whole pig in it. The Bluebird Club serves a modern interpretation of club food that actually makes it worth joining: whether chicken breast, wood-roasted vegetables, lemon oil; deep-fried lemon sole, chips and tartare sauce or cod with chickpeas and chorizo, one can usually count on things to be done well. Service is pretty near flawless. Some members can be a little pompous but then that is part of the fun and any disputes, usually about mobile telephones, are resolved with tact and charm by the enchanting social secretary Melissa Caruth. This is one of the best things Conran has done in a long time and I keep pestering him to open one nearer my house. By the way, the mysterious number 301.129 refers to a record-breaking speed achieved by one or other of the vehicles after which the club was named.

- **DRESS** *Smart but ties not required*
- **TUBE** *Sloane Square; South Kensington*
- **HOURS** *Lunch Mon–Fri 12.00–15.00; Sun 11.00–15.00;*
  (closed Sat)
  Dinner Mon–Sat 19.00–23.00; (closed Sun)
- **AVERAGE PRICE** *Lunch £25; Dinner £65*
- **CREDIT CARDS** *All major cards*
- **MOBILES** *Not allowed*
- **CIGARS** *Humidor*

BLUE PRINT CAFÉ
Design Museum, Butler's Wharf, London SE1
☎ 0171 378 7031

Even if you hate design and the earnest short-haired young men in black suits who could 'bore for Britain' on the subject, The Blue Print Café is still worth a visit. The place is no more or less 'designed' than any other Conran place and the sort of robust no-nonsense food that chef Jeremy Lee presents works rather well in the uncluttered yet often crowded and noisy surroundings. Paul Thomson, the surprisingly nice, normal and unpretentious director of the Design Museum eats here about four times a week. The best place to sit is on the covered balcony and the best thing to eat, in my opinion, is the gravadlax and pickled herrings with potato and cucumber salad if it is on the menu. However, Jean Pierre Martel the celebrated Iberian tastemaker who likes nothing better than a good pig's trotter or a plate of sweetbreads, was prolix in his praise of the uncompromising slabs of ox tongue that were put in front of him. The rest of the menu runs on similar lines: pork rillettes with gherkins and toast; salad of feta, anchovies, olives and French beans; halibut with parsley sauce and beetroot relish and fricassee of rabbit with prunes, pine kernels, almonds and white wine. Lee makes his own chutneys, preserves and jams and, this being a Conran outfit, I am surprised that this potential profit centre has not been harnessed and put to work for the greater financial good of Sir Terence's all-conquering gastronomic and business juggernaut. As with all Conran places, the food is not given away, but it is fairly priced and of course the smoking of the post-prandial cigar is welcomed heartily by the staff and Sir Terence himself.

- **DRESS** *Design aware*
- **TUBES** *Tower Hill; London Bridge*
- **HOURS** *Lunch Mon–Sun 12.00–15.00*
  Dinner Mon–Sat 18.00–23.00; (closed Sun)
- **AVERAGE PRICE** *Lunch/Dinner £35*
- **CREDIT CARDS** *All major cards*
- **MOBILES** *Allowed*
- **CIGARS** *Humidor*

BOMBAY BRASSERIE
Courtfield Close, Courtfield Road, London SW7
☎ 0171 370 4040

The Bombay Brasserie is a proper London landmark and to judge from the row of taxis stationed outside on a recent visit, it should be a part of the 'knowledge'. The Bombay Brasserie is annexed to the Bayley's Hotel. Bayley's used to have a wonderful bar at the back with high-peeling damp-stained walls and was the perfect place to hide away and drink. It has since been renovated beyond recognition, leaving the Bombay Brasserie as the hotel's sole draw – And what a draw ... it has been part of the London restaurant scene since 1982. That was a time when one's local curry house was a highly seasoned oasis of flocked wallpapered dignity and something like the Bombay Brasserie was a daring neologism. However, times change and so has the Bombay Brasserie – it has grown to accommodate an ever-increasing regiment of devotees. The menu is plastered with scrapbook-like snaps of the famous people who have popped by for a curry – apparently Tom Cruise liked it so much he arranged for a take-away to go to his film set in Italy. The main rooms can be a bit gloomy – so sit in the splendid conservatory. The place is famed for its buffet lunch which is heavily booked on Sundays. Evenings are à la carte and starters are particularly good, and include tangy prawns and a tasty crab dish billed as crab pepper fry. On no account miss the sev batata puri, described as a seaside attraction of Bombay, and consists of 'small biscuit-like puris topped with cubed boiled potatoes, gramflour straws, sprouted lentil coriander leaves and covered with a mix of mint, tamarind and chilli chutneys'. There are dishes from the tandoor and a selection of Goan specialities, which are not bad. The selection 'Some like it Hot' is a small testing ground of two hot dishes for macho palates, amongst which apparently Faye Dunaway is numbered – you live and learn.

- **DRESS** *As a film star*
- **TUBE** *Gloucester Road*
- **HOURS** *Lunch Mon–Sun 12.30–15.00*
     Dinner Mon–Sun 19.30–24.00
- **AVERAGE PRICE** *Lunch £18–20; Dinner £35*
- **CREDIT CARDS** *All major cards*
- **MOBILES** *Allowed*
- **CIGARS** *Humidor*

THE BRACKENBURY

129–131 Brackenbury Road, London W6
☎ 0181 748 0107

This former west London wine bar has become one of the best reasons for living in what estate agents insist on calling 'Brackenbury Village'. Now owned by the Kensington Place (qv) Mob, it is the sort of place where people who wear Boden clothes can go and eat clever West End food at suburban prices. The sort of things one might expect to eat include: steamed mussels and clams, chilli, lemon grass and lime butter; whole baked lemon sole with mushrooms, Riesling and new potatoes; steamed sea bass with noodles, bok choi, soy and ginger; roast chicken with grilled red onion, black olive and tomato salad; or venison stew with button mushrooms and mash. Puds are inventive and include, say, banana Yorkshire pudding with caramel ice-cream. Service is friendly and, like the surroundings, casual.

- **DRESS** *West London casual*
- **TUBE** *Goldhawk Road*
- **HOURS** *Lunch Mon–Fri 12.30–14.45; Sun 12.30–15.00;*
     (closed Sat)
     Dinner Mon–Fri 19.00–22.45; Sat 19.00–22.45;
     (closed Sun)

- **AVERAGE PRICE** *Lunch/Dinner £20–25*
- **CREDIT CARDS** *No Diners Club*
- **MOBILES** *Not encouraged*
- **CIGARS** *Not allowed*

LAS BRASAS
63b Clerkenwell Road, London EC1
☎ 0171 250 3401

This might be an attempt to provide a diffusion line of the cooking at Gaudi (qv). It does not live up to the standard of its neighbour, but it is much cheaper. The thing to do is treat the place like a Spanish brasserie, go there with a couple of friends and order one of the paellas (vegetarian, seafood, poultry and vegetables) and drink plenty of robust red wine. Other dishes are not half so appealing. The seafood crêpes are memorably unexciting and did the reputation of this restaurant no favours – and given the proximity of Gaudi, one might have hoped for more. However, things may improve with time.

- **DRESS** *Casual*
- **TUBE** *Farringdon*
- **HOURS** *Lunch Mon–Fri 11.30–15.00; Sat 12.00–14.30;*
       (closed Sun)
       Dinner Mon–Fri 18.30–22.00; Sat 18.00–23.00;
       (closed Sun)
- **AVERAGE PRICE** *Lunch £10; Dinner £12*
- **CREDIT CARDS** *All major cards*
- **MOBILES** *Allowed*
- **CIGARS** *Allowed*

BRASSERIE DU MARCHE AUX PUCES
349 Portobello Road, London W10
☎ 0181 968 5828

This is a charming little restaurant in the Notting Hill hinterland that really ought to go under the name of a bistro. It is the sort of menu that used to be all the rage about 10 or 20 years ago – sort of blanket French: snails with garlic and parsley butter; bleu d'Auvergne and roast pepper tart; chef's chicken liver parfait, red onion marmalade and toast, and chef's thinly sliced salmon gravadlax, lemon and dill cream. 'Chef's this' and 'chef's that' always reminds me of Fawlty Towers. The menu changes pretty regularly but things like the 'handmade Perigord sausages (lamb, red wine, mushrooms), horseradish mashed potatoes and shallot gravy' seldom come off. There is an intimate and unpretentious charm about the place that allows one to relax and take it a bit easy – not always possible in this fashion-conscious corner of town. However some guests were really throwing sartorial caution to the four winds on my last visit and I saw a man dressed entirely in denim, something I have not seen since the early eighties.

- **DRESS** *Faded jeans*
- **TUBE** *Ladbroke Grove*
- **HOURS** *Mon–Sat 10.00–23.00; Sun 11.00–17.00*
- **AVERAGE PRICE** *Lunch £15; Dinner £20–25*
- **CREDIT CARDS** *No Diners Club*
- **MOBILES** *Allowed*
- **CIGARS** *Allowed*

BRASSERIE ST QUENTIN
243 Brompton Road, London SW3
☎ 0171 589 8005

Brasserie St Quentin keeps on dishing up the same cocktail of trad. French surroundings and trad. dishes to the apparent satisfaction of locals and regulars. Things like assiette de charcuterie de Gascogne, snails in puff pastry, skate wing with capers, Sainte Maure grillé aux artichauts, must have seemed terribly new and daring once upon a time. But these days they and the continued presence of Brasserie St Quentin – although now owned by the omnipresent Laurence Isaacson (qv) – at the Oratory end of Brompton Road are comforting in an institutional sort of way. Although Brasserie St Quentin likes to bill itself as a neighbourhood restaurant, bear in mind that the neighbourhood is Knightsbridge and that you can expect to be billed accordingly – the lunch and early evening set menu is the value option.

- **DRESS** *Old Knightsbridge*
- **TUBE** *Knightsbridge*
- **HOURS** *Lunch Mon–Sat 12.00–15.00; Sun 12.00–15.30*
  Dinner Mon–Sun 18.30–23.00
- **AVERAGE PRICE** *£20–25*
- **CREDIT CARDS** *All major cards*
- **MOBILES** *Allowed*
- **CIGARS** *Not encouraged*

BROMPTON BAY

96 Draycott Avenue, London SW3
☎ 0171 225 2500

This perfectly acceptable, if largely personality-free, restaurant seems to attract middle-aged, puce-complexioned hoorays, who think they are a bit slick, lunching their ageing female companions. I am not quite sure what sort of restaurant this is trying to be. The sort of places that seem to typify the appeal of Draycott Avenue are places along the lines of Daphne's and Joe's Café. And if Brompton Bay is trying to appeal to lunching ladies, an overly buttery dish of ravioli of dolcelatte, artichokes, sage butter and panagratatto or butch food like marinated wild boar, stewed red cabbage and juniper sauce are unlikely to do it. To be fair, simple things can be done well here, for example, chargrilled squid with chilli jam and wild rocket, which manages to be both sweet and peppery. And some care has gone into the ingredients, for example, acorn-fed pork loin 'Iberico' with black figs and shaved parmesan; corn-fed chicken breast filled with goat's cheese and Leon chorizo with roasted Jerusalem artichokes, carrots and leeks. The back room with its conservatory-style roof is pleasant and the main room is bright. However, I cannot escape from the feeling that someone has just assembled the identikit elements of a vaguely fashionable, vaguely expensive restaurant and then hoped for the best.

- **DRESS** *Ladies and gents who lunch*
- **TUBE** *South Kensington*
- **HOURS** *Lunch Mon–Sat 12.00–15.00; Sun 12.00–16.00*
  Dinner Mon–Sat 19.00–22.30; (closed Sun)
- **AVERAGE PRICE** *Lunch/Dinner £25–30*
- **CREDIT CARDS** *All major cards*
- **MOBILES** *Allowed*
- **CIGARS** *Humidor*

BUTLERS WHARF CHOP HOUSE

36e Shad Thames, London SE1 2YE
☎ 0171 403 3403

At night the view of a floodlit Tower Bridge, is so unreally glamorous that it almost looks like a movie backdrop: not unlike those New York skylines that decorate the studios of American chat shows. The Chop House is my favourite part of Sir Terence's riparian gastrodrome. This place is one of the cradles of the renaissance of British food – the steak and kidney pudding, with the option of oysters on top, is one of those dishes about which some people dream. In fact the menu is littered with dishes to tempt the anglophile palate: pork chop with herb stuffing and gravy; the excellent fillet of pork, apples, chestnuts and cider sauce; lamb and mint sausages, mash and peas; fish and chips and mushy peas. A dish like roast sea bass with thyme and tomato tart is a hearty reinterpretation of a fish I adore but that has become a nineties cliché. The menu has witty touches like an exemplary prawn cocktail (served on a bed of shredded lettuce and in a metal goblet), a list of liqueur coffees and a Black Forest gateau that bears little resemblance to the dish that languishes in the freezer compartments of a thousand dowdy supermarkets. Indeed, puddings are excellent if unashamedly calorific and are matched with useful wine suggestions. I find it hard to believe that it opened as long ago as 1993: its scrubbed wood interior still looks clean and fresh. My only cavil is that the bar tends to get noisy.

- **DRESS** *Vaguely suited*
- **TUBES** *Tower Hill; London Bridge*
- **HOURS** *Lunch Mon–Sun 12.00–15.00*
       Dinner Mon–Sat 18.00–23.00; (closed Sun)
- **AVERAGE PRICE** *Lunch £35; Dinner £40*
- **CREDIT CARDS** *All major cards*
- **MOBILES** *Allowed*
- **CIGARS** *Humidor*

CAFÉ FISH

36–40 Rupert Street, London W1
☎ 0171 287 8989

Café Fish is laid out with an informal 'canteen' downstairs and a noisy restaurant with some interesting piscatorial engravings upstairs. Clever touches such as the starting times of performances at nearby theatres chalked up on a blackboard only heighten the disappointment when the food arrives – deep-fried spiced squid with gribiche sauce seemed to have been cooked in salt and the kedgeree, while not inedible, was not the pleasure giving-comforting dish that I know, love and enjoy at Kaspia (qv). Granted, one is not paying particularly high prices, and Café Fish is probably a perfectly adequate place for a plate of fish and chips – but there are better places for this kind of food, for example, Fish at Borough Market.

- **DRESS** *Casual*
- **TUBES** *Piccadilly Circus; Leicester Square*

- **HOURS** Lunch Mon–Fri 12.00–15.00; (closed Sat–Sun)
  Dinner Mon–Fri 17.30–23.30; Sat 12.00–23.30;
  Sun 12.00–22.30
- **AVERAGE PRICE** £25–30
- **CREDIT CARDS** All major cards
- **MOBILES** Allowed
- **CIGARS** Prohbited

CAFÉ LAZEEZ
93–95 Old Brompton Road, London SW7
☎ 0171 581 9993

Despite the slightly tired-looking surroundings at Old Brompton
Road, this is still an important Indian restaurant. Café Lazeez is
one of the pioneers of modern Indian cooking and Samar Hamid
seems like a terribly pleasant man. What is more, at the end of
'98, he poached a chef from Biki Oberoi's eponymous hotel
chain in India, so one can entertain reasonably high expectations
of the place. Certainly dishes like the red mullet masala, a dish
that might sound slightly odd, is tasty. Tikka Lazeez is a starter of
either chicken cubes, or tuna, swordfish and salmon, marinated
and then bunged in the tandoor. The section of the menu entitled
'Main Course – Evolved' lists dishes that are a progression of
traditional Indian dishes, including the evocatively named Officers
Chops – lamb chops marinated in a sauce of honey, soy and
garlic and then baked. Typical of the 'evolved dishes' is tuna
steak in a sauce of onions, tomatoes, fresh ginger, cinnamon,
cloves and black cardamom – to my mind less successful than
some of the more conventional offerings. However, fried jumbo
prawn coated in vermicelli for an intriguing porcupine effect is an
interesting and successful experiment. There is a cocktail bar but
stick to Cobra or Czech Bud while you eat or order numerous
glasses of the refreshing lime and sparkling water.

- **DRESS** Blazer – the owner wears one
- **TUBE** South Kensington
- **HOURS** Mon–Sat 11.00–01.00 am; Sun 11.00–22.30
- **AVERAGE PRICE** Lunch £15–18; Dinner £20–25
- **CREDIT CARDS** All major cards
- **MOBILES** Allowed
- **CIGARS** Allowed

ALSO AT
CAFÉ CITY LAZEEZ, 88 St John Street, London EC1;
 0171 253 2224 TUBE Farringdon

CAFÉ MED

184a Kensington Park Road, London W11
☎ 0171 221 1150

Mediterranean cooking is one of those terms that has come into use in current years. To my mind such nomenclature is inexact at the best of times and ludicrously meaningless in this case. The Mediterranean is a large chunk of water: Monte Carlo and Barcelona are cities that find themselves on it, as are Tripoli and Port Said. To imply that these and other places are linked by a shared gastronomic culture any more defined than the need to eat to live is, in my view, cobblers. The Café Med chain is the *de facto* inheritor of the mantle of the wine bar – remember them? Surroundings are best described as bold, battered, and baroque. As far as food is concerned, simple predictability would seem to be Café Med's forte with generously-sized salads, pasta dishes and goats' cheese among the starters and cheesecake among the puds. The simple grills are something of a keynote and the chips come in wooden bowls almost big enough to do your washing up in.

- **DRESS** *Casual*
- **TUBE** *Earl's Court*
- **HOURS** *Mon–Sat 10.00–23.30; Sun 12.00–22.30*
- **AVERAGE PRICE** *Lunch £16; Dinner £22*
- **CREDIT CARDS** *All major cards*
- **MOBILES** *Allowed*
- **CIGARS** *Not encouraged*

ALSO AT

370 St John's Street, London EC1;
   0171 278 1199 TUBE Angel
22–25 Dean Street, London W1;
   0171 287 9007 TUBE Tottenham Court Road
320 Goldhawk Road, London W6;
   0181 741 1994 TUBE Stamford Brook
2 Hollywood Road, London SW10;
   0171 823 3355 TUBE Fulham Broadway
2 Northside Road, London SW18;
   0171 228 0914 TUBE Clapham Common
21 Loudoun Road, London NW8;
   0171 625 1222 TUBE St John's Wood

CAFÉ MILAN
312–314 King's Road, London SW3
☎ 0171 351 0101

The waiters and greeters are pleasant and pretty, the surroundings are agreeably modern and include a wood-fired pizza oven finished in a funky mosaic and a suitably decadent downstairs bar. There is even a little deli-style shop and ice-cream bar. This operation opened at the very end of 1998 and the idea of a slick-looking Italian lounge/foodstore/restaurant/bar on the King's Road should work. However, if it does, it will not be on the strength of the food, which is at best competent. There are some interesting ideas, such as the selection of the menu entitled salumeria della casa, but what might be an intriguing array of Italian meats amounts to little more than speck, Parma ham, bresaola and salami. A pasta dish of orecchiette with anchovies, broccoli and chilli boasted very few anchovies; however the waiter made a gallant case for the few specks that might have been anchovy flesh and it was agreeably highly seasoned. Spaghetti vongole was better. The list of pizzas is encouraging and they come with poppadum-thin bases. However the good idea of lobster pizza as a daily special was marred by letting the pizza stand about long enough to let the lobster flesh wrinkle and rubberise. Nevertheless the atmosphere is lively and the customers dress the part.

- **DRESS** King's Road Euro
- **TUBES** South Kensington; Sloane Square
- **HOURS** Brunch Sat–Sun 11.30–15.30; (closed Mon–Fri)
  Lunch Mon–Fri 12.00–15.00; (closed Sat–Sun)
  Dinner Mon–Sat 18.00–23.30; (closed Sun)
- **AVERAGE PRICE** Lunch/Dinner £25
- **CREDIT CARDS** All major cards
- **MOBILES** Allowed
- **CIGARS** Humidor

CAFÉ SPICE NAMASTE
16 Prescot Street, London E1
☎ 0171 488 9242

Cyrus Todiwala has a reputation as an Indian chef of note and this is something that he does not go out of his way to disguise – his agreeable mug beams out at one from the labels decorating his jars of pickle that one can buy to enjoy at home. Certainly his menu challenges traditional perceptions of the curry house, everything from wild boar to ostrich winds up being spiced up. Beside them, dishes such as Goan prawn curry seem decidedly unadventurous. Pickles too are interesting and could bring a minor sub continental revolution to one's domestic catering arrangements – cheese and swordfish pickle sandwiches anyone? The Prescot Street branch is located in what is a former law court, but it struck me as a slightly depressing, acoustically incorrect nineteenth century hall, notwithstanding the brightly-coloured banners in which the place was swathed. Given its proximity to the Square Mile, there is a tendency for the place to fill up with loud red-faced young men with loosened ties and foaming lagers. City boys might view the proximity of their ilk comforting, others might think otherwise.

- **DRESS** *South London City boy*
- **TUBES** *Aldgate East; Tower Hill*
- **HOURS** *Lunch Mon–Fri 12.00–15.00; (closed Sat–Sun)*
      Dinner Mon–Fri 18.15–22.30; Sat 18.30–22.00;
      (closed Sun)
- **AVERAGE PRICE** *Lunch/Dinner £22–25*
- **CREDIT CARDS** *All major cards*
- **MOBILES** *Allowed*
- **CIGARS** *Humidor*

ALSO AT
247 Lavender Hill, London SW11;
    0171 738 1717 TUBE Clapham Junction

CALZONE
352a King's Road, London SW3
☎ 0171 352 9790

This excellent modern pizza chain has been growing slowly in London over the last couple of years, and the newest location is near Sir Terence Conran's Bluebird complex (qv). Calzone is a slightly superior version of Pizza Express and specialises in the *calzone* (folded pizza), whereby the pizza topping, or more accurately filling, is steamed rather than scorched. I like pizzas and I like visiting Calzone, especially if hungry. The frutti di mare is particularly good and has fresh, tangy anchovies. Indeed the pizza list includes many favourites that benefit from the Calzone treatment, however with some, for example the Fiorentina (spinach and egg), it is difficult not to overcook the egg inside the calzone. Pasta dishes include some attractive offerings such as penne carpigliana (spinach, toasted pine nuts, gorgonzola and mascarpone) and it is possible to get a decent rocket and parmesan salad. Puddings are all right and there is a well thought out little children's menu. Calzone is a welcome and valid addition to a crowded sector.

- **DRESS** *Casual*
- **TUBE** *Sloane Square*
- **HOURS** *Mon–Sun 10.00–23.45*
- **AVERAGE PRICE** *Lunch/Dinner £15*
- **CREDIT CARDS** *No Diners Club*
- **MOBILES** *Allowed*
- **CIGARS** *Prohibited*

ALSO AT

2a Kensington Park Road, London W11;
   0171 243 2003   TUBE Notting Hill Gate
335 Fulham Road, London SW10;
   0171 352 9797   TUBE South Kensington
35 Upper Street, London N1;
   0171 359 9191   TUBE Angel
66 Heath Street, London NW3;
   0171 794 6775   TUBE Hampstead

CANTALOUPE
35 Charlotte Road, London EC2
☎ 0171 613 4411

One of the first of the groovy Shoredith eateries, Cantaloupe is a weird hybrid of a place that with its pub/garage/restaurant décor delivers a blast of weirdness not too far removed from the Cantina in Star Wars. Food is however recognisable as a style that is probably known as modern Mediterranean: braised squid provençale, herb & garlic roast aubergine; grilled sour dough, fried chorizo, poached egg, chilli oil; roast free-range chicken breast, pickled lemon couscous, Mediterranean salsa; chargrilled grey mullet chermoula, tabbouleh, piperade and to finish, a plate of munchego, with oat cakes and quince jelly. The surroundings may not make this the most relaxing meal, nevertheless, the place has its devotees.

- **DRESS** *Relaxed urban trendy*
- **TUBE** *Old Street*
- **HOURS** *Lunch Mon–Fri, Sun 12.00–15.00; (closed Sat)*
         Dinner Mon–Fri 18.00–23.30; Sat 19.00–23.30;
         Sun 12.00–15.00 (in the bar only)
- **AVERAGE PRICE** *Lunch/Dinner £25–30*
- **CREDIT CARDS** *No American Express*
- **MOBILES** *Allowed*
- **CIGARS** *Humidor*

THE CANTEEN

Chelsea Harbour, London SW10
☎ 0171 351 7330

If you cannot get away to St Tropez or Puerto Banus, then you can always book one of the conservatory tables at the Canteen in Chelsea Harbour, with their views of the marina. Granted the gin palaces of SW10 are nowhere near as impressive as they are on the Riviera or the Costa del Sol, but the place does have an air of cosmopolitan glamour to it, as does the design of Michael Caine and Claudio Pulze's restaurant. John Pawson would hate it. I however rather warm to the banquettes covered with playing card fabric, the forties-style French mirrors and all the other shiny bits. The place got its reputation when Marco Pierre White was running it. He is long gone, but the food by Raymond P Brown remains more than competent, with such dishes as pappardelle with field mushrooms and truffle oil and the amusing crêpe suzette soufflé, building a loyal fan club. Care has gone into the wine list with such interesting oddities as Californian Sangiovese being brought to a wider audience. Service too, run by the inimitable Bob – a sort of Eastern European Jeeves who used to work at Riva (qv) – is friendly and knowledgeable. When Caine is in residence at Chelsea Harbour, the place apparently fills up with his celebrity chums.

- **DRESS** *Chelsea Harbour*
- **TUBES** *Earls Court; Fulham Broadway*
- **HOURS** *Lunch Mon–Fri 12.00–15.00; (closed Sat–Sun)*
        Dinner Mon–Fri 18.30–23.00; Sat 18.30–24.00
        (closed Sun)
- **AVERAGE PRICE** *Lunch £25–30; Dinner £35–40*
- **CREDIT CARDS** *No Diners Club*
- **MOBILES** *Allowed*
- **CIGARS** *Humidor*

CANTINA DEL PONTE

Butlers Wharf Building, Shad Thames, London SE1
☎ 0171 403 5403

I still have the letter that Sir Terence Conran fired off when I first reviewed Cantina del Ponte. Most of it was taken up defending his then henchman Joel Kissin. As a 'PS' he added, 'I do think that if you were to look again at the menu, you would feel that you have wrongly described Cantina as a pizzeria or a pizza and pasta restaurant.' As I look at the menu a couple of years later, there is other stuff: Tuscan bean soup; chargrilled vegetable bruschetta; roast mackerel crostini; osso bucco; roast dorade; grilled tuna and collateral dishes to bear out the legend 'Mediterranean food and wine' that runs along the bottom of the menu. However I am not someone who thinks or believes pizzeria to be a pejorative term. A good pizza is a great thing. I would like to write the definitive guide to pizza, I have eaten pizza in Rome, in the Alpes Maritimes and even in the Dominican Republic. But back to Cantina. It has to be said that the list of pizzas seems to owe something to the Cal-Ital school of cooking, for example: spiced chorizo sausage; asparagus and goats' cheese; marinated swordfish, tomato, oregano and pecorino. The dough however is not always perfect. Nevertheless, the Cantina is a jolly, and relatively inexpensive, if noisy, place to visit.

- **DRESS** *Casual*
- **TUBES** *Tower Hill; London Bridge*
- **HOURS** *Lunch Mon–Sun 12.00–15.00*
  Dinner Mon–Sat 18.00–23.00; Sun 18.00–22.00
- **AVERAGE PRICE** *Lunch £25; Dinner £30*
- **CREDIT CARDS** *All credit cards*
- **MOBILES** *Allowed*
- **CIGARS** *Humidor*

CANYON

Riverside, Richmond, Surrey TW10 (near Richmond Bridge)
☎ 0181 948 2944

Canyon is a sibling of the terribly trendy Dakota (qv) and its mission is apparently to bring modern restaurant methods to Richmond. It is all cool, pale and modern with the coat-check person storing one's outergarment in zip-up body bags that make it a little difficult to tell whose clothes are where, when it is time to go home. The menu is unabashedly fashion-conscious and seems to delight in obscure nomenclature. On my first visit, the charming if slightly chummy waiter, said that there would be plenty of strange words on the menu and he was right. How about banana leaf wrapped kingsnapper; yucatan marinade; pineapple chipotle salsa; oaxacan lentil salad? Other dishes are simpler to deconstruct, witness chargrilled Iowa rib eye of beef, duo of potato gratin, cinammon jus, caramelized shallots; wood-smoked spring chicken, adobo rub, citrus glaze, herb-cracked wheat salad. The upside of the upmarket Tex-Mexicanisation of the food is genuinely intriguing confections such as ceviche of scallops, tortilla wedges, avocado cream, tomato citrus salsa; roasted rack of lamb with a pecan mustard crust, jalapeno and mint jelly, and roast corn chipotle mash. The downside is that many things seem to arrive blackened in some way or other, which I find tedious after a while. The wine list is compiled under headings like 'Crisp Clean and Elegant' and 'Medium-bodied and Moderately oaked' with a strong leaning to the New World, hence the appearance of such wines as Bonny Doon Pacific Rim Dry Riesling.

- **DRESS** *Thirty-something suburban trendy*
- **TUBE** *Richmond*
- **HOURS** *Mon–Fri 10.30–23.30; Sat 9.00–23.30; Sun 9.00–22.30*
- **AVERAGE PRICE** *Lunch £20; Dinner £34*
- **CREDIT CARDS** *No Diners Club*
- **MOBILES** *Allowed*
- **CIGARS** *Humidor*

LE CAPRICE
Arlington House, Arlington Street, London SW1
☎ 0171 629 2239

Le Caprice and its sister establishment the Ivy (qv) crop up on everyone's list of favourite London restaurants. It is almost a convention amongst restaurateurs, food critics and anyone else keen to demonstrate their conversancy with the London restaurant scene, to rhapsodise about Jeremy King, Chris Corbin and their preternatural skill as restaurateurs. Although little has changed in appearance since its brief ownership by the fashion retailer Joseph Ettedgui in the early eighties, Le Caprice is always the fashionable place to lunch. Customers include MPs, thespians, pop stars, authors and the late Saint Diana. The reasons for its sustained success are simple to identify, if difficult to replicate. Service is usually faultless to the point of being psychic. Almost every customer tends to be known by name and treated as the most important person in the room. The menu is sufficiently fashionable as to reassure customers that they are being kept abreast of culinary trends while also offering delicious chips, Caesar salad, chopped steak Americain (hamburger) and the finest fish cake in the civilised world. Prices are not as rapacious as they might be. During service either one or other of the owners tend to tour the restaurant and engage in conversation if appropriate. The constant attention of Jesus the delightful Bolivian maitre d' and his evening counterpart Angelo (also Bolivian) that ensure continued excellence.

- **DRESS** *Smart*
- **TUBE** *Green Park*
- **HOURS** *Lunch Mon–Sat 12.00–15.00; Sun 12.00–15.30*
        Dinner Mon–Sun 17.30–24.00
- **AVERAGE PRICE** *Lunch/Dinner £35*
- **CREDIT CARDS** *All major cards*
- **MOBILES** *Not encouraged*
- **CIGARS** *Allowed*

CAVE
161 Piccadilly, London W1
☎ 0171 409 0445

People have said many clever things about caviar over the years, but the one that springs to my mind, was uttered by Tatler's former restaurant critic, Rory Ross. Ross's thoughts went along the lines that rich people do not like to chew and this is why foods requiring little mastication are so expensive: foie gras is of course one and caviar is of course another. If you want to drop well over 1500 quid on 125 g of Almas caviar (served with blinis, sour cream and Jersey potatoes), then you will be made most welcome at Cave. With its ostrich egg chandeliers and large tanks of bubbling water suspended in the windows, this Piccadilly outpost of the Caviar House empire does not pander to olde worlde notions of the pomp and pageantry that attend caviar consumption. It is light, bright and well-located for that restorative dollop of beluga or that lobster salad with black truffle dressing that is so necessary after a heavy morning shopping on Bond Street. Cave sells seven types of caviar – as a man of simple tastes, I am quite happy with a large tin of sevruga – and operates a prix fixe lunch menu (mousse of crab with Mediterranean prawns and white asparagus; grilled tuna with crispy baby squid and ratatouille). Dinner is priced à la carte and offers slightly more elaborate dishes. As well as sturgeon roe, Caviar House also offers Balik salmon: this is smoked by Hans Gerd Kubel in Switzerland's Toggenburg mountains, in a style that allegedly used to be enjoyed by the Tsars. The best is the Tsar Nikolaj fillet, served in little medallions. The wine list is almost entirely French and not too steep provided you steer clear of Cristal, DP, Corton Charlemagne, Petrus and La Tache. On the way in – and out – one passes through a smart little corner shop selling caviar, vodka, foie gras, fine wine, all manner of caviar-serving implements and countless other essentials.

- **DRESS** *As you would for a shopping binge on Bond Street*
- **TUBE** *Green Park*
- **HOURS** *Lunch Mon–Sat 12.00–15.00; (closed Sun)*
     Dinner Mon–Sat 19.00–22.30; (closed Sun)
- **AVERAGE PRICE** *Lunch £25–40; Dinner £50–60*
- **CREDIT CARDS** *All major cards*
- **MOBILES** *Allowed*
- **CIGARS** *Humidor*

CHADA THAI
16–17 Picton Place, London W1
☎ 0171 935 8212

There is immense charm about this husband and wife-run operation. The original Chada Thai nestles in the shadow of a monolithic towerblock and if you are interested in studying the variety of net curtains that can be displayed over a dozen or two storeys of brutalist concrete, come for lunch and ask for a window table. Other attractions include the opportunity to spot Tatler's social editor, the fragrant Marchioness of Milfordhaven, who often pops in for a take-away curry to bolster the strength of her polo-playing marquess. The charming and caring service aside, the food is also memorably good. If you are undecided about starters, there is a combination platter that offers a variety of the generally exemplary first courses. Curries are delicious and other dishes worth ordering are the invigorating phud phed talay (mixed seafood cooked in red chilli curry paste with bamboo shoot and lime leaves) and the priew wharn pla (cod fillet topped with onion, cucumber, tomato, pineapple, green and red pepper and spring onion in a sweet and sour sauce). Chada Thai also has an interesting way with vegetables: for example, broccoli and oyster sauce. The Central London outpost offers a quicker, more metropolitan pace of lunch than the rather stately progress through the midday repast in SW11.

- **DRESS** *Casual*
- **TUBE** *Bond Street*
- **HOURS** *Lunch Mon–Sat 12.00–15.00; (closed Sun)*
     Dinner Mon–Sat 18.00–23.00; (closed Sun)
- **AVERAGE PRICE** *Lunch £10; Dinner £20*
- **CREDIT CARDS** *All major cards*
- **MOBILES** *Allowed*
- **CIGARS** *Allowed*

ALSO AT
CHADA THAI CUISINE, 208–210 Battersea Park Road, London SW11; 0171 622 2209 RAIL Battersea Park

CHAPTER TWO
43–45 Montpelier Vale, Blackheath Village, London SE3
☎ 0181 333 2666

Any restaurant that actually bills itself as a 'modern European restaurant' on its awning, is I feel, asking for it. Chapter Two is apparently the sister restaurant to the 'award winning' Chapter One, of Locksbottom, near Bromley in Kent. As regards the design of the Chapter Two, it is a sufficiently competent clone of many a modern London restaurant and the majority of tables do not seem to suffer overly from being located in a basement accessed by a spiral staircase. The food, for instance, sea bass, foie gras mash, and leek fritters is the sort of thing that might once have seemed innovative and out here, on the very borders of London, maybe it still is. Light and dark breads presented with a flourish are made with olive oil and treacle respectively. Service is of a high standard and dishes are well presented. However both the salmon confit, crab risotto, baby spinach and maize-fed chicken, sweetbread, morels (shredded almost out of existence) and fondant potato, were judged to be so delicately flavoured as to be nearly tasteless. Who knows? Perhaps this is what the smart inhabitants of Blackheath, many of whom seemed to be thoroughly enjoying themselves, want from a restaurant: smart décor, good service, a good, well-priced wine list and food that sounds good but does not offend with obtrusive flavours.

- **DRESS** *Dreaded smart casual*
- **RAIL** *Blackheath Village*
- **HOURS** *Lunch Mon–Sat 12.00–14.30; Sun 12.00–15.30*
       Dinner Mon–Sat 18.30–22.30; Sun 18.30–21.30
- **AVERAGE PRICE** *Lunch/Dinner £20–25*
- **CREDIT CARDS** *All major cards*
- **MOBILES** *Allowed*
- **CIGARS** *Prohibited*

CHE
23 St James's Street, London SW1
☎ 0171 747 9380

A friend of mine who toils on the wildest frontiers of the information prairie setting up web sites and so on almost got it right when he said 'Some German clients took us to Che – I bet it cost them a packet.' To be fair, this place can be as cheap or as expensive as you want – for the West End. Che is located in a culturally important piece of sixties architecture next to the Economist. It was set up by a suave reformed rake, Michael

Naylor Neyland, for a charming, young entrepreneur and cigar-enthusiast called Hani Farsi. On the food side, the formula can be described as chips to caviar punctuated by the sort of dishes popular in modern millenial London: Thai spiced tiger prawns; Caesar salad; scrambled eggs with truffles; seared tuna steak with soy ginger and garlic dressing and bok choy; roast lobster; calf's liver; Thai green chicken curry; steak and kidney pudding; bangers and mash; sticky toffee pudding and so on. While competent, the food has been criticised for being too polyglot. Where the place really scores is on the cigar and booze front – the ground floor is divided into two rooms, in the front is a well-stocked bar with some of the most eccentric and expensive bourbons and tequilas that I have ever seen. One wall of the back room is a glass-fronted humidor, behind which are stacked boxes and boxes of cigars. The regular list covers most sizes of most Cuban marques and is impressive enough for a restaurant. But the list of historic cigars is outstanding: Henry Clay petit coronas from before the thirties, pre-Embargo Montecristos, a good selection of cigars from the sixties and seventies, and some of the fabled Davidoff Chateau series from Cuba. Although cashing in on the popularity of cigars in recent years, this is the best and least cynical cigar-oriented restaurant I have yet encountered in London; I very much doubt that it will be bettered on that score. In its early days the place was still finding its feet and lacked a little sparkle, but it would be good to see it succeed.

- **DRESS** *Suits and cigars*
- **TUBE** *Green Park*
- **HOURS** *Lunch Mon–Fri 12.00–15.00; (closed Sat–Sun)*
  Dinner Mon–Sat 17.30–23.30; (closed Sun)
- **AVERAGE PRICE** *Lunch £35; Dinner £45*
- **CREDIT CARDS** *All major cards*
- **MOBILES** *Allowed*
- **CIGARS** *Humidor*

CHEZ BRUCE

2 Bellevue Road, London SW17
☎ 0181 672 0114

Bruce Poole has become famous for offering a West End level of cooking in a suburban, well Wandsworth, setting. The grande assiette de charcuterie is a dish of renown; roast cod with olive oil mash rarely comes off the menu; the grilled sea bass with seafood salsa, a summer dish, is a clever idea and well executed; while at the other end of the seasonal spectrum is roast guinea fowl with braised leeks and Béarnaise sauce. Ballotine of chicken with foie gras and onion confit is a typical starter and a dish of potato and egg ravioli with fontina and pancetta shows that Bruce's influences are not exclusively French. The hot chocolate pudding with praline parfait remains on the menu constantly and Bruce is proud of his cheeseboard. The room itself is nothing special to look at but boasts a bizarre beamed bit of ceiling. In fact the only interesting thing about the site, is that it was the location of Harvey's, Marco Pierre White's first place.

- **DRESS** *Rugger club v-necks give way to blazers and ties*
- **RAIL** *Wandsworth Common*
- **HOURS** *Lunch Mon–Fri 12.00–14.00; Sat 12.30–14.30; (closed Sun)*
  Dinner Mon–Sat 19.00–22.30; (closed Sun)
- **AVERAGE PRICE** *Lunch £30–35; Dinner £45–50*
- **CREDIT CARDS** *All major cards*
- **MOBILES** *Allowed*
- **CIGARS** *Prohibited*

CHEZ GERARD
8 Charlotte Street, London W1
☎ 0171 636 4975

This ever-expanding chain of themed and allegedly French steakhouses, where steak 'n' chips is called steak frites, is the mainstay of the great Laurence Isaacson's mid-market restaurant empire. Chez Gerard is not particularly French, instead it is run rather as a chain of étapes for carnivores. If a decent steak, competent chips, lashings of Béarnaise and a bottle or two of perfectly palatable French red wine are what you want from a restaurant, then you probably have a favourite table at your local Chez Gerard already. I mean it is a compliment that these are the Berni Inns of the new millenium. More recent examples, such as the Roseberry Avenue branch, have been given the attentions of a trendy interior designer called David Collins. The well-located Chez Gerard at the Opera Terrace becomes crowded in the warm weather. Most of them seem to exist to serve lunch to middle management on expenses.

- **DRESS** *As you would at the office*
- **TUBES** *Tottenham Court Road; Goodge Street*
- **HOURS** *Lunch Mon–Fri 12.00–15.00; Sun 12.00–15.00; (closed Sat)*
  Dinner Mon–Sun 18.00–23.30
- **AVERAGE PRICE** *Lunch/Dinner £15–25*

- **CREDIT CARDS** *All major cards*
- **MOBILES** *Allowed*
- **CIGARS** *Allowed*

ALSO AT

THE OPERA TERRACE, The Market, The Piazza, London WC2;
    0171 379 0666 TUBE Covent Garden
119 Chancery Lane, London WC2;
    0171 405 0290 TUBE Chancery Lane
84–86 Rosebery Avenue, London EC1;
    0171 833 1515 TUBES Angel; Farringdon
64 Bishopsgate, London EC2;
    0171 588 1200 TUBE Liverpool Street
14 Trinity Square, London EC3;
    0171 480 5500 TUBE Tower Hill
31 Dover Street, London W1;
    0171 499 8171 TUBE Green Park
3 Yeoman's Row, London SW3;
    0171 581 8377 TUBE South Kensington

CHEZ MOI

1 Addison Avenue, London W11
☎ 0171 603 8267

Chez Moi has been a part of the Holland Park landscape for
more than three decades. This year it scooped a Carlton
Restaurant Award for the quality of its host, Colin Smith. The
video clip that accompanied the bestowal of this award was a
spectacularly saccharine reconstruction of a proposal of marriage
– which should give you some idea about the kind of place that
this is. Typical dishes include: spinach and chicken liver salad;
quails' eggs in hollandaise sauce; Japanese seared scallops with
futo-maki rolls; rack of lamb à la diable; Thai chicken, and grilled
oriental sea bass with pak-choy braised in oyster sauce.

- **DRESS** *Camp; smart*
- **TUBE** *Holland Park*
- **HOURS** *Lunch Mon–Fri 12.30–14.00; (closed Sat–Sun)*
       Dinner Mon–Sat 19.00–23.00; (closed Sun)
- **AVERAGE PRICE** *Lunch/Dinner £35*
- **CREDIT CARDS** *All major cards*
- **MOBILES** *Allowed*
- **CIGARS** *Prohibited*

CHEZ NICO

Ninety Park Lane, London W1
☎ 0171 409 1290

This is the way traditional Michelin-starred fine dining ought to
be: an understated room, subdued yet formal well-judged service,
and well-flavoured excellent food. The set menus can offer really
good value. But what is special about the place is the sense of a
solid, 24 carat reliability that makes it a little like the restaurant
world's riposte to the Rolls Royce – comfortable, traditional, well-
engineered and reassuring in every way, including the price.
And as with the Rolls Royce, there is the suspicion that some
people come to Chez Nico to be able to show that they can
afford it – but where's the harm in that? The lobster ravioli, more
of a raviolo or pasta covered lump of lobster flesh, was a triumph
of deceptively casual construction and intensity of flavour, that
defies proper description. Seared fillet of sea bass with basil-
flavoured pomme purée with confit of fennel was almost as
good – and that is saying a lot. And the intoxicating aromas
of a dish of breast of corn-fed chicken with wild mushroom
sauce and ravioli of foie gras were a rich and sustaining repast
in themselves. There is a confidence about Chez Nico that one
rarely sees outside France.

- **DRESS** *Suits*
- **TUBES** *Marble Arch; Hyde Park*
- **HOURS** *Lunch Mon–Fri 12.00–14.00; (closed Sat–Sun)*
  Dinner Mon–Sat 19.00–23.00; (closed Sun)
- **AVERAGE PRICE** *Lunch £25–40; Dinner £50–75*
- **CREDIT CARDS** *All major cards*
- **MOBILES** *With consideration*
- **CIGARS** *Humidor*

CHINA JAZZ

12 Berkeley Square, London W1
☎ 0171 499 9933

There is something highly enjoyable, if not kitsch, about China
Jazz; it is a sort of themed restaurant for adults. The theme is art
deco ocean liner, movie set Shanghai of the twenties or thirties or
something like that. The Berkeley Square entrance with its fake
silk flames, theatrical entrance hall and ornamental fish pond set
the scene. The dining room has no natural light, but is panelled
in reflective glass so it looks as though it is a couple of hundred
yards long; waiters hover in white tie and a songstress warbles

away. Customers are not required to wear evening dress, but dark suits are mandatory for men, although, apparently, lighter suits are tolerated in the summer. Sake comes in decanters so ornate that one half expects a genie to pop out of the top, but most people drink cocktails with names like the Scoundrel. Food is obviously not the most thing important here, but it is nice enough. It pays to pick starters with care, for example, skewers of prawns and scallops: two skewers, two prawns and two scallops might be judged to be a little parsimonious – especially for the prices. Main courses tend to do better, for example, wild sea bass wrapped in lotus leaves, baked in sea salt, served with French beans and noodles is an interesting idea. Lamb cutlets barbecued with fresh mint and a selection of spices served with straw mushrooms and asparagus is the sort of dish that Lord Lucan (a notorious lamb cutlet fan) might have liked in one of his more adventurous moments. Sunday night is Salsa night (£6 entrance fee).

- **DRESS** *Dark suits mandatory*
- **TUBE** *Green Park*
- **HOURS** *Lunch Mon–Fri 12.00–14.30; (closed Sat–Sun)*
        Dinner Mon–Sat 18.00–23.30; Sun 18.00–24.00
- **AVERAGE PRICE** *Lunch/Dinner £30–£50*
- **CREDIT CARDS** *All major cards*
- **MOBILES** *Not allowed*
- **CIGARS** *Humidor*

CHOR BIZARRE
16 Albemarle Street, London W1
☎ 0171 629 9802

Chor Bizarre and it is. If this looks like a sub continental riposte to Steptoe's Yard, then that is the idea: apparently a Chor bazaar is an Indian thieves' market and this Indian restaurant's eclectic décor is the distillation of numerous Indian flea markets. Almost everything is for sale and it is just my luck that the pair of wall sconces I fancied were too tightly bolted to the wall. Chor Bizarre is supposed to be something of a legend in New Delhi – never having visited I would find it difficult to verify, but the Mayfair branch seems to have established a reasonably loyal following. What is more, when salmon tikka is described as 'velvety morsels of salmon flavoured with a unique blend of royal cumin and herbs', it is fairly near the truth – they really are velvety and very moreish. Much ado is made about the thalis and these multi-

course platters are generous in scale, offering a good way of
sampling numerous dishes. The kerala prawn curry is delicious.
In fact the only cavil I have is that breads were not the best. Now
about those sconces...

- **DRESS** *Impossible to compete with the décor so don't even try*
- **TUBE** *Green Park*
- **HOURS** *Lunch Mon–Sun 12.00–15.00*
        Dinner Mon–Sat 18.00–23.30; Sun 18.00–22.30
- **AVERAGE PRICE** *Lunch/Dinner £28*
- **CREDIT CARDS** *All major cards*
- **MOBILES** *Not allowed*
- **CIGARS** *Allowed*

CHRISTOPHER'S THE AMERICAN GRILL
18 Wellington Street, London WC2
☎ 0171 240 4222

The Hon. Christopher Gilmour is the kind of man who gives toffs
a good name. Kind and jovial to the point of being a soft touch,
Gilmour has made this agreeably un-American restaurant
something of a London landmark. The restaurant sprawls over
three floors with a basement bar, a ground floor restaurant and
a splendid first floor dining room. Christopher used to trade pork
bellies and soy beans on the Chicago Futures Exchanges, but
became a restaurateur after eating in one too many East Coast
steak and lobster houses. The menu reflects the culinary genre
that inspired him, with a splendid array of different cuts of steak
(favourites are the blackened rib-eye and the 14oz New York
strip), lobsters from Maine and such stateside classics as
Maryland crab cakes, served with a red pepper mayo. However,
in its six years, Christopher's has developed its own classics
including, the lobster cobb salad, the warm lobster carpaccio and
the lobster coleslaw. On the whole, the dishes are commendably
simple, and along the lines of: swordfish with tomato and
angostura sauce; buttermilk fried sole with lemon mash and caper
aioli. At any one time, there are at least four dozen wines and
Champagnes by the glass and, as is fitting, there is a strong
emphasis on the New World.

- **DRESS** *Suits*
- **TUBE** *Covent Garden*
- **HOURS** *Lunch Mon–Sat 12.00–15.00; Sun 11.30–17.00*
        Dinner Mon–Sat 18.00–23.30; (closed Sun)

- **AVERAGE PRICE** Lunch/Dinner £35
- **CREDIT CARDS** All major cards
- **MOBILES** Not encouraged
- **CIGARS** Humidor

CHUTNEY MARY
535 King's Road, London SW10
☎ 0171 351 3113

When it opened almost ten years ago, Chutney Mary was presented as an Anglo-Indian restaurant. Back then, things like Jewel in the Crown were a part of the zeitgeist and dishes like Hill Station bread and butter pudding mixed nostalgic patriotism with a liking for Indian food. The term Chutney Mary referred to Indian women who copied English mores. As the years have passed, Chutney Mary has moved towards being a more straightforward Indian restaurant, leaning towards unusual regional dishes. Typical of the intriguing dishes that gather on the menu are green chicken curry from Goa; masala roast lamb shank (an Anglo-Indian speciality – slow-roasted in a curry of Goan spices); roast duck curry (Syrian Christian in origin from Kerala with coconut, tamarind and chilli) or mangalore prawn curry. 'The food is rarely found in restaurants even in India' trumpets Chutney Mary's propaganda, 'It is from gourmet homes, Maharajas' palaces and humble wayside stalls.' If, like me, you do not find the idea of eating at an Indian wayside stall overly appealing, do not worry, there cannot be many street vendors in India who can boast the talents of Eddie Khoo. Khoo is the man who raises Chutney Mary from being a good Indian restaurant to an outstanding one. Khoo is a man who will fearlessly recommend a 1982 Cheval Blanc to go with a curry and what is more he will be right – he is a genius. Under his aegis, Chutney Mary has consolidated its reputation and a new upper dining room has replaced the old verandah bar, cheering up the entrance floor of this otherwise anodyne complex of shops just up the road from Chelsea Harbour.

- **DRESS** Informal
- **TUBE** Fulham Broadway
- **HOURS** Lunch Mon–Sat 12.30–14.30; Sun 12.30–15.00
        Dinner Mon–Sat 19.00–23.15; Sun 19.00–22.15
- **AVERAGE PRICE** Lunch £25; Dinner £35
- **CREDIT CARDS** All major cards
- **MOBILES** Allowed
- **CIGARS** Permitted in the lounge

CICADA
132–136 St John Street, London EC1
☎ 0171 608 1550

Cicada opened in the Spring of 1997 in fashionable Clerkenwell and was therefore uniquely situated, both temporally and geographically, to surf the wave of Cool Britannia that washed over the capital. Cicada is the creation of Will Ricker (Great Eastern Dining Room), a man who in his own quiet way seems to be taking over much of this allegedly trendy part of town. The style of cooking here could loosely be described as Thai with influences from Vietnam to Japan. As at the Great Eastern Dining Room (qv), there is a £10.00 ceiling on dishes, which shows that interesting and tasty food can be had on a budget. Crispy duck salad with sweet fish sauce, cashews and watermelon is a witty idea and the sweet fish sauce makes another appearance in a side dish of quails' eggs. Here and there, such Eastern staples as salmon teriyaki and beef rendang make a reassuring appearance. Puddings range from the refreshing Cicada sorbet to fresh fruit to the indulgent chocolate and lemon grass brulée. This being trendy Clerkenwell, expect none of the odd Asian surroundings that manage to make so many restaurants look like a set for the local dramatic society's village performance of *The King and I*. Instead, a modern look with a large bar make it relaxed, if at times a little self-consciously fashionable.

- **DRESS** *Trendy*
- **TUBE** *Farringdon*
- **HOURS** *Lunch Mon–Fri 12.00–15.00; (closed Sat–Sun)*
        Dinner Mon–Sat 18.00–23.00; (closed Sun)
- **AVERAGE PRICE** *Lunch/Dinner £25*
- **CREDIT CARDS** *All major cards*
- **MOBILES** *Allowed*
- **CIGARS** *Allowed*

CIRCUS
Restaurant & Bar, 1 Upper James Street, London W1
☎ 0171 534 4000

The only really circus-like thing about this Soho sibling of the Avenue (qv) is that it was designed by a man called Chipperfield. Chipperfield has eschewed the fun and gaudiness of the big top and has created a cool and airy space with lots of glass, dark wood and soft light. It is a competent exercise in the identikit-style of restaurant minimalism. The menu is what might loosely be called modern British (but so might so many things). The food is good, and typical dishes include pan-fried risotto with smoked haddock and soft poached egg; seared salmon with mustard leaves and potato salad; roast quail with poached pear in mulled wine; seared tuna with wakame and cucumber with soy dressing; roast rabbit leg with lentils and braised cabbage and chicken breast wrapped in prosciutto with morels and leek mash. Puddings might run from raspberry tart to banana cannelloni with pecan nuts and butterscotch sauce. Those on the sauce of a different kind will be interested by the 'Christie's at Circus' collection of fine wines acquired from the illustrious auctioneer's wine sales. And for an evening of hedonism, there is a handsome and well-stocked membership bar in the basement.

- **DRESS** *Modern*
- **TUBE** *Piccadilly Circus*
- **HOURS** *Lunch Mon–Sat 12.00–15.00; (closed Sun)*
  Dinner Mon–Sat 18.00–24.00; (closed Sun)
- **AVERAGE PRICE** *Lunch/Dinner £35*
- **CREDIT CARDS** *All major cards*
- **MOBILES** *Discouraged*
- **CIGARS** *Humidor*

CITY RHODES
New Street Square, London EC4
☎ 0171 583 1313

This branch of the Rhodes empire is a shrine to the cult of the personality that encumbers modern cooking – Rhodes's books are on sale at the coat check and arty pics of the spikey-haired cheeky chappie adorn the walls of the place. The restaurant is on the first floor of a modern building and seems to have borrowed heavily from the visual lexicon of Coast (qv). The food is good and rather lighter than that on offer at Rhodes in the Square (qv). A cappuccino of artichokes as an amuse-bouche put one in exactly the right mood and the rest did not disappoint: caramelised shallot tart with a red wine butter was a good dish, warm escalope of smoked salmon on a crispy potato cake with a bitter lemon and caper dressing was better. Typical of main courses are steamed goujons of sole with a mustard and tarragon cream sauce and lightly steamed lobster casserole. However when it comes to puddings, Rhodes or his pastry chef pile on the calories with bread and butter pudding, sticky cranberry and walnut tart with vanilla ice cream and warm apple strudel with apple and butterscotch ice cream.

- **DRESS** *Suits*
- **TUBE** *Chancery Lane*
- **HOURS** *Lunch Mon–Fri 12.00–14.30; (closed Sat–Sun)*
  Dinner Mon–Fri 18.00–21.00; (closed Sat–Sun)
- **AVERAGE PRICE** *Lunch/Dinner £50–60*
- **CREDIT CARDS** *All major cards*
- **MOBILES** *Not allowed*
- **CIGARS** *Prohibited*

CLARIDGE'S
Brook Street, Mayfair, London W1
☎ 0171 629 8860

If Dame Barbara Cartland were a restaurant, she would be Claridge's. In the past I have enjoyed service that might have been amusing elsewhere, but which in Claridge's was downright impertinent. However, when I last went, in the company of the amusing aesthete and spear fisherman Yann Debelle de Montby, things seemed much improved. Debelle de Montby is a regular and the service accorded to us and our charming female companion was exemplary, as was the food. Starters are called Préludes and include a most agreeable salad of Cornish lobster and lime-dressed crab with roquette and asperla cream, while a more traditional, and less expensive way of consuming shellfish is the lobster bisque with Armaganac. In season, expect such things as pressed game and wild mushroom terrine with bramble and port wine jelly and roast breast of grouse with savoury pear tourte and pine jus. Nor is Claridge's afraid of putting tournedos rossini or chateaubriand on the menu. However when faced with such surroundings, liveried flunkies, cloches and everything else, I experience a powerful Pavlovian urge to order grilled Dover sole. Other than lunch, I am told that breakfast is well worth getting up for and I can highly recommend tea. In fact it could be said that Claridge's, with the sound of old Vienna being pumped out by a vaguely Ruritanian quartet is the finest venue for afternoon tea in the West End. I once brought Mademoiselle Colban, proprietress of Charvet, here for a mid-afternoon cuppa and she was fascinated by the Battenberg cake. And although I mourn the passing of the Causerie, its replacement cocktail bar, designed by David Collins, is a good spot for an early evening sharpener.

- **DRESS** *Smart*
- **TUBE** *Bond Street*

- **HOURS** *Breakfast Mon–Sat 7.00–10.30; Sun 8.00–11.00*
  Lunch Mon–Sun 12.30–15.15
  Tea Mon–Sun 15.00–17.30
  Dinner Mon–Sun 19.00–23.15
- **CREDIT CARDS** *All major cards*
- **AVERAGE PRICE** *Lunch/Dinner £50–55*
- **MOBILES** *Discouraged*
- **CIGARS** *Humidor*

CLARKE'S
124 Kensington Church Street, London W8
☎ 0171 221 9225

I have never agreed with the idea of a restaurant that dictates one's choices, but there are obviously plenty of people who adore being told what to eat as the continuing success of Sally Clarke's eponymous restaurant amply demonstrates. There is but one choice of menu. Sally Clarke brought Cal-Ital food to England and so started the evolution of a gastronomic strand that has formed an important part of what is now broadly known as Modern British. I would avoid eating at Clarke's for the reason I have stated above, however it is an important gastronomic site. But, I am a great fan of & Clarke's – the neighbouring café, delicatessen, bakery and wineshop. & Clarke's is a sort of Tesco Metro for *bien pensant* rich people, and is home to the smartest bread queues in London. On a Saturday morning *le tout* Notting Hill Gate, or at least that well-off bit of it that thinks it matters, comes here for coffee, cheeses, oils, rice, pre-ordered savoury tarts to take home for lunch, slices of tasty lopsided Cal-Ital pizzas to eat in, croissants, coffee, varietal apple juices and so on. I am sure that part of the reason for the outrageous cost of property in Notting Hill is due to the proximity of & Clarke's.

- **DRESS** *Smart relaxed and affluent*
- **TUBE** *Notting Hill Gate*
- **HOURS** *Lunch Mon–Fri 12.30–14.00; (closed Sat–Sun)*
  Dinner Mon–Fri 19.00–22.00; (closed Sat–Sun)
- **AVERAGE PRICE** *Lunch £40; Dinner £50*
- **CREDIT CARDS** *All major cards*
- **MOBILES** *Not allowed*
- **CIGARS** *Not allowed*

CAFE/BAKERY/DELI/SHOP AT
& CLARKES, 122 Kensington Church Street, London W8;
   0171 229 2190 TUBE Notting Hill Gate

THE CLERKENWELL

73 Clerkenwell Road, London EC1
☎ 0171 831 7595

This was one of the earlier examples of a fashionable Clerkenwell eatery; its hard-edged interior is wearing well and I have heard good reports of the food served here. So it was rather sad that my companion described the roast chicken broth with leeks julienne, vermicelli and poached egg as one of the most unpleasant soups he had ever consumed. And even though I am notoriously loath to say anything too detrimental, on the grounds that I could scarcely do better myself, the allegedly poached quail egg looked decidedly hardboiled. Nevertheless, we did arrive right at the end of the lunchtime service and this might have had something to do with a less than perfect soup. A dish of ravioli of salmon dressed with lobster meat and dill was correctly al dente and perfectly acceptable. Among those dishes that regulars apparently seldom allow to leave the menu are pan-fried calves' liver and chargrilled tuna (the latter served with a cassoulet of cannellini beans, aubergine and fennel relish).

- **DRESS** *Casual*
- **TUBES** *Farringdon; Chancery Lane*
- **HOURS** *Lunch Mon–Fri 12.00–15.00; (closed Sat–Sun) Dinner (from December 1999) Mon–Fri 18.00–23.00; (closed Sat–Sun)*
- **AVERAGE PRICE** *Lunch/Dinner £25*
- **CREDIT CARDS** *All major cards*
- **MOBILES** *Allowed*
- **CIGARS** *Prohibited*

CLUB GASCON

57 West Smithfield, London EC1
☎ 0171 253 5853

This was the restaurant that *le tout Londres* was raving about at the end of 1998. As the name suggests, and the rather flowery prose (all about romance food and France) on the back of the menu hammers home, this place is about the food of south west France, straying down into the Pays Basque and up into Bordeaux. Expect stacks of foie gras, especially as one of the partners is Vinvent Labeyrie, scion of the celebrated foie gras dynasty. The room is charming, an old Lyons Corner House with what I am told are listed marble walls, but one would have to be a complete heathen to want to rip them out. Prices are decidedly reasonable, so reasonable in fact that it was alleged that Nigel

Platts Martin of the Square (qv) was heard to say something along the lines of 'put your prices up or we'll all go out of business'. The atmosphere is a lot less sepulchral than at, say, the Square, but the food is sensational. Duck foie gras comes in about half a dozen different ways and goose gets a cameo role with charmingly-named tatin of goose foie gras with surprising turnips. Dishes like the crispy smoked eel and horseradish cream and turbot in seaweed sauce and delight of potatoes (mash to you and me) deserve not be overlooked and the selection of dishes from the market, scribbled on the main carte in pencil, repay deciphering. For those who like their food dead simple and trad, start with farmhouse jambon de Bayonne and then move on to the old-fashioned cassoulet Toulousain. If you order pudding only once, make it the original recipe almond pie from M Duclos which is served with a small cup of freshly squeezed apple juice. Finish with an Armagnac or two from the short but interesting list and then go home for a lie down.

- **DRESS** *Suity or foodie*
- **TUBE** *Barbican*
- **HOURS** *Lunch Mon–Fri 12.00–14.00; (closed Sat–Sun)*
      Dinner Mon–Sat 19.00–22.00; (closed Sun)
- **AVERAGE PRICE** *Lunch/Dinner £20–30*
- **CREDIT CARDS** *No Diners Club*
- **MOBILES** *Allowed*
- **CIGARS** *Humidor*

COAST

26b Albemarle Street, London W1
☎ 0171 495 2999

Coast is to my mind the apotheosis of the slick modern inner-city restaurant and out of the trio of London restaurants operated by Oliver Peyton, it is my favourite. It is designed by Marc Newson and may look a bit funny (it always reminds me of the Milk Bar in *Clockwork Orange*). The 'art' may not be to everyone's taste, but the cooking is innovative and the service, run by Vincent McGrath, is friendly, knowledgeable and attentive. The food is at times almost alarmingly neologistic, but never just for novelty's sake. There always seems to be a point to what the chef, under the guidance of Peyton's culinary director Bruno Loubet, is trying to do. Although flavours come from all quarters of the globe, this is more than just a gastronomic firework display. Coast repays frequent visits. Even side orders and self-effacing sounding dishes such as vine-ripened tarte tatin with soft goats' cheese are a delight. While more showy dishes such as Hereford duck glazed with Szechwan pepper and honey, served with stir-fried Asian greens seldom disappoint. Puddings, such as, a new way with baked Alaska, or apple tea jelly with butter biscuit and rosemary ice-cream favour the adventurous palate. A similar amount of effort and imagination seems to have been put into the wine list – a must for the groovy thirty-something oenophile with money to spend.

- **DRESS** *Modern and trendy*
- **TUBE** *Green Park*
- **HOURS** *Lunch Mon–Sat 12.00–15.00; Sun 12.00–15.30*
    Dinner Mon–Sat 18.00–24.00; Sun 18.00–22.30
- **AVERAGE PRICE** *Lunch/Dinner £40*
- **CREDIT CARDS** *All major cards*
- **MOBILES** *Allowed*
- **CIGARS** *Humidor*

THE COLLECTION
264 Brompton Road, London SW3
☎ 0171 225 1212

Huge bar and restaurant packed with Euro bankers eyeing up pretty girls. The bar offers high tone intoxicants like Laurent Perrier Grand Siècle Alexandra Rose 1988 and an engaging fivesome of Champagne cocktails. To ensure that only choice spirits are allowed in, bouncers have been known to police the long corridor-like entrance. The cooking, though not the point, is more than adequate. Food is split between the sustaining – eggs Benedict, Caesar salad, grilled rib-eye steak, chicken and coconut green curry which available in the lounge – and the more elaborate offerings of the Mezzanine restaurant, which flirts with Pacific Rim influences and functions as an amusement arcade for the palate. After a few Champagne cocktails or bottles of DP, one might well work up a taste for steamed foie gras and pork dumplings with chilli honey dip or rice paper-wrapped monkfish with coriander pesto and sticky rice. The crispy duck with yaki soba noodles and plum sauce has a loyal following. White peach and mascarpone tart is probably the most restrained of puddings: the rest are likely to be caramelised, chocolate or both.

- **DRESS** *Flashy – out to pull an 'It' Girl*
- **TUBE** *South Kensington*
- **HOURS** *Lunch Mon–Fri 12.00–15.00; Sat–Sun 12.00–15.30*
    Dinner Mon–Sat 18.30–23.30; Sun 19.00–22.30
- **AVERAGE PRICE** *Lunch £15–20; Dinner £35*

- **CREDIT CARDS** *All major cards*
- **MOBILES** *Allowed*
- **CIGARS** *Humidor*

LE COLOMBIER
145 Dovehouse Street, London SW3
☎ 0171 351 1155

Le Colombier is the kind of restaurant that my stepfather-in-law, the fabled Hampshire wine merchant, John Konig, would adore. It is the sort of genuine French corner restaurant that in Paris would be called 'Chez something or other', and be everyone's favourite local. It used to be Nicky Kerman's pub, the POW, and traces of Kerman, such as the bar covered with cigar labels, can still be seen, but Didier Garnier (brother of Eric of the Bank, (qv) has created a pleasant and very reasonably priced local restaurant. The staff are French, the menu is in French, even the grumpy old geezer sitting in the corner, eating on his own and looking up occasionally to scowl at the room, is French. The menu is classic not clever and to read it is to recognise many old friends like oeufs poches meurette, rillettes d'oie, loup de mer roti au thym and entrecôte pommes allumettes. The terrace is a treat when the sun shines and Didier is trying to get permission to have it enclosed for winter. The set lunch menu is a virtual give-away. In fact, Le Colombier must be one of the most powerful incentives for moving to this part of Chelsea.

- **DRESS** *Old affluent Chelsea*
- **TUBE** *South Kensington*
- **HOURS** *Lunch Mon–Sat 12.00–15.00; Sun 12.00–15.30*
        Dinner Mon–Sat 18.30–23.00; Sun 18.30–22.30
- **AVERAGE PRICE** *Lunch £20; Dinner £30*
- **CREDIT CARDS** *All major cards*
- **MOBILES** *Not allowed*
- **CIGARS** *Humidor*

COMO LARIO
22 Holbein Place, London SW1
☎ 0171 730 2954

Guido Campigotto, part-owner and front-of-house man runs this popular version of an updated Chelsea trattoria. Busy, at times noisy, and popular with the motor-racing fraternity, this is a good neighbourhood Italian restaurant tucked away in this quiet street

near such august businesses as Nicky Haslam's design practice
and David Linley Furniture, yet well within yomping distance of
the Sloane heartlands and cosmopolitan Belgravia. Food tends to
be broadly northern Italian: ravioli with walnut sauce; cannelloni
with crab and scampi; wild mushroom risotto wrapped in Parma
ham; wild boar bresaola; calf's kidneys and liver in red wine
served with grilled polenta; rabbit stew and, for the more
conservative customers, breaded lamb cutlet with anchovy
rosemary and white wine sauce. While not the most refined of
restaurants, it is a good place to sit with a plate of grilled
vegetables and a glass or two of Trebbiano.

- **DRESS** *Vaguely sloaney*
- **TUBE** *Sloane Square*
- **HOURS** *Lunch Mon–Sat 12.30–14.45; (closed Sun)*
       Dinner Mon–Sat 18.30–23.30; (closed Sun)
- **AVERAGE PRICE** *Lunch/Dinner £25*
- **CREDIT CARDS** *All major cards*
- **MOBILES** *Allowed*
- **CIGARS** *Humidor*

THE CONNAUGHT
Carlos Place, London W1
☎ 0171 499 7070

Apparently the Connaught was created as a place for the landed
gentry to stay when in town. That was in 1897, when to stay
at the Connaught, or the Coburg as it was then known, was an
admission of poverty as clearly one could not afford to maintain
a London house of one's own. My, how times have changed. The
Connaught – the name change came in 1917 when presumably
Coburg was too Germanic for patriotic tastes – is the grandest
of discreet hotels, or perhaps the most discreet of grand hotels –
either way, you get the picture. Its dining rooms, the restaurant
and more intimate grill, are both delightful, if slightly formal
places to eat: the roaring twenties, swinging sixties and Cool
Britannia all seem to have missed the Connaught. Michel Bourdin's
accomplished Michelin-starred cooking is deeply rooted in the
grand culinary tradition of Escoffier. The menu is a cracking read,
including consommé Prince of Wales; consommé en gelée Cole
Porter; sole Jubilee (created for Her Majesty The Queen Elizabeth
II during the Silver Jubilee of 1977 – and long may it be served
at the Connaught) and homard d'Ecosse 'My Way'. Those who
do not go in for fancy nomenclature can feast on kipper paté or
smoked Scotch salmon followed by roast sirloin of Scottish beef

'Old England', lamb cutlets, chicken pie or liver and bacon and a savoury, say welsh rarebit or the immortal sardines diablées. The Connaught is a fine institution that deserves to be preserved for the nation – after all, there cannot be many hotels that boast a top-hatted doorman who happens to be a conjurer to boot. I tend to like eating in smart hotels, but if I had to choose only one London hotel in which to eat, it would probably be the Connaught.

- **DRESS** *Suit and tie*
- **TUBES** *Green Park; Bond Street*
- **HOURS** *Lunch Mon–Sun 12.30–14.30*
      Dinner Mon–Sun 18.30–22.30
- **AVERAGE PRICE** *Lunch £45; Dinner £65*
- **CREDIT CARDS** *All major cards*
- **MOBILES** *Not allowed*
- **CIGARS** *Humidor*

COQ D'ARGENT
1 Poultry, London EC2
☎ 0171 395 5000

Inoffensive, expensive food – sauté foie gras with lentils, plenty of caviar, oysters, grilled Dover sole with maitre d'hotel butter, lobster sauté with tarragon and cream – is probably just what the City boys like after a hard day in front of the screens. Out of deference to the name, there is a selection of chicken dishes: spit roast chicken, chicken and foie gras boudin and Coq d'Argent chicken and bacon torte, Waldorf salad. The coq au vin is the pièce de résistance, served with much ceremony and the coxcomb. Nothing too fancy, just reassuringly pricey, is a formula that seems to work in this spectacular top floor restaurant, as the place is full in the evenings too. What is remarkable is just how unhealthy City people look – pasty, heavy-drinking chainsmokers; but at least they, or their employers, can afford to treat this wonderful space as a canteen. Still, I think it is a shame that such a place, with its carefully decorated dining rooms, numerous terraces and beautiful looking garden is squandered on a clientele which includes its share of drunken boors. This thought came as I watched two young men flicking bits of shellfish (from the plateau de fruits de mer) at each other, while another table proudly displayed a beer bottle which looked decidedly out of place among the crisp linen, smart candleholder, witty ashtray and so on. It is doubtless with the City drinker in mind that the list of post-prandial beverages runs to almost every spirituous intoxicant except four star petrol.

- **DRESS** *City slicker*
- **TUBE** *Bank*
- **HOURS** *Lunch Mon–Fri 11.30–14.30; Sun 12.00–14.30;*
    (closed Sat)
    Dinner Mon–Fri 18.00–21.30; Sat 18.30–21.30;
    (closed Sun)
- **AVERAGE PRICE** *Lunch/Dinner £40*
- **CREDIT CARDS** *All major cards*
- **MOBILES** *They don't like them*
- **CIGARS** *Humidor*

CORNEY & BARROW
44 Cannon Street, London EC4
☎ 0171 248 1700

Corney & Barrow have been flogging booze to City types for the last couple of centuries. In recent years Corney & Barrow wine bars have become a familiar sight in and around the Square Mile. As we know, alcoholic refreshment would seem to be a necessity for those in the financial sector. The pinstripe brigade always appear to be celebrating success or obliterating failure from their minds – either way, Corney & Barrow is as much, if not more, of an institution than the banks and stockbroking outfits it lubricates. Now they are making a play for the restaurant market. Adam Robinson who launched and then sold the Brackenbury (qv) is the executive head chef and the man masterminding Corney & Barrow's assault on our digestive tracts as well as our livers. The list of good wines and Champagnes by the glass at C&B is impressive and tempting. Typical dishes include: smoked haddock poached egg hollandaise; venison sausages and mash; warm duck breast, foie gras and rocket salad; steamed mussels; clams and squid with chickpeas and chorizo. St Martin's Lane is different in that it is outside the business district and therefore attracts evening restaurant customers to its brasserie as well as drinkers to its two bars. The chef, Andrew Green, is a veteran of London's restaurants and cooked for a couple of years at Adam Robinson's Brackenbury – his food would therefore seem to be a real West End bargain and could be served up in more serious and self-regarding surroundings. Thankfully, C&B is an unpretentious environment.

- **DRESS** *As you would for a drink after work*
- **TUBE** *Mansion House*
- **HOURS** *Mon–Sat 11.00–23.00; Sun 11.00–16.30*
- **AVERAGE PRICE** *Lunch/Dinner £20*

- **CREDIT CARDS** *All major cards*
- **MOBILES** *Allowed*
- **CIGARS** *Humidor*

ALSO AT

116 St Martin's Lane, London WC2;
   0171 655 9800 TUBE Leicester Square
111 Old Broad Street, London EC2;
   0171 638 9308 TUBES Liverpool Street; Bank
12 Mason's Avenue, Basinghall Street, London EC2;
   0171 726 6030 TUBES Bank; Moorgate
37 Jewry Street, London EC3;
   0171 680 8550 TUBE Aldgate
9 Cabot Square, London E14;
   0171 512 0397 DLR Canary Wharf

THE COW
89 Westbourne Park Road, London W2
☎ 0171 221 0021

This saloon bar and first floor dining room is a quintessential part
of the Notting Hill scene. The patron is Tom Conran, son of that
living god, Sir Terence (qv). The atmosphere downstairs is trad.
pub inhabited by youngish trendies. What is encouraging about
the place is that Tom can be seen hanging around here, in a
bizarre sleeveless T-shirt, or if not here, at his eponymous deli on
Westbourne Grove. The food on the first floor is not really sold at
pub prices, but then the surroundings are much nicer, as is the
food. Smoked haddock and Jerusalem artichokes with anchovy
and balsamic dressing was flavoursome and sophisticated. Tempura
of monkfish with roasted peanut, ginger and rice noodle salad
was well executed. However, this being a pub, it is also possible
to get steak and chips, or Scottish sirloin steak, fat chips with a
horseradish and smoked garlic mayonnaise and then there is a
chargrilled poussin with roast red onion, chargrilled courgette
and Linzer potato salad. Puddings are no-nonsense affairs like
fashionable rhubarb crumble with custard and clotted almond tart
with clotted cream, or if you prefer, there is Stilton with chutney and
oatcakes. There is a Sunday brunch, with poached, chargrilled
mushrooms, baked tomatoes or the sumo breakfast – a body-
building fry-up. As well as the Patrick Caulfield prints on the
walls, I was pleased to see a guide to the sizes of Havana cigars.

- **DRESS** *Trendily scruffy in the bar, less scruffy upstairs*
- **TUBE** *Royal Oak*

- **HOURS** *Lunch Mon–Sat 19.00–23.00; Sun 12.30–15.30*
  Dinner Mon–Sat 19.30–22.30; Sun 19.30–23.30
- **AVERAGE PRICE** *Dinner £20–25*
- **CREDIT CARDS** *No Diners Club or American Express*
- **MOBILES** *Allowed, but discouraged upstairs*
- **CIGARS** *Humidor*

THE CRITERION BRASSERIE
MARCO PIERRE WHITE

224 Piccadilly, London W1
☎ 0171 930 0488

The more I eat in Marco Pierre White's restaurants, the more I am impressed by the man's operations. He seems, on the whole, to be able to deliver a consistently good level of food, service and surroundings. The Criterion is no exception – the room is one of the most glamourous and subliminally decadent in London. The gold mosaic ceiling recalls the interior of an orthodox basilica and the Venetian standard lamps heighten this effect. The only reservation I have with the way the place looks is the slightly corny art – portraits of weird noblemen from something like Othello and substandard Victorian-looking stuff depicting street scenes in somewhere like Allepo. The food is good, asparagus risotto has just the right nutty quality to it – fine for me, a little too al dente for my associate Christian, but he is a young man and will in time learn that certain tastes are worth acquiring. A main course of smoked haddock with poached egg, Jersey Royals, grain mustard and beurre blanc was rich, comforting and almost addictive. The emphasis here is on simple-ish classics hence such starters as Bayonne ham and terrine of foie gras with green peppercorns and Sauternes gelée and a strong list of fish mains like grilled lobster with garlic and herbs, pommes frites and sauce Béarnaise and salmon fish cake with sorrel and watercress. Meat mains are similarly reassuring: escalope of veal Holstein and roast chicken anglais with bread sauce and 'jus gras'. The only slight let-down comes with pudding: sticky toffee pudding with caramel ice-cream was sufficiently rich but could have been warmer. However, lemon tart was served in generous portions and diplayed the required lemony tang. Prices for everything except cigars, are not unreasonable.

- **DRESS** *Relaxed smart*
- **TUBE** *Piccadilly Circus*
- **HOURS** *Lunch Mon–Sat 12.00–14.30; (closed Sun)*
  Dinner Mon–Sat 18.00–23.30; Sun 18.00–22.30

- **AVERAGE PRICE** Lunch/Dinner £35–40
- **CREDIT CARDS** All major cards
- **MOBILES** Allowed
- **CIGARS** Humidor

DAKOTA
127 Ledbury Road, London W11
☎ 0171 792 9191

A bizarre stockade-style of interior decoration with palisade walls, gives a distinctly Wild West feel to this corner of Notting Hill. Western styling continues on the menu, which seems to have been concocted with the sole aim of bewildering those who have not studied arcane American gastronomic nomenclature to Phd. level, majoring in the emerging cuisine of the south west. Typical of the offerings is a starter such as pecan wood-smoked rabbit and guajilla carnita, fig, apple and lemon salsa, sour cream; caramelised plantain tamale, molasses butter, Oaxacan lentil salad. Sandwiches are particularly good, for example, swordfish club, roasted peppers, vine tomatoes, and spiced tapenade vegetable crisps and the Cuban sandwich of pulled roasted pork, melted cheese, mojo sauce, pickled red onion and crusty bread. Puddings reinforce the New World nuances of the rest of the menu, for example, Nantucket pumpkin nutmeg cake, pumpkin seed brittle ice-cream (£4.75); New England apple and maple pie, vanilla bean ice-cream (£4.75). As one might expect, the New World influence does not let up when it comes to wines. Bottles are arranged under such headings as 'Spicy and Floral – intensely aromatic wines with stronger flavours' (for example, Stag's Leap White Riesling, Napa Valley 1996) or 'Medium-bodied & Moderately Oaked – Cruiserweights of all varieties. Predominantly fruity, seasoned with herbs and spice and well-integrated oak', (for example, Cline Cellars Cotes d'Oakley, Vin Rouge, 'whacky Rhone Red', California 1996). The place has integrated neatly into the trendy local attracting such customers as Madonna, Gwyneth Paltrow, Dinny Hall, Zoe Ball, who had her birthday here, Joan Collins, whose daughter Tara held her 'baby shower' here and Paul Smith who held a dinner here after the opening of his Notting Hill flagship store. Otherwise, it is the sort of place where you might stumble across a fashionable training-shoe-clad urban novelist moaning to his agent/editor/anyone who will listen about the success of rival urban novelists. A social highlight is the weekend brunch, which often turns into an all day affair with huevos rancheros, breakfast burritos and American newspapers.

- **DRESS** *Notting Hill casual*
- **TUBES** *Notting Hill; Westbourne Park*
- **HOURS** *Lunch Mon–Sat 12.00–15.30; Sun 11.00–15.30*
  Dinner Mon–Sat 19.00–23.00; Sun 19.00–22.30
- **AVERAGE PRICE** *Lunch £10; Dinner £25*
- **CREDIT CARDS** *No Diners Club*
- **MOBILES** *Allowed*
- **CIGARS** *Humidor*

DAPHNE'S
112 Draycott Avenue, London SW3
☎ 0171 589 4257

The restaurant where the It Girl thing started. Way back in the early 1990s, a little known Dane called Mogens Tholstrup bought an old Chelsea restaurant and reopened it as a fashionable vaguely Tuscan trat for the beautiful people of the Tara Palmer Tomkinson years. Daphne's was once described thus: no sun-dried tomatoes, only sun-dried people. As far as I can recall, I attended the opening party and will happy to regale my grandchildren with the fact. Daphne's is likely to remain Tholstrup's most remarkable achievement. It may no longer be the gossip column fodder that it was, instead it has now become a superior and fashionable local Italian, with a repertoire of properly and simply prepared dishes. The salads, in particular crab, avocado, tomato and pepper, are worth ordering. Pasta and risotto dishes are sound. Chargrilled swordfish with lemon, oregano and olive oil is a dish to be eaten in the garden room at the back when the sun is shining. One's fellow customers are inevitably richer and better looking than oneself but that is part of the point.

- **DRESS** *Young Sloane Street shopper*
- **TUBE** *South Kensington*
- **HOURS** *Lunch Mon–Sat 12.00–15.00; Sun 12.30–16.00*
  Dinner Mon–Sat 19.00–23.30; Sun 19.00–22.30
- **AVERAGE PRICE** *Lunch £30; Dinner £40*
- **CREDIT CARDS** *All major cards*
- **CIGARS** *Humidor*
- **MOBILES** *Prohibited*

DEALS

Chelsea Harbour, London SW10
☎ 0171 795 1001

The acronym stands for David (Linley), Eddie (Lim), Ahmed (Sultan of Pahang), (Patrick) Litchfield – the 'S' was added to make it sound better. Chelsea Harbour is the *locus classicus* of the Deals experience and it is here that Mr and Mrs Fulham bring Master and Miss Fulham for Sunday lunch. While the adults tuck into multicultural hangover-repairing ribs, chops, chilli, stir-fries, noodles, steaks, salads and burgers, the kiddies have their faces painted and marvel at the magician. As this sort of dining experience goes, the formula works and is less cynical than other similar operations. The menu even shelters a couple of dishes worth making the trek for, namely Chef Tong's Thai curries, of which there are two, prawn and chicken. The former is hot and flavoured with sweet basil, coriander and citrus leaves, the latter simmered in coconut milk with lemon grass and bamboo shoots.

- **DRESS** *Chinos*
- **TUBE** *Parsons Green*
- **HOURS** *Lunch Mon–Sat 12.00–15.30; Sun 12.00–17.00*
        Dinner Mon–Fri 17.30–23.00; Sat 12.00–23.30;
        (closed Sun)
- **AVERAGE PRICE** *£18–23*
- **CREDIT CARDS** *All major cards*
- **MOBILES** *Allowed*
- **CIGARS** *Allowed*

ALSO AT

14–16 Fouberts Place, London W1;
    0171 287 1001 TUBE Oxford Circus
Bradmore House, Queen Caroline Street, London W6;
    0181 563 1001 TUBE Hammersmith
Forte Crest Heathrow, Sipson Road, Middlesex UB7;
    0181 759 2323 TUBE Healthrow Terminals 1,2,3

DENIM

4a Upper St Martins Lane, London WC2
☎ 0171 497 0376

Denim is actually rather sweet. It is a bar and restaurant intended for young people, but has a real charm that can be appreciated by people of all ages. In the basement, there is a charming bar with padded (presumably sound-proofed) walls and on the occasion I visited, a charming young woman in a cowboy hat and Heidi plaits was acting as DJ. The restaurant, on a suspended mezzanine, seems to want to cram as many nationalities into one line as possible, for example, medallions of monkfish with black risotto, Andalouse aubergine, tempura scampi and ponzu sauce or pan-fried saddle of venison, Byron potato, Shanghai choi and a jus de reglisse'. The food itself is OK. The flavours of such dishes as Japanese beef, sweet pickled vegetables and wasabi or baked tomato, aubergine, prune and buffalo mozzarella gâteau, were not the most refined. However I do not think the nicer points of gastronomy cause the young people here to lose too much sleep, they are far more worried about the state of their Vivienne Westwood clobber.

- **DRESS** *Young and fashionable*
- **TUBE** *Leicester Square*
- **HOURS** *Mon–Sat 12.00–1.00 am; Sun 12.00–22.30*
- **AVERAGE PRICE** *Lunch £15; Dinner £25*
- **CREDIT CARDS** *No Diners Club*
- **MOBILES** *Allowed*
- **CIGARS** *Allowed*

DIVERSO
85 Piccadilly, London W1
☎ 0171 491 2222

I would surmise that this identikit smart Italian restaurant was intended as a West End Daphne's – it looks eerily similar, which is explained by the participation of Emily Todhunter in the design of both places. However, Diverso's success has not been total, in that it has never really managed to achieve the same recognition and fame as Daphne's. The food is, however, above-average and though one is able to order mozzarella cheese with fresh basil, rocket salad (albeit perked up with a raspberry vinaigrette) and escalope Milanese, the menu does repay further exploration, for example, wide ribbon pasta with wild duck and porcini sauce, and the fagottino stuffed with lobster and crab. The manager is enthusiastic and laden with designer knick-knacks – moonsphase Cartier Pasha watch, Louis Vuitton pen and a blazer that looks like Brioni. Dress like that and you will probably fit in.

- **DRESS** *Smart*
- **TUBE** *Green Park*
- **HOURS** *Lunch Mon–Sat 12.00–15.00; (closed Sun)*
  Dinner Mon–Sat 18.45–23.30; (closed Sun)

- **AVERAGE PRICE** *Lunch/Dinner £35*
- **CREDIT CARDS** *All major cards*
- **MOBILES** *Allowed*
- **CIGARS** *Humidor*

ECO PIZZERIA
162 Clapham High Street, London SW4
☎ 0171 978 1108

Eco is a good local pizzeria delivering a thinness of crust that eludes many similar operations. The self-consciously modern décor looks a little tired but the place is deservedly busy. It may interest you to know that the owner is Egyptian and he does not like aubergines – they make him sick. His best selling pizza? Aubergine and sun-dried tomato.

- **DRESS** *Casual*
- **TUBE** *Clapham Common*
- **HOURS** *Lunch Mon–Fri 12.00–16.00; Sat 12.00–17.00; Sun 12.00–17.00*
  Dinner Mon–Fri 18.30–23.00; Sat 18.00–23.30; Sun 18.30–23.00
- **AVERAGE PRICE** *Lunch/Dinner £12–15*
- **CREDIT CARDS** *No Diners Club*
- **MOBILES** *Allowed*
- **CIGARS** *Prohibited*

ELENA'S L'ETOILE
30 Charlotte Street, London W1
☎ 0171 636 7189

Elena Savoni is about the most famous maitresse d' ever to work in a London restaurant. She used to be a dressmaker, but with the wartime rationing of cloth, went to work in the restaurant business, starting at Café Bleu on Old Compton Street in 1940. From there she went to Bianchi's from which she retired in 1981. She was then brought out of retirement to run L'Escargot. She retired again, only to be brought to L'Etoile by Roy Ackerman. L'Etoile is one of those old London eating places that used to be patronised by the likes of Augustus John, Dylan Thomas and Graham Greene. Nowadays, this restaurant with its nicotine-coloured walls and photographs of the famous is popular with middle-ranking suits eating on expenses. Food is not going to twist anyone's head off with its thrilling newness but is good enough for Charlotte Street: salade de coquilles St Jacques roties and roast monkfish with white truffle oil mash and asparagus – that sort of thing. Puddings are unpretentious. The wine is solidly, classically French. And cigar historians should note a unique combined cigar and cognac trolley which dates from the early years of this century.

- **DRESS** *Suits*
- **TUBE** *Goodge Street*
- **HOURS** *Lunch Mon–Fri 12.00–14.45; (closed Sat–Sun)*
        Dinner Mon–Sat 18.00–22.45; (closed Sun)
- **AVERAGE PRICE** *Lunch/Dinner £35*
- **CREDIT CARDS** *All major cards*
- **MOBILES** *Allowed*
- **CIGARS** *Humidor*

ELISTANO

25–27 Elystan Street, London SW3
☎ 0171 584 5248

Elistano is the sort of, if not cheap, then certainly inexpensive and cheerful restaurant that everyone should have at the bottom of their road. The menu holds no surprises: rocket salad, salade Niçoise, mozzarella in carozza, satisfying pastas and so on. However it is impossible to eat Saturday lunch here without booking. What makes for a loyal following of the lively lunch scene, is that Elistano is several notches above the countless restaurants with similar menus in terms of décor (touches of the Pompeiian fresco school of design) and execution of simple yet tasty dishes. Rocket salad is a generous pile of leaves with large shavings of parmesan; a plate of fusilli with tomato, mozzarella and aubergines exhibits the correct balance of al dente pasta and melted cheese gooeyness. Elistano is a favourite with a youngish vaguely Euro-Chelsea crowd who require familiar yet good food to polish any remaining shreds of hangover before hitting the shops of nearby Brompton Cross.

- **DRESS** *Affluent casual*
- **TUBE** *South Kensington*
- **HOURS** *Lunch Mon–Sat 12.30–14.30; (closed Sun)*
        Dinner Mon–Sat 19.30–23.00; (closed Sun)
- **AVERAGE PRICE** *Lunch/Dinner £15*
- **CREDIT CARDS** *All major cards*
- **MOBILES** *Allowed*
- **CIGARS** *Allowed*

EMPORIO ARMANI EXPRESS
191 Brompton Road, London SW3
☎ 0171 581 0854

One of the first, and still one of best, of the new wave in-store restaurants. Although now something of an old hand, the Armani café can still deliver good casual Italian food: Bresaola with grilled herb potatoes and truffle oil; fusilli with tomato and basil sauce; beef carpaccio with mustard dressing and rocket salad; red wine risotto; corn-fed chicken with prosciutto, sage and roasted pumpkin. The surroundings have worn well, and if you get a well-positioned table, the view out onto the first floor women's department can be diverting. But just because you have to be petite to fit into Giorgio's skimpy frocks, do not expect the portions at the Armani Café to help you achieve that perfect size eight – tempting tiramisu is served in generously-proportioned slabs.

- **DRESS** *Armani*
- **TUBES** *Knightsbridge; South Kensington*
- **HOURS** *Mon–Tues 10.00–18.00; Wed 10.00–19.00; Thurs–Sat 10.00–18.00; (closed Sun)*
- **AVERAGE PRICE** *£25*
- **CREDIT CARDS** *All major cards*
- **MOBILES** *Allowed*
- **CIGARS** *Prohibited*

THE ENTERPRISE
35 Walton Street, London SW3
☎ 0171 584 3148

This intriguing style hybrid of pub, country house hotel and bordello is often packed with Manolo-heeled shoppers who do not seem deterred by the decidedly un-pub prices charged for such modern urban staples as salmon fish cake, braised shank of lamb, seared scallops and chargrilled scallops. This stylish outpost of the Firmdale hotel empire, which includes among other chic London B&Bs the Pelham and the Covent Garden hotel, chimes in well with the aspirations of those who live, work, and most importantly, shop along the polite, cosmopolitan shopping mall that is Walton Street.

- **DRESS** *Superior pub*
- **TUBES** *South Kensington; Knightsbridge*
- **HOURS** *Mon–Sun 12.00–24.00*
- **AVERAGE PRICE** *Lunch/Dinner £20–25*

- **CREDIT CARDS** *All major cards*
- **MOBILES** *Allowed*
- **CIGARS** *Humidor*

EUPHORIUM
203 Upper Street, London N1
☎ 0171 704 6909

The 'far' end of Upper street has become gastronomically synonymous with this ever-expanding adventurous eatery. Shaven-headed Mawan, a cheery cove if ever there was one, is the creator of this genuinely innovative restaurant that teeters on destination status. The extensive and extremely smart, vaguely Frank Lloyd Wright restaurant is the venue for a Sunday brunch few will ever want to leave when, climatic conditions permitting, the garden opens for business. Yet even in the depths of winter there is a wit and warmth about Euphorium that is extremely winning – the menu carries the footnote 'pheasant dishes may contain lead shots (sic) – this is simply part of the game!!!' And if you thought game was just for old farts in tweed jackets and Brigade ties, think again – pheasant consommé, shrimp wontons and pak choy would have even the crustiest of Colonels sitting up and taking notice. In deference to my Teutonic antecedence, I feel obliged to praise charred sweet-cured salmon, sauerkraut and sour cream – where the salmon is adroitly dealt with to be both pink and black. From coq au vin through to fillet of beef, gorgonzola polenta and oyster mushrooms to the intriguingly flavoured monkfish, baby aubergine, tomato, tamarind and tarragon – main courses, like the customers, run the gamut from traditional to trendy. A similar touch is evident on the wine list, where vintage Green Point is the sparkler offered by the glass; while the less adventurous can take refuge in the lower rungs of classed growth Bordeaux. Although not cheap, the atmosphere is certainly lively and cheerful.

- **DRESS** *Islington trendy*
- **TUBES** *Highbury; Islington*
- **HOURS** *Lunch Mon–Sat 12.00–14.30; Sun 12.00–15.30 Dinner Mon–Sat 18.00–22.30; (closed Sun)*
- **AVERAGE PRICE** *Lunch £22–27; Dinner £25–30*
- **CREDIT CARDS** *All major cards*
- **MOBILES** *Not allowed*
- **CIGARS** *Allowed*

FAKHRELDINE

85 Piccadilly, London W1
☎ 0171 493 3424

This Lebanese restaurant evinces a remarkable style of décor that is perhaps best described as a high-glitz late seventies/early eighties hotel lobby. The view over Green Park from the window tables is also pleasant. The restaurant's namesake is one Prince Fakhreldine II, apparently one of the most generous hosts of the ancient world. I am fond of eating Lebanese food. Fakhreldine offers the long familiar menu that gives you the option to eat fresh lamb's liver (raw or fried), lamb brains, lamb tongues, lamb testicles (fried or grilled with lemon). I always order at least one plate of kalaje jibne (grilled halloumi on Lebanese bread) and fatayer (pastry parcels of spinach, onion and lemon) and then build on these foundations according to mood. Farouj Fakhreldine is a house speciality of baby chicken, cooked in the oven and served with oriental bread, onion spices and olive oil. Fakhreldine may not be right at the cutting edge of restaurants in London, but there is something charming about a restaurant that still has a menu section entitled 'European Dishes' including such things as steak au poivre and escalope of veal cordon bleu.

- **DRESS** *As you would for a night out in Beirut before the troubles*
- **TUBE** *Green Park*
- **HOURS** *Mon–Sun 12.00–24.00*
- **AVERAGE PRICE** *Lunch/Dinner £30*
- **CREDIT CARDS** *All major cards*
- **MOBILES** *Allowed*
- **CIGARS** *Allowed*

LA FAMIGLIA

7 Langton Street, London SW10
☎ 0171 351 0761

Alvaro Maccioni did not actually invent the London trattoria as we know it today, but he has spent the last three decades and more perfecting it. He used to work for Mario and Franco and then opened his own place, Alvaro's, on the Kings Road in 1966. A year later he opened the Aretusa, a key part of the mythology of the Swinging Chelsea of the 1960s. The Aretusa was a nightclub, restaurant, boutique, poste restante, business centre and generally fab hang-out for the groovers of the day. By the early seventies, Alvaro had 20 restaurants, all of which he sold in 1972. He then left the country, got bored, came back, opened La Famiglia at the World's End end of the King's Road and has been here ever since. La Famiglia's menu does not need to be self-consciously clever. Alongside such jewels of classic 'trat' cooking – for example that sixties staple mozzarella in Carrozza (fried cheese with bread in spicy tomato sauce, garlic and parsley) – there is a discernible Tuscan influence at work: for example, crostini di pollo (chopped chicken livers, capers, garlic on toast) and fagioli al fiasco (beans cooked in a flask with extra virgin olive oil, and panzanella). If you want risotto, be prepared to wait, as it takes 25 minutes to prepare. Fish dishes are simple but tasty, for example, pesce spada all'agrodolce, a sort of sweet and sour swordfish with onions, courgette and balsamic vinegar sauce. And the wild boar sausages are such a delicacy that Princess Michael of Kent wants to buy them to cook at home. Torta di ricotta (a rustic type of cheesecake) is one of the stars of the pudding trolley. The wine list is concise with all the things you would expect to see, like Ornellaia and Sassicaia as well as the nice touch of half a dozen Italian sparkling wines, including three types of the celebrated Bellavista. The atmosphere is the kind of thing that old sixties roués, their children and grandchildren can relate to.

- **DRESS** *Chelsea*
- **TUBE** *Sloane Square*
- **HOURS** *Lunch Mon–Sun 12.00–14.45*
        Dinner Mon–Sun 19.00–23.45
- **AVERAGE PRICE** *Lunch £22–27; Dinner £25–30*
- **CREDIT CARDS** *All major cards*
- **MOBILES** *Allowed*
- **CIGARS** *Allowed*

FIFTH FLOOR

Harvey Nichols, Knightsbridge, London SW1
☎ 0171 235 5250

I have to say that I am not an immense fan of Fifth Floor. Staff have always been pleasant, the views can be good and the bar is certainly lively enough, but there have been times when I have not wanted to eat a thing on the menu. However Henry Harris's robust brand of cooking has its staunch devotees and a publisher has seen fit to commission a cookbook, which Henry has written with Hugo Arnold; therefore I have come to the quite logical conclusion that I must be missing the point. Almost any chef will tell you that he places great emphasis on the freshness of his ingredients, but one of Harris's fans says that his ingredients are

incredibly English and fresh to the point of being supersonic –
whatever that might mean. In menu terms, this translates as
dishes like six native oysters with grilled spicy sausages; smoked
haddock with black pudding hash; halibut with meat juices, black
trumpet mushrooms and saffron; grilled veal chop, Roquefort
butter; rabbit with spinach, chickpeas, paprika-cured bacon and
mustard sauce. Puddings such as baked cherry sponge with port
and cherry compote come with individual wine suggestions – a
clever way of boosting sales of sweet wines, in fact the wine list
is well worth examining. I have a feeling I would like Henry
Harris, his parents used to run a restaurant in Brighton called
the Grandgousier, which I remember my parents used to visit.
Besides, any man who puts Bismarck herrings on a menu has
to be sound.

- **DRESS** *Smart*
- **TUBE** *Knightsbridge*
- **HOURS** *Lunch Mon–Fri 12.00–15.00; Sun 12.00–15.30;*
        (closed Sat)
        Dinner Mon–Sun 18.30–23.30
- **AVERAGE PRICE** *Lunch £30; Dinner £35–40*
- **CREDIT CARDS** *All major cards*
- **MOBILES** *No mobiles*
- **CIGARS** *Humidor*

FISH!

Cathedral Street, Borough Market, London SE1
☎ 0171 836 3236

This clever café-like approach to piscine dining is brought to us
by the people who gave us Bank (qv). That they also happen
to be fishmongers helps. Located in what looks like a former
greenhouse in a railway arch in South London, Fish! is a bustling,
bright, modern no-frills fish restaurant. You can either sit at a large
central section which surrounds the open kitchen or at clothless
tables. The glasshouse and hard edges makes Fish! a noisy
experience but then it is not a place to linger inordinately. One
orders off the menu printed on the place-mat and food arrives
promptly. A column called 'piscivore' lists starters and mains,
such as devilled whitebait (crisp and delicious), smoked haddock
with Welsh rarebit (comforting in the extreme) and what might be
billed as piscine fast food: tuna burger; swordfish club sandwich
etc. Fish on a long list ticked to denote daily availability, can
be served steamed or grilled and with salsa, hollandaise, herb
butter, olive oil dressing or red wine fish gravy. And talking of

wines, the list is small and chosen with fish eaters in mind –
witness the presence of not one, but two, chilled reds. Fish! is
the sort of place that one would be glad to have near one's
home or place of work and would suit many areas in and
around London.

- **DRESS** *Casual*
- **TUBE** *Tower Bridge*
- **HOURS** *Lunch Mon–Sat 11.30–15.00; (closed Sun)*
      Dinner Mon–Sat 17.30–23.00; (closed Sun)
- **AVERAGE PRICE** *£30*
- **CREDIT CARDS** *All major cards*
- **MOBILES** *Allowed*
- **CIGARS** *Humidor*

FLORIANA

15 Beauchamp Place, London SW3
☎ 0171 858 1500

I knew something was up when I asked for a rocket and
parmesan salad and was told that such a dish would not be
made available to me. I felt like saying that this was Beauchamp
Place, that I was in an Italian restaurant (one of the partners is
Riccardo Mazzucchelli – the former Mr Ivana Trump), that I was
having lunch with a delightful blonde who was wearing an
extremely expensive wrist watch, and that I thought if such
conditions prevailed I was virtually obliged by law to toy with a
few leaves. Instead, being the coward that I am, I acquiesced
and meekly ordered steamed Scottish lobster with celeriac ravioli,
pan-fried baby artichoke and sorrel – it was extremely good,
concentrated in flavour and more memorable than any rocket and
parmesan salad. Floriana is neither cheap, nor 'on the occasion
that I visited' particularly cheerful, yet it is indisputably smart,
in a sleekly expensive, cosmopolitan, furs, jewellery and 'no this
comely young woman is not my mistress she is my niece' sort of
way. The talented interior designer Emily Todhunter has created
a space of considerable elegance and if I were trying to impress
my arms dealer, I would bring him here for lunch. The menu may
be printed in Italian (with useful English translations), but the food
– elaborate and put together with great care – is not what one
tends to expect from an Italian restaurant; for instance, warm corn
crêpes with roasted Bresse pigeon in shallot sauce and chutney
of quince apple. Instead, the gastronomic language is probably
best described as international luxury. Typical dishes include:
trio of scallops, cured salmon and marinated crab tartar with

tomato confit; rosti of potato and sevruga caviar; tagliolini with pan-fried foie gras de Landes, green lentils and Madeira jus; sea bass steamed in lettuce seaweed, in a caviar and lemon sauce; Scottish beef fillet with pan-fried foie gras de Landes in a Sautern (sic) wine sauce flavoured with star anis. My personal favourite is a description of a dish of pan-fried John Dory fillet in a potato waistcoat – not a potato jerkin, dinner jacket, or overcoat – with leek purée in a Riesling wine and squid ink sauce. Those with simple tastes have the option to order unadorned caviar.

- **DRESS** *Up*
- **TUBE** *Knightsbridge*
- **HOURS** *Lunch Mon–Sat 12.30–15.00; (closed Sun)*
      Dinner Mon–Sat 19.00–23.00; (closed Sun)
- **AVERAGE PRICE** *Lunch/Dinner £50*
- **CREDIT CARDS** *All major cards*
- **MOBILES** *Allowed*
- **CIGARS** *Humidor*

FORTNUM & MASON
181 Piccadilly, London W1
☎ 0171 734 8040

This, the Queen's corner shop, is one of the world's smartest grocers. It has three restaurants. The Fountain restaurant is a street level eatery with its own entrance onto Jermyn Street. The Patio, a mezzanine restaurant overlooking the main grocery floor is the least formal of the three. The St James's, the grandest and most traditional, is on the fourth floor. Its feel is somewhere between genteel fifties dining room and unisex Pall Mall club. The food is traditional, well executed and British. First-time visitors to this delightful place should choose from the selection of 'St James's Classics' which includes Fortnum & Mason's London smoked salmon and roast sirloin of Angus beef and Yorkshire pudding from the trolley. Things like grilled Dover sole are tarted up ever so slightly. As befits the dignity of the shop, puddings are called Sandringham coffee ice-cream coupe and the cheese trolley of the St James's Restaurant is one of the wonders of the West End. It trundles about the restaurant in an incredibly stately fashion, the port swaying gently in the decanters at either end. The point of the St James's is to become a regular – if things such as, say, caviar and smoked venison do not appear on the menu, then regulars know to ask for them to be brought up from the ground floor food store. And although the wine list is perfectly respectable,

those who know ask for a bottle of fine claret to be sent up from
Fortnum's well-stocked wine department and decanted in advance
of their arrival. A token corkage charge of a couple of pounds
for fine wines bought from the ground floor wine shop, mean
that this is an excellent place to enjoy fine wines without the
usual restaurant mark-up. For those in search of less intoxicating
beverages, afternoon tea is served from 3pm in the St James's
Restaurant, but you can order a cuppa at any time in the Patio.

- **DRESS** *Up from the country for the day*
- **TUBE** *Piccadilly Circus*
- **HOURS** *(St. James's restaurant) Mon–Sat 9.30–18.00;
  (closed Sun)*
- **AVERAGE PRICE** *Lunch £25; Tea £16.50*
- **CREDIT CARDS** *All major cards*
- **MOBILES** *With discretion*
- **CIGARS** *Humidor*

FOUNDATION
Harvey Nichols, Knightsbridge, London SW1
☎ 0171 201 8000

This smart basement restaurant is a paradigm of the new wave
of in-store café-restaurants, offering fashionable, inoffensive
food at prices that veer on the high side of reasonable for the
surroundings. The place is an inoffensively groovy basement
of polished concrete, sleek wood and a water wall. The food
includes: risottos; couscous; salad of smoked wild pigeon breast;
warm oak smoked salmon; goats' cheese; mains of smoked
haddock, roast cod, pan-fried scallops, grilled chicken breast,
roast duck breast etc. Puddings are naughty but nice. If you
regard lunch as an opportunity to push a few leaves about a
plate for a limited time before doing some serious damage to
the credit card on the floors of designer clothes above you, then
I am sure Harvey Nix would like you to feel at home here.

- **DRESS** *Trendily seasoned shopper*
- **TUBE** *Knightsbridge*
- **HOURS** *Lunch Mon–Sun 12.00–16.00*
- **AVERAGE PRICE** *£20*
- **CREDIT CARDS** *All major cards*
- **MOBILES** *Don't work very well*
- **CIGARS** *Humidor*

FOUR SEASONS

84 Queensway, London W2
☎ 0171 229 4320

The Four Seasons is one of the places that bears out the old, if rather condescending, truism that a Chinese restaurant packed with Chinese people (and with a queue stretching into the street) is usually a good bet. Four Seasons is famous for its duck, which is apparently almost addictive: aficionados speak of it having a lightness and an absence of fattiness that is quite exemplary. The trick here is to ignore the menu and order whatever happens to be in the window: pork, duck etc. However, it has to be said that a dish like the sweet and sour fish is worth a try, if only to marvel at the quite vivid orange hue of the sauce.

- **DRESS** *Informal*
- **TUBE** *Bayswater*
- **HOURS** *Mon–Sat 12.00–23.30; Sun 12.00–23.00*
- **AVERAGE PRICE** *Lunch/Dinner £10–15*
- **CREDIT CARDS** *No Diners Club*
- **MOBILES** *Not allowed*
- **CIGARS** *Allowed*

FOXTROT OSCAR

79 Royal Hospital Road, London SW3
☎ 0171 352 7179

Foxtrot became famous as a burger bar in Chelsea, much in the way that Enzo Ferrari could be described as making his name as an Italian grease monkey. Culinary refinement is not and never was the name of the game here and in both establishments every expense has been spared vis-à-vis decoration. Nevertheless, Foxtrot celebrates its 20th birthday in the year 2000 and still attracts the same invigorating social cocktail of customers. Dai Llewellyn, the most most famous son of Wales since Lloyd George (who sold his family a baronetcy), is the prototypical Foxtrot customer, or at least so I would like to believe. However, the Old Etonian co-owner Michale Proudlock likes to play down the place's reputation as a retirement home for old roués and stress the fact that these same roués now bring their young children and even younger girlfriends here to eat. Foxtrot's Eggs Benedict are still considered the best in London by a few people whose opinion I value. Other things to order are steak and kidney pie, bangers and mash, steak, chips and, of course, burgers. Wash it down with a case of perfectly acceptable Bordeaux Superieur.

And in case you were wondering, the man with the short hair, dark glasses and menacing mien is Dan Meinertzhagen – backgammon and casino veteran.

- **DRESS** *Jeans*
- **TUBE** *Sloane Square*
- **HOURS** *Lunch Mon–Fri 12.30–14.30; Sat–Sun 12.30–15.30 Dinner Mon–Sat 19.00–23.00; Sun 19.00–22.00*
- **AVERAGE PRICE** *Lunch/Dinner £20*
- **CREDIT CARDS** *All major cards*
- **MOBILES** *Allowed*
- **CIGARS** *Allowed*

ALSO AT
16 Byward Street, London EC3
☎ 0171 481 2700 TUBE *Tower Hill*

GAUDI

63 Clerkenwell Road, London EC1
☎ 0171 608 3220

Gaudi is located in gloomy surroundings that do their best to recall the architectural highlights of Barcelona, but the chef, Nacho Martinez-Jimenez, a powerfully-built man with a shaven head is from Huelva in Andalucia. While the venue (above the famous Turnmills nightclub) may be depressing, the food can be truly outstanding. There is a lightness and delicacy about such dishes as pimientos de piquillo rellenos de brandada de bacalao (roasted Spanish pepper stuffed with salt cod brandade) that is exemplary: the brandade is more like a cappuccino of salt cod than the coarse paste that is its usual incarnation. Grilled baby calamari stuffed with spinach, pine nuts and sultanas, served with a little saffron rice and surrounded with its ink was exquisite, the flesh of the squid yielding and breaking beneath the merest pressure of the knife. There are also more hearty dishes such as Iberian pork fillet marinated with paprika with poached potatoes and roasted peppers and plain offerings such as mixed baby vegetables with virgin olive oil and Idiazabal cheese. This, at last, is a restaurant that shows what can be done with Iberian cuisine without distorting it into some 'modern European' parody. It exceeds expectations that have hitherto been founded on souped-up tapas bars.

- **DRESS** *It's so gloomy it hardly matters*
- **TUBE** *Farringdon*

- **HOURS** *Lunch Mon–Fri 12.00–14.30; (closed Sat–Sun)*
     Dinner Mon–Thurs 19.00–22.30; Fri 19.00–21.00;
     (closed Sat–Sun)
- **AVERAGE PRICE** *Lunch £15–20; Dinner £35–40*
- **CREDIT CARDS** *All major cards*
- **MOBILES** *Not allowed*
- **CIGARS** *Allowed*

LE GAVROCHE
43 Upper Brook Street, London W1
☎ 0171 408 0881

This old Mayfair dreadnought cruises on, with captaincy now transferred from father Albert to son Michel and a Michelin star dropped in the process. The place has its devotees and this year it garnered a Carlton Restaurant Award for all round excellence. Typical dishes here include: soufflé Suissesse (cheese soufflé cooked on double cream); cassoulet d'escargots et cuisses de grenouilles aux herbes (snails and frogs' legs served in little pots flavoured with herbs); mousseline de homard au Champagne (lobster mousse with caviar and Champagne butter sauce); râble de lapin et galette au parmesan (roast saddle of rabbit with crispy potatoes and parmesan); palet au chocolat amer et praline croustillante (bitter chocolate and praline indulgence) and parfait au chocolat blanc et gelée de framboises (white chocolate mousse filled with poached raspberries).

- **DRESS** *Suits*
- **TUBE** *Marble Arch*
- **HOURS** *Lunch Mon–Fri 11.00–14.00; (closed Sat–Sun)*
     Dinner Mon–Fri 19.00–23.00; (closed Sat–Sun)
- **AVERAGE PRICE** *Lunch £80–90*
- **CREDIT CARDS** *All major cards*
- **MOBILES** *Allowed with discretion*
- **CIGARS** *Humidor; in the bar or lounge only*

GORDON RAMSAY
68 Royal Hospital Road, London SW3
☎ 0171 352 4441

Located on holy ground, the site formerly known as La Tante Claire, Pierre Koffman's Chelsea fine dining room, Ramsay's sprung to national prominence when Sunday Times restaurant critic AA Gill was asked to leave … before he had written his review. Such was the importance of this gastronomic spot that it wiped the Balkans, the Russian economic meltdown and Clinton's troubles off the front pages. Formerly an aspirant Association footballer, a high-earning career with Glasgow Rangers eluded him, so Ramsay took to the kitchen. In his time, he has worked for Joel Robuchon, Guy Savoy, Marco Pierre White and Pierre Koffman (so there is symmetry to his return to Royal Hospital Road). He rocketed to fame with the Aubergine, which he quit in 1998 to open this eponynmous place. He is the man most people tend to compare with Marco Pierre White, in terms of temperament and culinary ability. I have a theory that there are two Gordon Ramsays. One is the charming, if plainly spoken, man who has always treated me courteously. The other is a psychopath who makes King Herod look like Saint Esther of Childline, and is known for the summary execution of his staff and acts of random brutality to his customers. A hint of the art deco lingers about this pale room. Chairs are covered in taupe suede and the wall on the way in is covered with a large silvered mural depicting athletic nudes which are mirrored in the etched glass panels that enclose the restaurant. The effect is comfortable but subdued, allowing the sensationally good food to make the statements. Salad of crispy pig's trotters with calves' sweetbreads, fried quails eggs and cream vinaigrette appears on the menu homage à Koffman. Foie gras three ways (sautéed with quince, mi-cuit with an Earl Grey consommé and pressed with truffle peelings) should tempt all but the most jaded of plutocrat's palates. Sautéed breast of quail with roasted ceps, braised kohl-rabi served with a velouté of pumpkin is a popular starter. The food can be complicated, for example, pigeon from Bresse, poached then grilled and served with a pizza of foie gras, celeriac and a truffle sauce – however nothing is done without a reason: the poaching reduces the fat before the grilling. The cheese trolley is almost as much of a miracle as the wagon that ferries the digestifs around the room. And while on the subject of booze, Thierry Berson is the perennially youthful sommelier, who peddles well-chosen wines with an enthusiasm that is quite unique. His tip for a top sweet white is the 1947 Vouvray from Marc Bredif and when it comes to classed growth clarets, the top wines are well represented and Thierry will happily talk to you about them until, as the Bordelais are fond of saying, *les vaches rentrent chez eux.*

- DRESS *Smart*
- TUBE *Sloane Square*
- HOURS *Lunch Mon–Fri 12.00–14.30; (closed Sat–Sun)*
  Dinner Mon–Fri 18.45–22.30; (closed Sat–Sun)

- **AVERAGE PRICE** *Lunch £50; Dinner £75*
- **CREDIT CARDS** *All major cards*
- **MOBILES** *Can be left at reception*
- **CIGARS** *Humidor; cigar smoking in the lounge*

GRACELANDS PALACE

881–883 Old Kent Road, London SE15
☎ 0171 639 3961

No London restaurant guide that even pretends to take itself
seriously can miss out Paul Chan's inimitable Chinese restaurant.
Nestling in the lee of some of the Old Kent Road's least
appealing tower blocks, across the road from a derelict house
and benefitting from the shade of a nearby railway bridge, this is
a restaurant that everyone should visit at least once before they
die. If I remember correctly, it was the great AA Gill who in a
rare flash of extreme kindness once described the food here as
not the kind of thing for which one would walk on one's knees
over broken glass. As ever, it is difficult to improve upon the
observations of the great Gill. A typical 'Elvis Set Menu B',
headed with the words 'Good Music' and 'Fun' might run thus:
crispy seaweed, smoked shredded chicken, aromatic crispy lamb,
deep-fried king prawns in shells with salt and pepper, kung po
chilli chicken, beef fillet steak cantonese-style, sweet and sour
pork fillet, quick-fried four mixed vegetables, and yeung chow
special fried rice. Gracelands Palace is all about atmosphere and
this set of low-ceilinged rooms plastered with Elvis ephemera and
dozens of framed press clippings has it in abundance. And when
finally Paul Chan descends in full Elvis regalia to run through his
Elvis tribute session, the effect is intoxicating. I still remember my
first visit when I was accompanied by the Tara Palmer Tomkinson
of South London, Gaynor Wetherall, and ended up singing along
with the great Mr Chan and two of Millwall FC's staunchest
supporters, who said if I 'lost the cravat' I would apparently fit in
rather well at the 'Den'. Every aspect of that memorable evening
(including the concomitant hangover) is forever etched into my
memory.

- **DRESS** *Dress as Elvis*
- **TUBES** *Elephant & Castle; New Cross Gate*
- **HOURS** *Lunch Fri–Sat 12.00–14.30; (closed Mon–Thurs, Sun)*
        Dinner Mon–Sat 18.00–24.00; (closed Sun)
- **AVERAGE PRICE** *Lunch £10; Dinner £20*
- **CREDIT CARDS** *All major cards*
- **MOBILES** *Allowed*
- **CIGARS** *Allowed*

GRANITA

127 Upper Street, London N1
☎ 0171 226 3222

Granita is to New Labour what the Osteria Italiana in Munich was to National Socialism or, as Stephen Bayley puts it in his wonderful svelte book, Labour Camp, 'comparable in its way to the role of the Deux Magots in the development and popular perception of Parisian existentialism'. As Bayley records, 'It was here, perhaps over a little salad of red oak leaf, shredded Gruyère and croûtons, that Gordon Brown famously conceded leadership that fateful night of 31st May 1994 and old Labour was, in an environment of harsh furniture, forever after translated into New'. Since then, the Blairs have moved from Barnsbury to Westminster, but the harsh furniture and prim modernity of the surroundings remain. Granita is a good restaurant that is deservedly busy and should be remembered in spite of its Blairite associations. That Old Labour red oak leaf still appears, in a starter that is a symphony of colour coordination: salad of red oak, aubergine, black olives, green grapes, feta, chunky tomato and cucumber dressing. Scrambled eggs (free range of course) come with oyster mushrooms, manchego and sourdough toast. Wok-seared squid, tamarind, chilli, garlic and Chinese watercress is a controlled, yet powerful, explosion of flavour across the palate – the squid cleverly avoiding the rubberiness that is all too often achieved. Middle Eastern overtones inform the main courses, for example: chickpea, spinach, Moroccan spice, steamed rice; tuna chargrilled rare, tabbouleh, olive oil mash, chermoula; quail chargrilled, aubergine caviare, green beans, preserved lemon, and coriander dressing. Service administered by young women in Mao-like ensembles is firm, yet kindly and helpful. Customers demonstrate the social variety of the area, from the rich and groomed to the merely affluent and tousled.

- **DRESS** *Any colour, as long as it is black*
- **TUBES** *Angel; Highbury; Islington*
- **HOURS** *Lunch Wed–Sun 12.30–14.30; (closed Mon–Tues) Dinner Tues–Sat 18.30–22.30; Sun 18.30–22.00; (closed Mon)*
- **AVERAGE PRICE** *Lunch £15; Dinner £25*
- **CREDIT CARDS** *Visa; Mastercard; Switch*
- **MOBILES** *Allowed*
- **CIGARS** *Prohibited*

GREAT EASTERN DINING ROOM
54–56 Great Eastern Street, London EC2
☎ 0171 613 4545

Not to be confused with Terence Conran's Great Eastern Hotel, the Great Eastern Dining room is a much more humble operation on Great Eastern Street and is the work of Will Ricker, the creator of Cicada (qv). The Great Eastern dining room is a paradigm of the groovy rebirth of Shoreditch. The ground floor is divided between a bar, which serves drinks at pub prices and has Guinness, Kronenbourg 1664 and Leffe beer and a smart-looking dining room with dark wood walls (actually US white oak stained nearly black), dark wood chairs and booths upholstered in dark leather. The food is rustic northern Italian with a fusion twist – for example, warm salad of new potatoes, green beans, orange and anchovy. Typical dishes are bruschetta of piquillo peppers and fennel with parmesan; salted cod mash and nutmeg with pickled tomatoes; lemon myrtle pasta with caper berries and battered lemon; spicy tomato and mussel stew, grilled ciabatta; grilled lamb steak with garlic and white bean mash, mint pesto; caramel panacotta with home-made raspberry wine. What is more, food is keenly priced with no dish costing more than £10.00. Unfortunately, drinks are not similarly priced, nevertheless there is a good range of wines, which, like customers including Jay Jopling, Peter Doig, Alexander McQueen and Katie England, tend to be very fashionable.

- **DRESS** *Inner city fashionable*
- **TUBE** *Old Street*
- **HOURS** *Lunch Mon–Fri 12.00–15.00; (closed Sat–Sun)*
          Dinner Mon–Sat 18.00–24.00; (closed Sun)
- **AVERAGE PRICE** *Lunch/Dinner £20–25*
- **CREDIT CARDS** *All major cards*
- **MOBILES** *In bar only*
- **CIGARS** *Allowed*

GREEN'S RESTAURANT AND OYSTER BAR
36 Duke Street, St. James's, London SW1
☎ 0171 930 4566

Green's is about as close as it gets to eating at Whites (just around a couple of corners) without actually being a member. For 16 years, Simon Parker Bowles has presided over what is a serious rival to nearby Wilton's and a destination restaurant for students of the turf. There is nothing deceptive about the menu; it is just plain and simple. This is the sort of restaurant where it is perfectly acceptable, in fact almost mandatory, to order smoked salmon and scrambled eggs as a starter or main. Once one has found one's favourite dishes one tends to stick to them – if smoked cod's roe and grilled sole is what I feel like, there are few places I would rather go. And the Haddock Parker Bowles, (a dish devised by Simon's father) with chive mash, soft poached egg and creamy white wine sauce is the very apotheosis of comfort food and the best thing of its kind to be had in London. In season, oysters are the thing and to sit in a booth at Green's and watch the pin-striped grandees tip them down their gullets is one of the great pleasures of life in London. Salmon fish cake with roast pepper and tomato sauce (available in both starter and main sizes) is a seminal Green's dish. Other classics include the Dorset crab salad, bangers and mash with onion gravy, and calf's liver and bacon with mash and onion gravy. Puddings are reassuring dishes like Bakewell tart, steamed lemon pudding with lemon curd and warm Eccles cakes and vanilla ice–cream. Cheeses are from Paxton and Whitfield. Wines are of the sort that would be equally at home in a grand country house cellar.

- **DRESS** *Pinstripes*
- **TUBE** *Green Park*
- **HOURS** *Lunch Mon–Sat 12.15–15.00; Sun 12.30–15.00 Dinner Mon–Sat 17.30–23.00; Sun 17.30–21.00*
- **AVERAGE PRICE** *Lunch/Dinner £40*
- **CREDIT CARDS** *All major cards*
- **MOBILES** *Not allowed*
- **CIGARS** *Humidor*

THE GRILL ROOM
The Dorchester, Park Lane, London W1
☎ 0171 629 8888

The Dorchester Grill is unlike the grillrooms of most grand hotels in that it does not aspire to the all-male club/public school dining hall look. Instead it has remained faithful to the Spanish style in which it was launched in 1931. However, if it looks like you are dining in the great hall of some Spanish hidalgo's mansion, the food tends to be decidedly classic. Smoked salmon; dressed crab; cream of lobster soup; grilled Dover sole with brown butter and capers; steak and kidney pie and rack of lamb are among the dishes highlighted as Grill Room classics. Slightly more adventurous are such dishes as the salad of pan-fried warm scallops on a confit of tomatoes flavoured with coriander –

delicious. There is a confidence and assurance about the Dorchester grill that is satisfying – cooking, service, almost everything in fact, tends to be done with great aplomb. Trolleys move about the room with dignity and staff execute the at-table preparation of certain dishes, for example, the caper butter, with élan. What impresses about the place is the confidence of the operation: ask for tartare sauce with your grilled sole and you will be told, in the nicest possible way, that tartare is fine for battered fish, but that a delicate Béarnaise is altogether more in tune with the sole – what is more, such advice is given so delicately that it is almost a pleasure to be corrected.

- **DRESS** *Smart*
- **TUBE** *Hyde Park Corner*
- **HOURS** *Lunch Mon–Sun 12.30–14.30*
       Dinner Mon–Sat 18.00–23.00; Sun 19.00–22.30
- **AVERAGE PRICE** *Lunch/Dinner £65*
- **CREDIT CARDS** *All major cards*
- **MOBILES** *Allowed*
- **CIGARS** *Allowed*

GRISSINI LONDON

The Hyatt Carlton Tower, Cadogan Place, London SW1
☎ 0171 858 7171

The pleasant looks of this well made-over space on the first floor of the Hyatt Carlton Tower are easy on the eye and the view down Cadogan Place is agreeable too. It is all a little unimaginative and as such is probably perfectly correct in a large upmarket international hotel, for those guests who might not want to stray out of the hotel but want to enjoy competent Italian food. The only vaguely interesting starter was oven-baked cheese soufflé, roasted peppers and figs – otherwise it was all stuff that has been seen before, albeit nicely done. If you are after a lunch of salad and pasta that will neither offend nor distract from the serious business of shopping or gossiping, then Grissini London is the place for you. The name suggests that there might be Grissinis in all sorts of major cities; having visited this one, I have to admit to not being fired with the immediate desire to seek them out.

- **DRESS** *As for serious shopping on Sloane Street*
- **TUBE** *Knightsbridge*
- **HOURS** *Breakfast Mon–Sat 7.00–11.00; Sun 8.00–11.00*
       Lunch Mon–Fri, Sun 12.30–14.45; (closed Sat)
       Dinner Mon–Sat 18.30–22.45; (closed Sun)
- **AVERAGE PRICE** *Lunch £25–30; Dinner £36*

- **CREDIT CARDS** *All major cards*
- **MOBILES** *Allowed*
- **CIGARS** *Humidor*

HALEPI
18 Leinster Terrace, London W2
☎ 0171 262 1070

Halepi is the schizophrenic face of Greek restaurants in London. The Bayswater branch is a throwback to the sixties. Halepi opened in 1966 and has changed about as little as the menu – as well as kebabs, dolmades, hummous and tzatziki, there is Steak Diane, Escalope Paillard and fresh scampi fried in butter with orange and brandy sauce, served with rice. Halepi in Bayswater is a relic of a time when restaurants were not delineated according to gastronomic appellations or hyped according to their design, but were nice cosy places to go and eat. The décor is of the checked tablecloth and candle-jammed-in-wine-bottle school: turn up on a chilly night and there might be a fan heater whirring away by the front door. Halepi Belsize Park is more of what might, I daresay, become known as contemporary Greek or Modern Pelopponesian cuisine. The place itself is clean, white and unpretentious looking and the food, though not radically different – hummous, tahini, taramosalata, halloumi, saganaki, kalamari and good warm dolmades – benefits from modern presentation. The more contemporary approach is increasingly evident with such dishes as: scallops served grilled on a bed of cabbage; giant prawns split, charcoal grilled and served with lemon oil, spring onions and garlic sauce (delicious). Indeed much is made of the freshness of the fish. The aim is apparently to educate customers into an appreciation of Cypriot peasant cooking, which means that dishes such as stuffed squid with pine kernels are likely to appear on the menu.

- **DRESS** *Casual*
- **TUBES** *Lancaster Gate; Queensway*
- **HOURS** *Mon–Sun 12.00–1.00 am*
- **AVERAGE PRICE** *Lunch/Dinner £25–£30*
- **CREDIT CARDS** *All major cards*
- **MOBILES** *Allowed*
- **CIGARS** *Humidor*

ALSO AT
HALEPI, 48–50 Belsize Lane, London NW3;
0171 431 5855 TUBES Belsize Park; Swiss Cottage

HARRY'S BAR

26 South Audley Street, London W1

☎ 0171 408 0844

Arguably the most luxurious Italian restaurant in the world, and priced accordingly, Mark Birley's Mayfair private dining club is in danger of becoming more famous than its Venetian namesake, with which it shares the dish of tagliolini verdi gratinati al prosciutto. With its small but delightful bar, and dining room hung with dozens of Arno cartoons, Harry's Bar manages to make even the surrounding purlieus of Mayfair seem barbaric by comparison. Chef Alberico Penati is a man for whom cooking is a vocation rather than a job or a stepping stone to a television career. Penati is someone who can discourse with the eloquence of a latterday d'Anunzio on risotto and can enthral one for hours with his thoughtful observations on the nature of the marriage between the tartufo and the porcino. His food is indescribably good and, along with the offerings of Riva in Barnes, it is to my mind some of the finest Italian cooking in London. The menu is noted for its pasta and risotto dishes. But everything is worth eating and the versatility of the kitchen is quite outstanding, considering that for many customers the menu is only a guide and many of them order off it. Rice dishes can range from a hearty risotto of pesto and scarmoza to an almost ethereally light confection of seafood with chopped tomatoes. A daily special pasta dish might be langoustine ravioli and if your taste is a simple tranche of steamed turbot then that is no problem. The predominantly Italian wine list runs to almost 150 bins including an impressive array of Barolo wines, dating back over half a century. If you only ever eat here once, order the chocolate ice-cream as pudding – it is one of Mark Birley's most enduring contributions to life. Members only.

- **DRESS** *Men in suits, women in jewels*
- **TUBES** *Bond Street; Green Park*
- **HOURS** *Lunch Mon–Fri 12.00–15.00; (closed Sat–Sun)*
  Dinner Mon–Fri 18.00–24.00; (closed Sat–Sun)
- **AVERAGE PRICE** *£60–70*
- **CREDIT CARDS** *All major cards*
- **MOBILES** *Not allowed*
- **CIGARS** *Humidor*

THE HOUSE ON ROSSLYN HILL

34 Rosslyn Hill, London NW3
☎ 0171 435 8037

This is allegedly a north London landmark, and is full of young
north Londoners, giving public demonstrations of affection. The
last time I went, I saw a young man with a beard, sunglasses
(it was midnight), shaggy hairdo, anorak and cigar, swill
champagne and give a passable impression of a surly
Britpopper. On a nearby table was another young man who
looked exactly like a young Richard Branson. The place is
apparently close to Air Studios. Food hits and misses with dishes
like pan-fried king prawns in a Moroccan marinade proving spicy
enough to be noticed by the most booze-anaesthetised palate,
yet retaining some elegance. However, the idea of putting fish
cake with ginger and wasabi, as if it were some sort of sushi,
seems pointless. Otherwise, expect the standard multicultural
millenial brasserie fare: sausage and mash, lamb shank, Greek
salad, beef and chicken stir-fry, carpaccio, and gyoza (steam
grilled Japanese beef dumplings accompanied with soya sauce).
Next door is a coffee shop that seems to borrow from the Harvey
Nichols food hall and Pret a Manger. The House is undeniably
busy, undeniably lively and undeniably a scene. The only
debatable aspect is whether one wants to be a part of it.

- **DRESS** *Up in a sort of casual North London way*
- **TUBE** *Hampstead*
- **HOURS** *Mon–Fri 11.00–24.00; Sat 10.00–24.00;
          Sun 10.00–23.30*
- **AVERAGE PRICE** *Lunch £10; Dinner £20*
- **CREDIT CARDS** *No Diners Club or American Express*
- **MOBILES** *Allowed*
- **CIGARS** *Allowed*

THE ICON

21 Elystan Street, London SW3
☎ 0171 589 3718

Although opened only relatively recently, this Chelsea restaurant
has already established itself as a key Eurotrash étape. Part of
the place's attraction is its front woman, Yasemin Olcay, who
was once described by Taki as the prettiest Turk west of Ankara.
The food is actually rather accomplished; the chef used to work
at Le Gavroche – he is called Thierry Laborde. Lunch is light and
includes such dishes as poached asparagus, truffle vinaigrette,

tart of tomato and mozzarella, tapenade vinaigrette, tuna steak Niçoise, brill marinière, mixed vegetables, steak and chips with sauce Choron (Béarnaise with tomato). In the evenings, dishes become a little more complex and expensive, for example, roasted sea scallops with tomato confit and basil, ballotine of foie gras and chicken liver, roasted monkfish wrapped in Parma ham, confit of vegetables and grilled veal with girolle mushrooms and fresh pasta. Favourite puddings are assiette of chocolate and fresh fruit basket with crème diplomate and mango coulis. Krug is competitively priced at a shade under a ton a bottle and other wines are well chosen. This is the sort of place where one wears Tod's, jeans, blazers, pashminas, cashmere, Bulgari sunglasses, black tie and any other old thing you just happen to throw on.

- **DRESS** Eurotrash
- **TUBE** South Kensington
- **HOURS** Lunch Mon–Sat 12.00–15.00; (closed Sun)
  Dinner Mon–Sat 19.00–23.30; (closed Sun)
- **AVERAGE PRICE** Lunch £18–20; Dinner £35
- **CREDIT CARDS** All major cards
- **MOBILES** Not in the evening
- **CIGARS** Humidor

INAHO
4 Hereford Road, London W2
☎ 0171 221 8495

This tiny Japanese restaurant has for some reason always suggested the interior of a cuckoo clock. It has the dimensions and the wall coverings of a domestic sauna, yet it is a splendid place to settle down for an evening of good, reasonably priced Japanese food. There are set lunches listed on the menu, but somehow I have always wound up eating in this bizzare little cocooon of place in the evenings and enjoyed it thoroughly. It is not the longest of menus, but most of the elements are in place: noodles (soba and udon), soups, tempura, sashimi, teryaki and so on. And there are also interesting detours to be enjoyed, such as kaki fry (deep-fried oysters in breadcrumbs) and sunomono (marinated fish and seaweed). At a time when more Japanese restaurants are appearing as ultra modern and laden with gimmicks, Inaho is a charming and eccentric venue to be treasured.

- **DRESS** Hardly matters
- **TUBES** Bayswater; Notting Hill Gate

- **HOURS** Lunch Mon–Fri 12.30–14.30; (closed Sat–Sun)
    Dinner Mon–Sat 19.00–23.00; (closed Sun)
- **AVERAGE PRICE** Lunch £12; Dinner £25
- **CREDIT CARDS** Visa; Mastercard
- **MOBILES** Not allowed
- **CIGARS** Not allowed

L'INCONTRO
87 Pimlico Road, London SW1
☎ 0171 730 6327

This pricey but pleasant, slick, modern Italian local restaurant offers a well-honed version of the kind of light and easy Italian food that became popular at the end of the eighties. Dishes include: spagetti all'aragosta (spagetti with lobster); branzino alla aceto balsamic (poached sea bass in balsamic vinegar sauce); cape sante alla Veneea (Venician-style scallops); galleggo inferocito (grilled baby chicken in a spicy sauce); l'incontro di pasta (selection of three vegetarian pastas) and sfogliatina di mele (warm apple millefeuille with a vanilla sauce).

- **DRESS** Affluent casual
- **TUBE** Sloane Square
- **HOURS** Lunch Mon–Fri 12.30–14.30; (closed Sat–Sun)
    Dinner Mon–Sat 19.00–23.30; Sun 19.00–22.30
- **AVERAGE PRICE** Lunch/Dinner £40–45
- **CREDIT CARDS** All major cards
- **MOBILES** Not allowed
- **CIGARS** Humidor

INDIGO
One Aldwych, London WC2
☎ 0171 300 0400

Gordon Campbell Gray, boss of One Aldwych, is berated for calling his basement restaurant Axis and is branded a heel-clicking fascist. And it is in this jackbooted caricature that I can see him haranguing the crowds in the lobby of his smart hotel, from the galleried area that houses Indigo. The lobby of One Aldwych is a glamorous space, with the exception of an appalling sculpture of a man in a rowing boat which Gray really ought to put out of its misery, Indigo is a lively little restaurant, from which one can vicariously participate in the buzz while also enjoying a certain amount of detachment. It is a good place for a late supper, and service is impeccable. And as a nice thoughtful touch, each table is provided with a notepad headed 'notes taken at Indigo'. It is doubtless such attention to detail and anticipation of customers' needs that has made One Aldwych such a success. Food is variable, crab cakes with sweetcorn and coriander relish might be good, mature cheddar and spinach soufflé is edible but far from outstanding and best avoided. Had I noticed the small list of pizzettas, for example, lobster, tomato, asparagus and tarragon or goats' cheese, grilled aubergine and chilli, I would have ordered one of these instead. The 60 bin wine list, while teetering on the side of expensive, offers a reasonable world tour.

- **DRESS** *Jackboots*
- **TUBE** *Charing Cross*
- **HOURS** *Lunch Mon–Sun 12.00–15.00*
      Dinner Mon–Sun 18.00–23.15
- **AVERAGE PRICE** *Lunch/Dinner £40*
- **CREDIT CARDS** *All major cards*
- **MOBILES** *Not allowed*
- **CIGARS** *Prohibited*

I–THAI

The Hempel, 31–35 Craven Hill Gardens, London W2
☎ 0171 298 9000

Poor old Lady Weinberg got a bit of drubbing for the epic exercise in pretension that is the Hempel. I am the only person I know who is actually impressed by the James Bond villain-style lobby. The Hempel is a minimalist, Oriental-inspired hotel that seems out of place in this Bayswater backwater. What is more, punning aside (a bit Italian a bit Thai, in all a bit I-Thai) I have a fondness for the restaurant. The room is a symphony of floating walls, suspended screens and something that can only be described as a black stone diving board jutting into the room. Like the place settings, the food is precious – it seems sacrilegious to plunge knife, fork, spoon or chopstick into it. Billed as 'spa cuisine at lunch time', the food is weird, sometimes wonderful and not unlike the sort of stuff one gets at Vong or Nobu with Italian overtones. Once decoded and ordered, the food is more filling than you might think, for example, spiced stone bread with mountain leaves and kaffir lime dressing which turns out to be what others might call vegetarian pizza and jolly good it is too. Other dishes are more straightforward: seared tuna sushi with ginger and ponzu is what it claims to be. Dinner might offer up such things as tom khar phed (chicken coconut and foie gras soup flavoured with Thai basil), phad thai goong (stir-fried cellophane noodles with tiger prawns in black ink parcel) and saffron and truffle risotto. Puddings are bewildering and ostentatiously complex, for example ginger tiramisu pandan pudding garnished with blueberries. The wine list favours the typical Hempel guest: a big spending (Cristal '89) novelty hunter (Tasmanian Chardonnay).

- **DRESS** *One of the few places in town where you could wear an Anoushka Hempel ballgown to lunch*
- **TUBES** *Lancaster Gate; Queensway; Bayswater*
- **HOURS** *Lunch Mon–Sun 12.00–14.30*
  Dinner Mon–Sun 19.00–22.45
- **AVERAGE PRICE** *Lunch £50; Dinner £60*
- **CREDIT CARDS** *All major cards*
- **MOBILES** *Not encouraged*
- **CIGARS** *Humidor*

THE IVY
1 West Street, London WC2
☎ 0171 836 4751

This panelled, curiously intimate, room is as much of a London landmark as the Mousetrap which plays opposite its front door. As the creation of Messrs King and Corbin, the people who brought you Le Caprice (qv), The Ivy is the restaurant of choice in Theatreland and many other people besides. For the record: if I had to choose between the two, I would go for Le Caprice, nevertheless The Ivy is what I believe is called a 'Class Act'. AA Gill wrote the book, Mark Hix superintends the kitchen, luvvies, movie stars and those with pretensions to importance in publishing and the performing arts, pile in. This is the sort of restaurant where people come and eat early before going to the theatre. Therefore, the place is often full by 6 pm and seldom thins out until after midnight. As at Le Caprice, service is slick and attentive. And the menu has the kind of food that almost everyone likes: Mexican griddled chicken salad with guacamole and piquillo peppers; sautéed foie gras with peppered figs; the exemplary fish cake (eat with allumettes), risotto nero, seared yellow fin tuna with spiced lentils and wild rocket, rib eye steak Béarnaise – that sort of thing. The list of puddings shares similarities with Le Caprice; a classic is the Scandinavian iced berries with hot white chocolate sauce, but when I am lucky enough to get a table here I always close with Welsh rarebit.

- **DRESS** *Smart*
- **TUBE** *Leicester Square*
- **HOURS** *Lunch Mon–Sat 12.00–15.00; Sun 12.00–15.30*
        Dinner Mon–Sun 17.30–24.00
- **CREDIT CARDS** *All major cards*
- **AVERAGE PRICE** *Lunch/Dinner £40*
- **MOBILES** *Not encouraged*
- **CIGARS** *Allowed*

JAPANESE CANTEEN
21 Exmouth Market, London EC1
☎ 0171 833 3521

This no-frills small chain of Japanese restaurants is slightly more comfortable in feel than the overly antiseptic and rather grating MTV modernity of Yo Sushi! Two other good points include the solid black boxes in which some dishes are served and the bottles of La Yu chilli oil on the tables and counters. The concept is well thought out and dishes include: salmon rolls; chicken and miso soup; seafood salad; noodle soups; donburi (lunch only); bento boxes and deluxe bento boxes. When it comes to sushi, there are two options: sets or pick your own. There are about half a dozen bottles of wine but those seekers-after-authenticity should stick to beers (Sapporo and Asahi), sake or tea.

- **DRESS** *Casual*
- **TUBE** *Angel*
- **HOURS** *Lunch Mon–Fri 12.00–14.30; Sat 12.00–22.30;*
        (closed Sun)
        Dinner Mon–Fri 17.30–22.30; Sat 12.00–22.30;
        Sun 18.00–22.30
- **AVERAGE PRICE** *£10*
- **CREDIT CARDS** *Visa, Delta, Mastercard*
- **MOBILES** *Allowed*
- **CIGARS** *Allowed*

ALSO AT
5 Thayer Street, London W1; (take-away only)
    0171 487 5505 TUBE Bond Street
305 Portobello, London W10;
    0181 968 9988 TUBE Ladbroke Grove
394 St John Street, London EC1;
    0171 833 3222 TUBE Angel

JOE'S

126 Draycott Avenue, London SW3
☎ 0171 225 2217

Joseph Ettedgui is well known as a fashion retailer with
eponymous stores everywhere from London to Miami. His fashion
interests have tended to obscure his restaurant career – he was
the man behind the relaunch of Le Caprice (qv) and hired Messrs
King and Corbin to front it for him. These days, his role as a
restauranteur is confined to three branches of Joe's: one in the
basement of Joseph in Sloane Street and another in Fenwick.
His longest established restaurant is also his best, and is located
on Joseph corner (aka the top of Draycott Avenue). It used to be
a split-level black, chrome and brushed steel temple to eighties
chic, but was given a pale cream and tan leather makeover three
years ago. The food has calmed down a lot in the last year with
the focus moving on to simple dishes such as fresh Cornish crab,
chicken Caesar, wild mushroom risotto, beer-battered cod and
chips, Joe's burger and the perennially popular salmon fish cakes.
Puddings are similarly low-key and run along such lines as warm
blueberry tart or Joe's ice-cream with home-made cookies. If the
menu has been simplified, the wine list has been expanded to
include a number of reasonably grand French wines, but most
people still drink Joe's Champagne straight up or in a cocktail.
Having endured something like 30 seasons in the fashion world,
Joe's is still a trendy place to lunch on leaves, mineral water and
Marlboro Lights.

- **DRESS** *Joseph*
- **TUBE** *South Kensington*
- **HOURS** *Breakfast Mon–Sat 9.30–12.00; (closed Sun)*
  Lunch Mon–Sat 12.30–17.30; (closed Sun)
  Tea Mon–Sat 15.00–18.00; (closed Sun)
- **AVERAGE PRICE** *Lunch £24*
- **CREDIT CARDS** *All major cards*
- **MOBILES** *Not allowed*
- **CIGARS** *Humidor*

ALSO AT
Fenwick of Bond Street, London W1;
  0171 495 5402 TUBE Bond Street
16 Sloane Street, London SW1;
  0171 235 9869 TUBE Sloane Square

JULIE'S
135 Portland Road, London W11
☎ 0171 229 8331

A generation of affluent West Londoners has grown up with Julie's: their parents met here, who knows, they might even have been conceived after a romantic dinner, and they themselves have attended stag and birthday dinners here. Julie's has an aura of the sixties about it – after all, it has been going for more than 30 years, but really it transcends the passage of time and is just itself. The curious interconnecting system of rooms and passageways still holds a charm that cannot be found anywhere else. The food may not be the latest word in grooviness or the stuff of which stratospherically-praiseworthy restaurant reviews are made, nevertheless, classics and favourites from the menu include: fish and shellfish chowder; English goats' cheese briks with watercress and red onion; king prawns with green mango, lime and coconut salad; baked b'stilla of aubergines, red peppers, spinach and almonds; fillet of sole with crab, lobster sauce and beetroot leaves; the classic fillet of lamb with timbale of chickpeas, raisins, harissa and mint oil; and Julie's steak and kidney pie. Wines are reasonably priced, with a small list of grand bottles if that is what you are after. On a winter weekend afternoon, if you are feeling pleasantly melancholic, Julie's is a good place to while away the time with a pot of tea, a piece of cake and a lover. There is something touching about a place that presents bills with the postscript 'We hope you had a lovely time'.

- **DRESS** *Romantic casual*
- **TUBE** *Holland Park*
- **HOURS** *Lunch Mon–Fri 12.30–14.45; Sun 12.00–15.00;*
  (closed Sat)
  Dinner Mon–Fri 19.30–22.15; Sat 19.30–23.15;
  Sun 19.30–22.15
- **AVERAGE PRICE** *Lunch £20–25; Dinner £35*
- **CREDIT CARDS** *All major cards*
- **MOBILES** *Allowed*
- **CIGARS** *Humidor*

KASPIA
18–18a Bruton Place, London W1
☎ 0171 493 2612

'The trouble always is,' James Bond explained to Vesper, 'not
how to get enough caviar but how to get enough toast with it.'
Ian Fleming always came across as a bit of a gastronome, but
this extract from his 1953 novel *Casino Royale* is one of my
favourites. Would that all our lives were beset with such problems
and would that I could spend more time, at least one dinner and
one lunch every week, eating at Kaspia in Bruton Place. This is,
to my mind, the best place in London to eat caviar. The room,
with its glass cabinets of Russian knick-knacks and its cloth-
covered walls, has a faintly louche, old-fashioned elegance to it.
The customers are either extremely smooth men in smart striped
suits, or attractive, well-dressed women of uncertain age. Service,
supervised by the delightful Michel, is hard to fault. Caviar and
blinis is the classic dish. However potatoes Kaspia (a baked
potato served with a dollop of one of five sorts of caviar) has a
dedicated following and the kedgeree, topped with a poached
egg, is a brilliantly comforting dish on a chilly winter day.
Smoked sturgeon is a good thing to order as an adjunct to a
caviar dish, and if you are kept waiting for your lunch or dinner
partner, order half a dozen quails eggs to take your mind off
your companion's tardiness. Kaspia is a delight.

- **DRESS** *Rich*
- **TUBE** *Green Park*
- **HOURS** *Lunch Mon–Sat 12.00–15.00; (closed Sun)*
        Dinner Mon–Sat 19.00–23.30; (closed Sun)
- **AVERAGE PRICE** *Lunch £30; Dinner £50*
- **CREDIT CARDS** *All major cards*
- **MOBILES** *Allowed*
- **CIGARS** *Humidor*

KEMPS BAR AND RESTAURANT
The Pelham Hotel, 15 Cromwell Place, London SW7
☎ 0171 589 8288

Kemps is located in the basement of the Pelham hotel. The
Pelham is comfortable, chintzy and, to my mind, one of London's
finest boutique hotels. Come the biannual frock-fest of London
Fashion Week up the road at the Natural History Museum,
Kemps is one of the most fashionable places to be. For those
wishing to fuel their Ab Fab fantasies, there is an exemplary

'capsule' Champagne list. If you don't like Champagne, the list of still wines is respectable enough. The Sea Breezes have garnered the approval of no less an authority than that weather vane of contemporary metropolitan taste, Simon Mills. Kemps is sublty decorated with fashion-world memorabilia. Food, too, is subtly fashionable. The menu is catholic and includes such things as Caesar salad; pan-fried calf's liver on a cauliflower mash with beetroot oil; lime leaf marinated rump of lamb served on an olive oil mash. There are times when the menu might be accused of trying to overeach itself and such dishes as, say, turbot fillet en paupiette with coconut cream and chilli noodles might not live up to the highest expectations. Nevertheless, it must be remembered that Kemps is a restaurant in the basement of a small hotel and many much grander London hotels would be lucky to have a restaurant as good.

- **DRESS** *Fashiony*
- **TUBE** *South Kensington*
- **HOURS** *Lunch Mon–Fri 12.30–14.30; Sun 11.00–14.00;*
  (closed Sat)
  Dinner Mon–Sat 18.30–22.30; (closed Sun)
- **AVERAGE PRICE** *Lunch £15–20; Dinner £20–25*
- **CREDIT CARDS** *No Diners Club*
- **MOBILES** *Allowed*
- **CIGARS** *Humidor*

KEN LO'S MEMORIES OF CHINA
67–69 Ebury Street, London SW1
☎ 0171 730 7734

This dependable Belgravia Chinese restaurant has quite remarkable staying power. Its eponymous founder may be gone, but customers are still attracted by the double act of TV's noodle king Kam Po But and manager Milan Kosanovic – the charismatic Yugoslav maitre d' who is as much of an attraction as the Canton, Peking and Szechwan cuisine. Indeed, so popular is it that the owners decided to open a Kensington branch a couple of years ago and that too does steady business. The often rather grand clientele demand consistent, competent Chinese food that will not give them too many surprises, and this on the whole tends to be what they get. Steamed ginger sea bass, Peking duck, the ginger and onion lobster (resting on a bed of Mr But's televised noodles) and some sort of sizzling platter are key dishes. Some thought has gone into puddings resulting in the appearance of such dishes as chilled lotus nut soup.

- **DRESS** *Smart casual*
- **TUBE** *Victoria*
- **HOURS** *Lunch Mon–Sat 12.00–14.15; (closed Sun)*
  Dinner Mon–Sat 19.00–23.00; (closed Sun)
- **AVERAGE PRICE** *£30*
- **CREDIT CARDS** *All major cards*
- **MOBILES** *Not allowed*
- **CIGARS** *Prohibited*

ALSO AT
353 Kensington High Street, London W8
    0171 603 6951   TUBE High Street Kensington

KENSINGTON PLACE
201 Kensington Church Street, London W8
☎ 0171 727 3184

This large, glass-walled, almost aquarium-like restaurant is so much a part of the topography of Kensington Church Street that it tends to be taken for granted. Yet before Nick Smallwood (all round nice guy), Simon Slater (husband of newsagent heiress Kate Menzies) and Rowley Leigh (Cambridge-educated media chef) opened here some time in 1987, it was believed to be a doomed site, a gastronomic graveyard. I still believe it to be one of the closest things that London has to an authentic brasserie appropriate to life in the capital. There is no bogus French theming, but there is bustle, activity, noise (sometimes too much) and plenty of tables placed close together. The result is a genuinely convivial atmosphere. The food is *sui generis*. Classic dishes include the grilled scallops with pea purée and mint vinaigrette (one of the great London restaurant concoctions of last 20 years) and the exemplary chicken and goats' cheese mousse. KP's reputation is founded on quality ingredients transformed into simple yet considered dishes. The daily set lunch menu is well worth studying as it offers the chance to eat three courses for less than the price of many of the main courses.

- **DRESS** *Smart*
- **TUBE** *Notting Hill Gate*
- **HOURS** *Lunch Mon–Fri 12.00–15.00; Sat–Sun 12.00–15.30*
  Dinner Mon–Sat 18.30–23.45; Sun 18.30–22.15
- **AVERAGE PRICE** *Lunch £20; Dinner £25–30*
- **CREDIT CARDS** *All major cards*
- **MOBILES** *Allowed*
- **CIGARS** *Humidor*

KETTNERS

29 Romilly Street, London W1
☎ 0171 437 6437

Kettners was apparently founded in 1867 by Auguste Kettner, Chef des Cuisines de Napoleon III. Well, if Napoleon III were around to see it now, he would be scratching his beard in curiosity. Kettners is now and has been for quite a while, well established as the flagship of Peter Boizot's empire. (Boizot was the Pizza Express pioneer: back in 1965, he opened the first one on Wardour Street and sold the chain a couple of years ago. He stills owns a number of restaurants, including Pizza on the Park and Condotti in Mayfair). These days, the fading Belle Epoque splendour of Kettners is the venue for a burger and pizza restaurant – that is fun, lively and still gives a good night out that does not necessarily bankrupt you. A bonus is the Champagne bar that offers almost three dozen different examples of the fizzy stuff.

- **DRESS** *To make an evening of it*
- **TUBE** *Leicester Square*
- **HOURS** *Mon–Sun 12.00–24.00*
- **AVERAGE PRICE** *£15–20*
- **CREDIT CARDS** *All major cards*
- **MOBILES** *Allowed*
- **CIGARS** *Humidor*

KHAN'S

3–15 Westbourne Grove, London W2
☎ 0171 727 5420

Khan's (est. 1977) is one of the miracles of Notting Hill. This completely fashion-resistant curry hall has something of the atmosphere of a school dining hall – right down to the metal water jugs. It is vast, located in what seems to be a former department store that has been brightened up with large metal palm trees that might not look too out of place in Brighton Pavilion. It is certainly not London's smartest restaurant; there is no pretence at chic; it was amusing to watch a party of extremely sleek Italian women deal with the utilitarian environment. Given the mind-numbing numbers of covers that must be done every day, the food is well above local curry house standards while the prices pass on economies of scale to the customers. The menu holds few surprises, but king prawn bhuna, almost the most expensive item on the menu and still under seven quid, is extremely tasty. There are over a dozen tandoori dishes as well as lists of dishes of meat, chicken and seafood (in reality, prawns or king prawns). 'Chef's recommendations' is a section that includes three chicken dishes (butter, jalfrezi and murgh tikka masala) and two thalis. Breads are good, if not beautifully presented, and a glimpse through the kitchen door revealed an immense arsenal of poppadums, waiting to be served with the no-nonense institutional chutney dishes. I am sure Khan's has its detractors, and the staff have been known to get harrassed on occasion, however I find it hard not to like an Indian restaurant that bowls the occasional googly-like prawn cocktail or Irish coffee, for no apparent reason.

- **DRESS** *Canteen casual*
- **TUBES** *Queensway; Bayswater; Royal Oak*
- **HOURS** *Lunch Mon–Sun 12.00–15.00*
       Dinner Mon–Sun 18.00–23.45
- **AVERAGE PRICE** *Lunch/Dinner £10*
- **CREDIT CARDS** *All major cards*
- **MOBILES** *Allowed*
- **CIGARS** *Allowed*

THE LANESBOROUGH
No 1 Lanesborough Place, London SW1
☎ 0171 259 5599

When it completed its transformation from hospital to hotel, the Lanesborough used to have the most wonderful fine-dining room. One sat on extravagantly-upholstered, vaguely Napoleonic sofas and there was a dish of potted crab that I used to dream about. The fine dining room closed, largely I suspect because I often had the room pretty much to myself. The Conservatory Restaurant at the back, while perfectly good, has never managed to come near to eclipsing the memory of the fine-dining room. The menu is that pan global assembly of dishes that often tends to be associated with an expensive cosmopolitan venue: Caesar salad; sardine bruschetta with fennel caponata, goats' cheese and truffle oil; Moroccan carrot soup with chermoula; duck prosciutto with foie gras and celery jam; walnut gnocchi with Swiss chard, porcini and parmesan; North African spiced lamb shank, chickpea polenta and cumin root vegetables. Look hard and it is possible to find evidence of almost every gastronomic trend to have washed over London in the last seven or eight years. I have a rather soft spot for the Library Bar at the Lanesborough. It is presided over by Salvatore Calabrese, who has assembled a drinkers' museum of old spirits stretching back centuries and although he has probably run through the patter a thousand times, he is a great showman. The bar is also a great place for substantial snacks, good sandwiches, caviar and so on. Fashion victims will be interested to note that the bar at the Lanesborough is a favourite lunch spot for staff at Connolly (the people who gave London the ultimate driving shoe and have their shop in the mews behind). As an added attraction the cigar selection is remarkable.

- **DRESS** *As you would if a guest in an expensive hotel*
- **TUBE** *Hyde Park Corner*
- **HOURS** *Lunch Mon–Sun 12.00–14.30*
        Dinner Mon–Sun 18.30–24.00
- **AVERAGE PRICE** *Lunch/Dinner £28*
- **CREDIT CARDS** *All major cards*
- **MOBILES** *Bad reception*
- **CIGARS** *Humidor*

LANGAN'S COQ D'OR
254–260 Old Bromton Road, London SW5
☎ 0171 259 2599

Friendly staff and generous portions characterise the approach to eating at this Earl's Court brasserie-style operation. It looks and feels like one of those sad and slightly neglected neighbourhood restaurants in Paris, except prices are London – but reasonable London at least. Asparagus vinaigrette; gravadlax; Bayonne ham and melon; soupe de poisson, rouille and croûtons are among the usual suspects that have been rounded up as starters. Salads are big and hearty and then it is stuff like Langan's bangers and mash; cod, chips and tartare sauce; roast chicken and stuffing and bread sauce; grilled sole and so on. The place presumably trades on the Langan's name – but I doubt if that means much to anybody other than middle-ranking time-warp execs. The place is useful enough, given its location, but compared to something like, say, Didier Garnier's Le Colombier (qv), it is decidedly lack-lustre.

- **DRESS** *Businessmen in suits*
- **TUBE** *Earls Court*
- **HOURS** *Breakfast Tues–Sun 9.30–12.00; (closed Mon)*
        Lunch/Dinner Tues–Sun 12.00–23.00; (closed Mon)
- **AVERAGE PRICE** *Lunch/Dinner £35*

- **CREDIT CARDS** *All major cards*
- **MOBILES** *Allowed*
- **CIGARS** *Humidor*

THE LAUGHING BUDDHA

41 Montpelier Vale, Blackheath Village, London SE3
☎ 0181 852 4161

The only reason I feel like including this Chinese is because of the amusing name, the sparkly silver waistcoat and bow tie combos sported by the staff, and the fact that it seems a lot more relaxed than the nearby Chapter II (qv).

- **DRESS** *Relaxed*
- **RAIL** *Blackheath Village*
- **HOURS** *Lunch Mon–Sat 12.00–14.30; (closed Sun)*
  Dinner Mon–Sat 18.00–24.00; Sun 18.00–23.30
- **AVERAGE PRICE** *Lunch £8; Dinner £12–15*
- **CREDIT CARDS** *No American Express*
- **MOBILES** *Allowed*
- **CIGARS** *Allowed*

LAUNCESTON PLACE

1a Launceston Place, London W8
☎ 0171 937 6912

The cosy, clubby, country housey arm of the Slater and Smallwood empire, Launceston Place offers cooking appropriate to denizens of the area's stucco-fronted villas: well-mannered, agreeably presented and reassuring. The menu, customers and setting are more staid than at Kensington Place. The set lunch and early supper menus are reasonably priced and sufficiently appealing not to have one looking longingly across at the à la carte selection of dishes (as I find is sometimes the case at Kensington Place). At its most conservative, it is possible to come here, kick off with foie gras, move on to roast grouse, bread sauce and game chips and finish up with plum and almond tart and custard. But to bill Launceston Place as a nursery food ghetto would be unfair. Although not ground-breaking, it is possible to eat moderately fashionably here too, for example, with tempura of oysters with spiced mango and cucumber relish and pan-fried cod wrapped in pancetta and rosemary with tomato and olive stew. Wines include some New World stalwarts, Frog's Leap, Bonny Doon, Leeuwin, Hawk Crest. Launceston Place used to run

a late night supper menu of things like scrambled eggs – I wish
they would bring it back.

- **DRESS** *Smart-ageing Kensington*
- **TUBES** *Gloucester Road; High Street Kensington*
- **HOURS** *Lunch Mon–Fri 12.30–14.30; Sun 12.30–15.00;*
  (closed Sat)
  Dinner Mon–Sat 19.00–23.30; (closed Sun)
- **AVERAGE PRICE** *Lunch/Dinner £35–40*
- **CREDIT CARDS** *No Diners Club*
- **MOBILES** *Not encouraged*
- **CIGARS** *Allowed*

LAWN

1 Lawn Terrace, Blackheath Village, London SE3
☎ 0171 379 0724

This south London outpost of the Bank (qv) Empire, is an extremely
useful addition to the amenities of Blackheath. Located in
premises that are best described as an industrial village hall,
with exposed piping and a floating mezzanine, this place is a
genuine shot of uncondescending metropolitan grooviness – far,
far away from the West End. Nice touches included a coat-check
girl reading Madame Bovary and a soundtrack that included
Tom Browne's Funking for Jamaica. That the Bank group is
trying to build itself a corporate identity becomes evident when
scanning the menu and seeing such dishes as 'Bank Fish and
Chips'. Otherwise, the menu lists such standard modern London
confections as roasted cod with bok choy and ginger; grilled
salmon herb crust courgette salsa; duck confit, wok vegetables
and plum sauce and such fashion-conscious nods to hearty
rusticity as grilled rib-eye steak and rump of lamb with
mediterranean vegetables. The Thai-spiced fish and crab cakes
(a dish that I imagine one sees far more of in London than
Thailand) with sweet chilli sauce, came across as tough little
rissoles with a sweetish sauce, zigzagging across the plate.
However, creamy salt cod, bacon and poached egg was a
wonderful dish – the egg soft, the bacon crisped and looking
a little like crisps that I used to enjoy as a nipper. Wines, while
not cheap, are carefully chosen and helpfully categorised under
headings like Dry Fruity and Full Firm.

- **DRESS** *Suprisingly trendy for the suburbs*
- **RAIL** *Blackheath*

- **HOURS** *Brunch Sat 11.30–14.00; Sun 11.30–17.00;*
  (closed Mon–Fri)
  Lunch Mon–Fri 12.00–14.30; (closed Sat–Sun)
  Dinner Mon–Sat 18.00–23.00; (closed Sun)
- **AVERAGE PRICE** *Lunch/Dinner £30*
- **CREDIT CARDS** *All major cards*
- **MOBILES** *Allowed*
- **CIGARS** *Humidor*

LEITH'S
41 Beak Street, London W1
☎ 0171 287 2057

This West End outpost of the Notting Hill old-timer, is perfectly
all right, if not dazzlingly exciting. Staff are attentive and the
room is made versatile through large wood-framed translucent
screens on wheels, which can be moved about. The Leith's prawn
cocktail is the thing to order off the list of starters – it comes on
perfectly shredded lettuce and is just as delicious as it used to
be, before the prawn cocktail became an ironic postmodern icon.
A pea and black trumpet mushroom risotto with crème fraîche
and bitter leaves was all right, but the rice could have been a
bit nuttier and the whole a thing a little more al dente – but
maybe that is not how they eat their risotto in Soho. Most of the
menu is quite straightforward, and lists such dishes as cod and
smoked haddock cake with tomato and caper butter sauce; slow
roast shank of English Lamb, fried dauphinois potato, Provençal
vegetables and black olives; and pan-fried calf's liver with
sage crumbs, cauliflower and garlic cream. However I heartily
approve of the lines printed at the top, which read, 'If you'd
like something really simple please ask. If we have the ingredients
in our kitchen, we'll only be too pleased to prepare it for you.'
If more restaurants adopted this approach which veers close
to the now seemingly unfashionable maxim 'the customer is
always right', eating out would be considerably less stressful.
The wine list is good and well-edited, with helpful descriptions
that make an instant wine buff of even the least vinously-aware
individual.

- **DRESS** *Smartish*
- **TUBE** *Piccadilly Circus*
- **HOURS** *Lunch Mon–Fri 12.00–14.30; (closed Sat–Sun)*
  Dinner Mon–Sat 18.00–23.15; (closed Sun)
- **AVERAGE PRICE** *Lunch/Dinner £35*

- CREDIT CARDS *All major cards*
- MOBILES *Must be diverted to the restaurant*
- CIGARS *Allowed*

ALSO AT
92 Kensington Park Road, London W11
    0171 229 4481 TUBE Notting Hill Gate

THE LEXINGTON
45 Lexington Street, London W1
☎ 0171 434 3401

A Soho restaurant serving dishes along the lines of: piquillo peppers filled with salt cod on a saffron sauce – a noticeably coarser version of the dish served at Gaudi, (qv); tiger prawn and chicken salad; seared salmon on a lemon and pistachio risotto; warm chocolate brownie and lemon and passionfruit tart. The food is good, the service is friendly and the prices are not too greedy. But the tables are sometimes little bigger than a large ashtray and attempts at floral enchancement of the long narrow room can be pusillanimous. While neither particularly smart nor remotely destinational, the Lexington is a useful and unpretentious place amongst the gastronomic maelstrom of Soho.

- DRESS *Sotto voce Soho*
- TUBES *Piccadilly Circus; Oxford Circus; Tottenham Court Road*
- HOURS *Lunch Mon–Fri 12.30–15.00; (closed Sat–Sun)*
        Dinner Mon–Sat 18.30–23.00; (closed Sun)
- AVERAGE PRICE *Lunch/Dinner £30*
- CREDIT CARDS *All major cards*
- MOBILES *Allowed*
- CIGARS *Not allowed*

LIVEBAIT
43 The Cut, London SE1
☎ 0171 928 7211

As far as I was concerned, Livebait was one of the best things to happen to fish restaurants when it opened in the mid-nineties. This odd little restaurant with its tiled walls, cramped booths and wonderful way with fish is one of the best reasons I can think of for visiting the otherwise less-than-fragrant purlieus of Waterloo. It is also gratifying when one's opinions are endorsed by someone much richer than oneself: Laurence Isaacson, joint head honcho at Groupe Chez Gerard (qv), liked it so much that he bought it and promptly opened another one in Covent Garden next to the Lyceum Theatre. The Covent Garden branch has a lively bar and an exotic fast-changing menu that features most things from East Anglian monkfish to Honolulu mahi mahi. However I prefer the south London original, even if the booths are too small to be truly comfortable. Down at Livebait SE1, dishes like pan-fried blue-fin tuna with red chilli blini and Indian-scented fennel relish are everyday fare. Whether it is stir-fried Cornish squid in oriental vinaigrette with glass noodles, shredded mangetout and a preserved chilli or barbecued whole mackerel with a salad of roast vine tomato butternut squash and baba ganoush, it is unlikely to disappoint. If you like your seafood plain and unadorned, order a shellfish platter or a bowl of whelks – or go somewhere else. If you are inspired to give it a go yourself at home, there is a Livebait cookbook.

- **DRESS** *Surprisingly suity*
- **TUBE** *Waterloo*
- **HOURS** *Lunch Mon–Sat 12.00–15.00; (closed Sun)*
      Dinner Mon–Sat 17.30–23.30; (closed Sun)
- **AVERAGE PRICE** *Lunch/Dinner £28–32*
- **CREDIT CARDS** *All major cards*
- **MOBILES** *Allowed*
- **CIGARS** *Prohibited*

ALSO AT
21 Wellington Street, London WC2;
    0171 836 7161 TUBE Covent Garden

LOLA'S
The Mall Building, Camden Passage, 359 Upper Street, London N1
☎ 0171 359 1932

A couple of years ago, a petite blonde called 'M' (short for something long, Welsh and unpronounceable) and Carol, a tall brunette, quit Le Caprice (qv), where they had tirelessly worked front of house, and started Lola's. Going from Arlington Street to Camden Passage must have been quite a culture shock. Nevertheless, in premises that in a previous existence served as a tram shed, these two women have built up a good following for food prepared by Juliet Peston, who used to work for Alastair Little. A typical starter is a potato pancake, topped perhaps with cured salmon, sevruga caviar, crème fraîche and chives. And I could happily eat nothing but the Roquefort, red onion and rosemary pizza for several days. Main courses show a slight leaning towards classicism: fillet steak, chips and Caesar salad; grilled lamb cutlets, patatass bravas, spinach and olive gravy; salmis of guinea fowl. And the pain perdu, or 'lost bread' as it is billed, is never off the list of puddings. As a bonus to the well-prepared food, there is the well-drilled service that is a natural by-product of a background that includes Le Caprice.

- **DRESS** *Vaguely smart*
- **TUBE** *Angel*
- **HOURS** *Lunch Mon–Fri 12.00–14.30; Sat–Sun 12.00–15.00*
        Dinner Mon–Sat 18.30–23.00; Sun 19.00–22.00
- **AVERAGE PRICE** *Lunch/Dinner £25–30*
- **CREDIT CARDS** *All major cards*
- **MOBILES** *With discretion*
- **CIGARS** *With discretion*

1 LOMBARD STREET
1 Lombard Street, London EC3
☎ 0171 929 6611

Apparently the restaurant's proprietor found inspiration for this place in Titian's Rape of Europa – I have no idea how. However, what I do know is that Herbert Berger, the chef here, used to prepare me some quite splendid lunches when he worked at the Café Royal; sadly, the night I visited I fear he might have been out of the kitchen. The food was perfectly good, but not outstanding – a pity as I had always hoped that Berger would get the recognition I believe he deserves and was excited to visit his new berth. Perhaps we arrived a little late since the smart dining room, was thinning out – nevertheless, a very apologetic breadbasket and an allegedly-carbonated beverage that was served as flat as Tara P-T's chest did not augur well. The menu included: carpaccio of tuna and scallops with roasted sesame seeds, oriental spices, black radish and lime; warm salad of wood pigeon with braised endive beetroot and juniper vinaigrette; pot-roasted turbot with woodland mushrooms and thyme velouté; caramelised sea bass with fennel seeds, basil mash and saffron jus; Angus steak, seared foie gras, shallot confit and acidulated Madeira sauce; and poached fillet of lamb, summer vegetables and mint broth. Puddings are inventive, including feuillantine of caramelised Granny Smith; Guinness ice-cream and glazed hazelnuts; hot figs in red wine and port with liquorice parfait; treacle sauce and fromage blanc sorbet. My sister, a sort of Ally McBeal figure who works for a City law firm, has described the food as memorably forgettable, which is a pity as I feel Berger ought to be remembered. Nevertheless, the place seemed to be doing great business.

The noisy brasserie at the front of the building – which serves salads, pasta, and various grilled and blackened dishes – was thronged with City folk enjoying themselves and sending each other e-mails on the screens that are dotted about the place and display market movements etc. Friendly staff contributed to the jolly atmosphere.

- **DRESS** *Suits*
- **TUBE** *Bank*
- **HOURS** *Lunch Mon–Fri 11.00–15.00; (closed Sat–Sun)*
  Dinner Mon–Fri 18.00–22.00; (closed Sat–Sun)
- **AVERAGE PRICE** *Lunch £30 (brasserie), £40 (restaurant);*
  Dinner £50
- **CREDIT CARDS** *All major cards*
- **MOBILES** *Allowed*
- **CIGARS** *Humidor*

LUNDUM'S

The Danish Restaurant, 119 Old Brompton Road, London SW7
☎ 0171 373 7774

As I was growing up – a process still under way – in Brighton during the seventies, I remember a restaurant called the Danske Hus. It has taken me over twenty years to come across another restaurant that actively bills itself as a Danish restaurant and, as the definite article infers, the Lundum family are pretty sure of their unique status. The place, on the site of the sadly-missed Chanterelle, is a real find. The room, white with a blue ceiling, manages to be cosy yet smart and is superintended by Clint Lundum. The food is simple and straightforward, unlike that most famous of Danes, Hamlet. At lunch, order one of around a dozen 'Danish Open Face Sandwiches', ranging from herring with onion and capers through smoked eel with scrambled eggs to roasted loin of pork with prunes and red cabbage. A more substantial lunch might be 'A Danish platter with herrings, Danish meatblass, pan-fried fillet of plaice, chicken salad & Danish cheese'. Salmon dishes, listed under the endearing heading 'Lundum's Symphony of Salmons' are viewed, justifiably, as something of a speciality by Kay Lundum, the paterfamilias, a man with a splendid set of whiskers, who used to manage the restaurant at the Danish Club and presides over the kitchen here. The wine list is bigger and more ambitious than one might

at first expect and be prepared to down a slug or two of iced
Aalborg Aquavit. Neither big nor flashy, and certainly not overly
complex, Lundum's has the charm of a real family-run restaurant:
an increasingly rare commodity in inner London these days.
Perhaps Modern Danish will become this year's trendy cuisine.

- **DRESS** *Affluent local*
- **TUBES** *South Kensington; Gloucester Road*
- **HOURS** *Mon–Sat 11.00–23.00; Sun 12.00–16.00*
- **AVERAGE PRICE** *£30*
- **CREDIT CARDS** *All major cards*
- **MOBILES** *Allowed*
- **CIGARS** *Allowed*

MAISON NOVELLI
See NOVELLI page 160

MANDARIN ORIENTAL HYDE PARK
66 Knightsbridge, London SW1
☎ 0171 235 2000

This grand hotel has a dining room with one of the best views
in London: out over Hyde Park. Since the Mandarin have taken
over and set about rebuilding the place, standards and prices
have risen. There is a precision about the Mandarin operation
that is quite breath-taking – the staff are encouraged to study
polaroids of the contents of a minibar, so that they too can
standardise the arrangement of the contents. Food prepared
by David Nicholls, late of the Ritz, is similarly precise and he
is not a man afraid of doing simple things well – his crab cake
garnished with a chunk of lobster and almost geometric pile of
leaves is a delight. Seared tuna with spinach, aubergine, caviar
and five spice sauce is good, but not quite as good it sounds;
pavé of cod with parmesan mashed potatoes, olives and
minestrone of autumn vegetables is hearty without being
overbearing. And for those who might find a dinner of duck
tortellini with roast parsnip cappuccino followed by roast fillet
of turbot, pan-fried foie gras, potato gallette and ceps a little
too challenging, there is a list of grills, roasts and simple dishes:
smoked Scottish salmon, Dover sole, roast English duck etc.
Similarly simple and genuinely appetising is the brunch menu:
Caesar salad or creamed scrambled egg with smoked salmon
and chives are just two of a long list of good things to chase
away weekend hangovers. It is such touches that mark this place

out as somewhere where the customer is king and if he asks for something simple, the chef is not going to come out and insult him. Under the aegis of GM Brian Williams, this place is shaping up to be one of the best, and priciest, London hotels of the turn of the century.

- **DRESS** *Smart*
- **TUBES** *Knightsbridge; Hyde Park Corner*
- **HOURS** *Lunch Mon–Sun 12.00–14.30*
       Dinner Mon–Sat 18.30–23.00; Sun 18.30–22.30
- **AVERAGE PRICE** *Lunch £25–30; Dinner £40–45*
- **CREDIT CARDS** *All major cards*
- **MOBILES** *Allowed*
- **CIGARS** *Humidor*

MANZI'S

1–2 Leicester Street, London WC2
☎ 0171 734 0224

For seven decades, the Manzi family has been serving fish on this West End street corner. Manzi's is really two restaurants: the ground floor houses 'Manzi's Seafood Restaurant' while the first floor is home to the 'The Cabin Room at Manzi's'. With checked tablecloths, pale walls and a ceiling painted brasserie-style with dancing girls, the ground floor is the simpler side of the Manzi's offer. The fact that the list of starters includes such humble dishes as bread and butter, priced at 95 pence, points to a robustly unpretentious way with seafood. There are four seafood cocktails: oyster, lobster, prawn and crab. Other first courses include classics like smoked eel, smoked cod's roe and whitebait. Main courses tend to be grilled or fried, and there is a piscine mixed grill for two. Upstairs cooking is much more fancy, saucy and probably of most interest to culinary historians interested in experiencing the kind of fish dishes served during the fifties and sixties. For example, there are eleven ways with Dover sole, from plain grilled, through Dover sole Walewska (steamed with slices of lobster, mornay sauce and grated cheese) to sole Manzi (meunière with white wine, prawns and pommes Parisiennes). There are six lobster dishes, four turbot, four halibut, three skate, two plaice, three scallop, two salmon, four scampi and one meat (fillet steak). Puddings include cheesecake and crème caramel.

- **DRESS** *Varied*
- **TUBES** *Leicester Square; Piccadilly Circus*

- **HOURS** *Lunch Mon–Sat 12.00–14.45; (closed Sun)*
  Dinner Mon–Sat 17.30–23.45; Sun 18.00–22.45
- **AVERAGE PRICE** *Lunch/Dinner £28*
- **CREDIT CARDS** *All major cards*
- **MOBILES** *Allowed*
- **CIGARS** *Humidor*

MARK'S CLUB
46 Charles Street, London W1
☎ 0171 499 2936

This, to my mind, is Mark Birley's crowning achievement. Marks Club has done more to preserve civilisation, or at least to arrest its decline, than any other institution in London that springs to mind. It is the sort of thing that ought to have guaranteed Birley's elevation to the peerage years ago and his continuing absence from the House of Lords has dented my faith in the honours' system. I rather dislike the term 'gentleman's club', but it is reasonable, if inevitably inadequate, shorthand for the unique experience that is Mark's Club. If you want fusion-inspired-rustic-Italian-Pacific-Rim nosh, stay away from Marks Club. However if you like potted shrimp, haddock Monte Carlo, the best chocolate ice-cream in the civilised world and a post-prandial pre-Christian Havana cigar served amidst a sea of Landseer animal art, then the chances are that you will never want to leave this elegant Mayfair house. Service is faultless. Bruno, whose family also runs a restaurant called Giovanni in Montecatini near Pisa, superintends the two dining rooms; the front room is the more cosy and intimate, the second, lighter. The entrance hall is Terry's domain. The first floor bar and drawing rooms are run by one of London's great double acts, Barry and Roy, who dispense everything from tankards of beer to flutes of the finest Champagne with unique aplomb. But be warned – even if you can get to be a member, Mark's Club is an extremely expensive habit. Members only.

- **DRESS** *Like chairman of FTSE 100 company*
- **TUBE** *Green Park*
- **HOURS** *Lunch Mon–Fri 12.00–14.30; (closed Sat–Sun)*
  Dinner Mon–Fri 19.00–23.00; (closed Sat–Sun)
- **AVERAGE PRICE** *Lunch/Dinner £50–60*
- **CREDIT CARDS** *All major cards*
- **MOBILES** *Certainly not*
- **CIGARS** *Humidor*

MAROUSH II

38 Beauchamp Place, London SW3
☎ 0171 581 5434

I can recall many happy early mornings spent at Maroush on
Beauchamp Place. For a while, during my ever-so-slightly
dissipated younger years, it was the place I used to go after
leaving Tramp. The downstairs counters also used to harbour
snacking paparazzi keeping watch over San Lorenzo (qv)
opposite. I like Lebanese food, or perhaps more accurately, I
enjoy visiting Lebanese restaurants in London. At the best of them,
like Maroush, there is a lively informality: people dropping in
and out, some merely popping in for sandwich, others settling
in for the evening. There is something rather comforting about
a half dozen or so mezze dishes spread out in front of you,
especially if you are hungry. Given that there are well over three
dozen starters, from boiled brains, through four types of fresh
raw minced meat, to delicious fatayer bi sabanekh (pastry filled
with spinach, onions, lemon juice and pine kernels), I seldom find
it necessary to move on to the main courses, which rely heavily
on the charcoal grill.

- **DRESS** *Expensive casual*
- **TUBE** *Knightsbridge*
- **HOURS** *Mon–Sun 12.00–4.00 am*
- **AVERAGE PRICE** *£18–20*
- **CREDIT CARDS** *All major cards*
- **MOBILES** *Allowed*
- **CIGARS** *Allowed*

ALSO AT

MAROUSH III, 62 Seymour Street, London W1;
　　0171 724 5024 TUBE Marble Arch
MAROUSH I, 21 Edgware Road, London W2;
　　0171 723 0773 TUBE Marble Arch
MAROUSH IV, 68 Edgware Road, London W2;
　　0171 224 9339 TUBE Marble Arch
RANOUSH, 43 Edgware Road, London W2;
　　0171 723 5929 TUBE Marble Arch
BEIRUT EXPRESS, 112–114 Edgware Road, London W2;
　　0171 724 2700 TUBE Marble Arch

MASH

19–21 Great Portland Street, London W1
☎ 0171 637 5555

This is the youngest and liveliest of Oliver Peyton's excursions into the London restaurant world. Mash is probably most famous for cameras which allow those using the ladies lavatories to monitor events in the gents. It is in essence a vast space age cocktail and bierkeller with alarming contemporary art and an upstairs restaurant. At the very back is the in-house microbrewery, which is responsible for the selection of weird flavoured beers, some of which work and some of which are best avoided by all but the most devoted students of the brewers art. Particularly worth ordering are the pizzas baked in the wood-fired oven and put together with a real sense of the baroque. Pizzas at times challenge the most eccentric excesses of the Cal-Ital days, for example: red onion marmalade, fresh thyme, olives, pickled anchovies and parmesan; or crispy duck, hoisin, cucumber and Asian greens. As well as pizzas, the wood-fired oven and grill create other dishes, fish en papillotte, suckling pig and so on. The wine list is thoughtful, large and as cheap or as expensive as you want. Mash was originally conceived as an informal no-bookings-taken style of eating house, but has matured into a slightly more formal but still lively and noisy restaurant, and prices have risen.

- **DRESS** *Trendy young office worker*
- **TUBE** *Oxford Circus*
- **HOURS** *Breakfast Mon–Fri 9.00–12.00; (closed Sat–Sun)*
      Brunch Sat 11.00–16.00; Sun 12.00–17.00
      Lunch Mon–Sun 12.00–15.00
      Dinner Mon–Sun 18.00–23.00
- **AVERAGE PRICE** *Lunch/Dinner £35*
- **CREDIT CARDS** *All major cards*
- **MOBILES** *Allowed*
- **CIGARS** *Humidor*

MATSURI

15 Bury Street, London SW1
☎ 0171 839 1101

This is the sort of place that bears out the condescending truism that it is a good thing to eat in an ethnic restaurant frequented by customers of the appropriate ethnic group. Matsuri is located in a charisma-free basement that seems not to have benefited from any concerted attempts at decoration. In the main room, one eats at counters located around Teppans, although there is a sushi bar and private dining. The sushi is excellent with some commendably exotic piscine life winding up in front of you, and top notch soups providing a change of texture. There is a good array of Teppan-yaki dishes: from lobster to duck. However the outstanding attraction of the Teppan is the intriguing, and misleadingly named, Okonomi-pizza Hiroshima-style. If you are hungry, try the Japanese pizza with seafood, it is nothing like a pizza, more like a pancake sandwich, but even that description fails to convey how good this dish is. Staff are charming as are the Japanese puddings – little jelly-like things. Drink tea. While you are unlikely to be able to fault the food, do not expect to be pleasantly surprised by the bill.

- **DRESS** *As if for a business meeting*
- **TUBES** *Green Park, Piccadilly Circus*
- **HOURS** *Lunch Mon–Sat 12.00–14.30; (closed Sun)*
  Dinner Mon–Sat 18.00–22.30; (closed Sun)
- **AVERAGE PRICE** *Lunch £23; Dinner £40*
- **CREDIT CARDS** *No Switch*
- **MOBILES** *Allowed in the bar but not at the table*
- **CIGARS** *Humidor*

MEDITERRANEO
37 Kensington Park Road, London W11
☎ 0171 792 3131

This restaurant is a sibling of nearby Osteria Basilico (qv). The menu is full of the staples that one has come to expect from such mid-market upwardly-mobile Italian restaurants: swordfish carpaccio; bufala mozzarella with Parma ham and marinated wild mushrooms; ribollita; grigliata mista di pesce; the recently rehabilitated veal cutlet alla Milanese; shank of lamb and so on. While not outstanding, the food is perfectly agreeable. An otherwise tasty dish of monkfish tails in saffron sauce, was marred in its presentation by the addition of a perfectly superfluous garnish of a few carrot gratings arranged on a piece of lollo rosso that looked like it had been put in a flower press. However, a pasta dish with chunks of fresh tuna was more of a success. The place is often packed.

- **DRESS** *Vaguely smart*
- **TUBE** *Ladbroke Grove*
- **HOURS** *Lunch Mon–Fri 12.30–15.00; Sat 12.30–16.00;*
  Sun 12.30–15.30
  Dinner Mon–Sat 18.30–23.30; Sun 18.30–22.30

- **AVERAGE PRICE** *Lunch £20; Dinner £30*
- **CREDIT CARDS** *No Diners Club*
- **MOBILES** *Not happy with mobiles*
- **CIGARS** *Allowed*

MEZZO; MEZZONINE
100 Wardour Street, London W1
☎ 0171 314 4000

Although I yield to no man in my admiration of Sir Terence
Conran, I have to say that neither Mezzo, nor Mezzonine are
much to my taste. I suppose my criticism of the place is perhaps a
distillation of a general dislike for Soho, in that it is too noisy and
brash. I have tended to view them as one gigantic restaurant,
which I am told is not the case at all. It basically splits up thus:
the ground floor is called Mezzonine, it has a large buzzy bar
and functions as an Oriental restaurant. Downstairs in Mezzo the
menu is contemporary European. Upstairs quite a bit of the food
is wok-fried: as in wok-fried scallops; black beans with coriander
and wok-fried monkfish with caramelised ginger; wok-fried King
crab with Thai herbs. Thai influences run throughout a list of
dishes that is offered under such titles as 'Amuse', 'Small Dishes
& Salads', 'Dishes for Two People', 'Larger Dishes', 'Side Dishes'
etc. On the lower floor, things take a more occidental turn, with
veal sweetbread and leek terrine; pan-fried risotto cake with salsa
verde; fillet of pork saltimbocca, polenta with Madeira jus; basil
gnocchi, Italian cabbage and slow-roast tomatoes. In the evening,
dishes for two, like Chateaubriand and plateau de fruits, make an
appearance as does a list of grills and rotisseries. There is also
live music. Neither Mezzo nor Mezzonine are places I would
recommend for a quiet romantic liaison, however if you are short
of conversation, the noise of the jazz or one's fellow customers
tends to soak up those awkward silences.

- **DRESS** *Brash*
- **TUBES** *Leicester Square; Piccadilly Circus*
- **HOURS** *Lunch Mon–Fri 12.00–14.30; Sun 12.30–15.00;*
  (closed Sat)
  Dinner Mon–Thurs 18.00–24.00; Fri–Sat 18.00–1.00 am;
  Sun 18.00–23.00; (Mezzonine closed Sun and opens
  at 17.30 for dinner Mon–Sat)
- **AVERAGE PRICE** *Lunch £25; Dinner £35*
- **CREDIT CARDS** *All major cards*
- **MOBILES** *Allowed*
- **CIGARS** *Humidor*

MIN'S

31 Beauchamp Place, London SW3
☎ 0171 589 5080

The people responsible for the nearby Enterprise (qv) also
bring you this small but exquisitely decorated Beauchamp
Place restaurant. The menu style is probably best described
as pasteurised trendy, perfect for middle-aged Knightsbridge
residents who do not want to be too adventurous with their
eating but still feel they ought to be aware of such trends as
the North African onslaught of recent years. Yes there might
be a couscous on the menu and a token sea bass with pesto
crust, stir-fried vegetables and linguini, but such notionally
fashion-conscious offerings tend to be balanced with things
like Min's chicken and mushroom pie and sirloin steak with
home-made chips and grilled tomatoes. The first floor room is
comfortable and cosily decadent and one can easily settle in
for the afternoon.

- **DRESS** *Twee*
- **TUBE** *Knightsbridge*
- **HOURS** *Brunch Sun 11.00–15.00*
      Lunch Mon–Sat 12.00–14.30
      Dinner Mon–Sat 19.00–22.30; (closed Sun)
- **AVERAGE PRICE** *Lunch £25; Dinner £35*
- **CREDIT CARDS** *All major cards*
- **MOBILES** *Not allowed*
- **CIGARS** *Not allowed*

MIRABELLE

56 Curzon Street, London W1
☎ 0171 499 4636

My favourite part of the Marco Pierre White empire, the
Mirabelle is a truly glamorous West End restaurant. The menu
is a vast oversized card of the sort you only ever see in films shot
in Eastman colour during the fifties. On it are printed the sort of
dishes that go with films of that era: veal escalope 'Holstein',
omelette 'Arnold Bennett' and a rather grand prawn cocktail,
'salad of tomato and fresh prawns – sauce cocktail'. The food
I have eaten here has been simply presented and skilfully, but
not showily, prepared. The wine list is preposterously large and
grand. It comes with an almost otiose note to the effect that even
smarter wines are available on request. For real show-offs, there
is a list of 50 different vintages of Chateau d'Yquem, reaching
back into the first half of the last century. The Mirabelle may be

in a basement, but it has been decorated with a light touch
and is superintended by Mr Louis, for years the major domo of
Annabel's. If I weren't so scared by Mr White and his reputation,
I would eat here more often.

- **DRESS** *Smart*
- **TUBE** *Green Park*
- **HOURS** *Lunch Mon–Fri 12.00–14.30; Sat–Sun 12.00–15.00*
        Dinner Mon–Sat 18.00–23.30; Sun 18.00–22.30
- **AVERAGE PRICE** *Lunch/Dinner £40–45*
- **CREDIT CARDS** *All major cards*
- **MOBILES** *Allowed*
- **CIGARS** *Humidor*

MOKARIS
61 Jermyn Street, London SW1
☎ 0171 495 5909

Central London brims with lots of café/restaurant/snack bars,
which pay almost no attention to passing trends in gastronomy
and decoration. Yet for many people, these are the restaurants
they use the most; be it for take-out sandwiches, cups of well-
made cappuccino, or the occasional hot dish of deep-fried
scampi, veal escalope alla Milanese, lamb cutlets, or chicken
Kiev. Almost everyone has their favourite and mine is Mokaris.
I was introduced to it by the great Edward Sahakian, proprietor
of Davidoff of St James's and am proud to have become a
regular here. I usually stop here for a coffee and cigar with the
great man once or twice a week. It is a splendid place from
which to watch the world go about its business. Sooner or later,
anyone of any importance will pass by the portals of Mokaris
and while you are waiting for them, the continuing pageant of
sheikhlings and princes pulling up in their vast Mercedes saloons
to shop at Vahe Manoukian's Vincci, is a pleasant diversion.

- **DRESS** *St James office worker*
- **TUBES** *Green Park; Piccadilly*
- **HOURS** *Lunch Mon–Sat 12.00–15.00; (closed Sun)*
        Dinner Mon–Sat 18.00–23.00; (closed Sun)
- **AVERAGE PRICE** *Lunch/Dinner £25–30*
- **CREDIT CARDS** *All major cards*
- **MOBILES** *Allowed*
- **CIGARS** *Humidor*

MOMO

25 Heddon Street, London W1
☎ 0171 434 4040

For a while in the late nineties, this was the most fashionable
restaurant in the most fashionable city in the world. The basement
bar with its souk-like ambience and membership card that was a
medallion was where the froth at the top of Cappuccino Society
wanted to spend its evenings. But groovy atmosphere and
iconic status were compensated for by less than brilliant food.
Nowadays suits are coming here for lunch, but the food has
improved under the aegis of a new chef. What is more, the old,
vaguely conical plates which looked rather good, but militated
against attractive food presentation, have been replaced by
something rather flatter. Classics like the starter of briquat de
légumes croquants aux herbes fraîches have improved with
particular reference to the quality of the pastry, ditto the pastilla
aux fruits de mer. Pan-fried sea bream on a hot tabbouleh with
citrus fruit juice is, for Momo, a delicate dish that benefits from
being presented on a flat plate rather than merely gathering in
the bottom of a shallow cone. Good use is made of dried fruits,
as both a pudding and an ingredient in the lamb tagine. Staff
veer between helpful and stupid, charming and moody, but they
all look great as does the clothing designed by Momo.

- **DRESS** *As fashionably as you want but the staff will always look
      cooler than you do*
- **TUBE** *Piccadilly Circus*
- **HOURS** *Lunch Mon–Fri 12.00–14.15*
      Brunch Sat–Sun 12.00–16.30
      Dinner Mon–Sat 19.00–23.30; (closed Sun)
- **AVERAGE PRICE** *Lunch/Dinner £30–35*
- **CREDIT CARDS** *All major cards*
- **MOBILES** *Allowed, but reception is poor*
- **CIGARS** *Humidor*

MONTANA

125–129 Dawes Road, London SW6
☎ 0171 385 9500

Montana was the first of Drew Barwick's southwestern American
restaurants, the formula (crudely described as gourmet Tex Mex in
trendy surroundings) has proved successful, and others, Dakota
(qv) and Canyon (qv), have followed. The kind of dishes you
can expect at Montana are chilli-cured smoked kingfish with a

savoury yellow corn griddle cake and jalapeno crema; pecan-crusted goats' cheese with baby chard leaves, beetroot crackers and pear chutney; roasted pepper and aubergine tamale, red chilli basil pesto; chargrilled tuna steak, fire-roasted tomato and smoked shrimp salsa and spicy green rice; and grilled Iowa rib-eye steak, smoked bacon compote, mushroom, sweet potato red onion relish. Brunch at Montana is a good way to spend a Sunday – after a roast chicken burrito or a plate of huevos rancheros (toasted blue corn tortilla, black beans, fried eggs and chorizo with red chilli sauce), there can be few more pleasurable prospects than a steamed Mexican chocolate cinammon bread puddings with kumquat ice-cream; unless of course you want to order the delicious cheesecake of the day. Wines, as at the other restaurants in the group, are strongly New World-oriented and well arranged under headings relating to body, oakiness etc. On an aesthetic note, the hide-covered corner booth and the large canvases of prominent Native Americans (painted from photographs) are worth a glance.

- **DRESS** *Casual Ralph Lauren*
- **TUBE** *Fulham Broadway*
- **HOURS** *Lunch Fri–Sun 12.00–15.30; (closed Mon–Thurs)*
        Dinner Mon–Thurs 19.00–23.00; Fri–Sat 19.00–23.30;
        Sun 19.00–22.30
- **AVERAGE PRICE** *Lunch £15; Dinner £30*
- **CREDIT CARDS** *No Diners Club*
- **MOBILES** *Allowed*
- **CIGARS** *Allowed*

MONZA
6 Yeoman's Row, London SW3
☎ 0171 591 0210

Monza is run by the older brother of Guido at Como Lario (qv). While it has few pretensions to being smart, Monza is a useful addition to the area and the cramped Mews location, stuffed with model cars and motor racing memorabilia has a cosy charm. The place is popular with hungry shoppers, lunching hoorays, casual aristocrats and Prince William. The food is competent without being alarmingly neologistic and therefore suits its clientele perfectly. Arancini di riso allo zafferano (deep-fried saffron rice balls stuffed with mozzarella in a tomato and basil sauce) is a hearty and cheering starter for cold winter days. Otherwise one can fall back on straightforward things like Parma ham with buffalo mozzarella and tomato. Pasta dishes are good enough and the mixed grill of fish is a generous platter. Amongst puddings, the semifreddo al torroncino has a not unpleasant medicinal tang to it. As is usual with such places, it pays to become a regular as then the proprietor will go to considerable lengths to make you happy – for example keeping a favourite box of your Cohiba Esplendidos close at hand.

- **DRESS** *Cashmere crew necks or whatever Prince William wears*
- **TUBE** *South Kensington*
- **HOURS** *Lunch Tues–Sat 12.00–14.30; Sun 12.00–14.30;*
  (closed Mon)
  Dinner Mon–Sat 19.00–23.30; Sun 19.00–22.30
- **AVERAGE PRICE** *£20–28*
- **CREDIT CARDS** *All major cards*
- **MOBILES** *Allowed*
- **CIGARS** *Humidor*

MORO
34–36 Exmouth Market, London EC1
☎ 0171 833 8336

Moro was one of the places that opened in the late nineties and got everybody worked up into a frenzy of praise. It tapped into the trend for North African food, yet overlaid it with a strong Iberian identity; the result is a credible culinary genre that I daresay someone has dubbed West Mediterranean. After the hype that has attended the place, the large bare surroundings, closely-grouped tables and open kitchen are a bit of a disappointment. Moro is a de facto club and its stars are people like Zaha Hadid, the architect, who happened to be enjoying lunch on a recent visit I made to Moro. The food however is genuinely interesting and tasty without being a knock-off of some well-tried formula. The charcoal grill is evident in such dishes as pork fillet with cabbage and chestnuts and monkfish with sprouting broccoli, capers and lemon. Lamb tagine with preserved lemon is served with flatbread and herb salad and the flatbread crops up again in the starter of quail backed in flatbread with pistachio sauce. Starters like tuna roe with chickpeas, saffron and parsley (with the roe grated like bottarga) have an agreeable peasant-like quality. The grilled sardines with tahini sauce put me in mind of the outdoor grill of a little beach restaurant that I sometimes visit between San Pedro and Marbella. Puddings are interesting and keen to demonstrate their regionality, for example, rose water and cardamom ice-cream; Malaga raisin ice-cream with Pedro Ximenez; Seville

orange tart; yoghurt cake with pistachios. Moro also caters
to the snacking eater, with a bar menu of mezze or raciones
scrawled on a blackboard, for example, boquerones, chorizo
and so on. While on the subject of the bar, there is an interesting
array of Spanish liqueurs and it is good to see that quintessential
Spanish brew Cruzcampo available in London. There are also
a few interesting sherries and Cavas to enjoy while you wait for
your table in this inevitably busy restaurant.

- **DRESS** *As if you are an important architect with a social conscience*
- **TUBES** *Farringdon; Angel*
- **HOURS** *Lunch Mon–Fri 12.30–14.30; (closed Sat–Sun)*
  Tapas Mon–Fri 12.30–22.30; (closed Sat–Sun)
  Dinner Mon–Fri 19.30–22.30; (closed Sat–Sun)
- **AVERAGE PRICE** *Lunch/Dinner £30*
- **CREDIT CARDS** *No Diners Club*
- **MOBILES** *Allowed*
- **CIGARS** *Allowed*

MORTON'S
The Restaurant, 28 Berkeley Square, London W1
☎ 0171 493 7171

It could be argued that Morton's has one of the most beautiful
dining rooms in London, but until recently only club members
were able to enjoy the views down Berkeley Square. Now this
exquisite first floor room has been given a lick of paint, some
new furniture and has emerged in what the owners call an
interpretation of Art Deco elegance. I have no idea what this
means, but happily the person who interprets the Art Deco has
not been allowed near the kitchen. The food, which used to
be mediocre and expensive, has now become excellent and
expensive. Gary Hollihead, late of MPW is the consultant chef
here and it shows in such dishes as: pavé of tuna; beignets of
scallops; escalope of foie gras, roast mango, apple and ginger
Jacqueline; medallions of lobster and scallops, spring onion
risotto; and rabbit and langoustine tails, girolles, Sauternes butter.
The deft touch with which Hollihead executes dishes here seems
to indicate that he is out to impress – as he ought to be at
these prices (although the prix fixe menu at lunch is eminently
affordable). Service is well managed and if I have any complaints
they are about the fake Magritte that looms above the fireplace.
Those in search of the old Morton's can find it at the bar
downstairs, which is still a members-only zone, packed with an

invigorating social cocktail of second-hand Rolls Royce drivers, foxy women of a certain age and youngish men on the make.

- **DRESS** *Smart*
- **TUBE** *Green Park*
- **HOURS** *Lunch Mon–Fri 12.00–15.00; (closed Sat–Sun)*
    Dinner Mon–Fri 19.00–23.00; Sat 19.00–23.00;
    (closed Sun)
- **AVERAGE PRICE** *£50*
- **CREDIT CARDS** *All major cards*
- **MOBILES** *Not allowed*
- **CIGARS** *Humidor*

MOXON'S
14 Clapham Park Road, London SW4
☎ 0171 627 2468

Moxon's is a good restaurant in a curious location. Those of a morbid bent might find it amusing that Moxon's occupies the same stretch of road as 'Clapham's only independent family funeral directors'. Indeed one can spend a happy few minutes gazing in windows that boast promotional material from the Funeral Planning Council, sample headstones, a photograph of a horse-drawn, glass-sided hearse and a 24-hour emergency hotline – ideal no doubt for the corpse in a hurry. However, on a recent evening visit to Moxon's, the emergency hotline must have been quiet as I saw no evidence of high speed hearses tearing around the streets of south London. I imagine being an undertaker must be hungry work, therefore the presence of Moxon's so close to one's place of work must be a bonus. This is a bona fide, good, reasonably-priced, smartish fish restaurant of a type all too absent from many parts of London. It strikes me as unfair that south London should have both the original Livebait and Moxon's. At Moxon's, there is a passionate understanding about fish that appeals to the serious gastronome and the informed lay restaurant visitor alike. Even simple and deceptively predictable dishes are executed with flair and imagination, for example, the salmon in the dish of gravadlax with smoked haddock and asparagus salad, sweet mustard and dill dressing came in richly-flavoured, chunky medallions. A starter of ravioli (acutally one big raviolo) of dressed crab with seared scallops was of a size and richness that might well have allowed it to be presented as a main course. There will be a token meat dish on the menu, but typical of the mains are grilled fillet of Irish salmon with lime-scented mash and parmesan-baked chicory and roast cod

with sage and gruyère crust with risotto a la (sic) carbonara.
The list of puddings is an unashamed calorie-fest, including
such dishes as Toblerone parfait with glazed bananas; warm
chocolate and pecan brownie; Belgian chocolate ice-cream and
cinnamon sabayon. The room is large and uncluttered and has
charming fish-print fabric blinds.

- **DRESS** *As if going on to a funeral*
- **TUBE** *Clapham Common*
- **HOURS** *Lunch Sun 12.00–16.00; (closed Mon–Sat)*
        Dinner Mon–Sun 18.30–22.30
- **AVERAGE PRICE** *Lunch £15–20; Dinner £25*
- **CREDIT CARDS** *No Diners Club or American Express*
- **MOBILES** *Allowed*
- **CIGARS** *With respect to others*

MR CHOW

151 Knightsbridge, London SW1
☎ 0171 589 7347

Mr Chow has undergone a revival. A couple of years ago it was
all but forgotten about, a relic of a past age, frequented by a few
sad but rich tourists influenced by guidebooks compiled in some
seventies time-warp. Then it perked up. First Mr Chow himself
began to take an interest. Next the Tatler held a few parties there.
Suddenly Mr Chow is hip again. Which is, all in all, no bad
thing as the food is actually good and it is a restaurant landmark.
I have no real idea whether Mr Chow is taken particularly
seriously by those who have devoted their lives to sampling
Chinese food – nor do I particularly care. That is not the point,
Mr Chow is Mr Chow and the food should be judged by its
own standards and as part of the Mr Chow experience. Green
prawns are a personal favourite but they come in other colours
too. The kitchen usually has an interesting way with sea bass
and the starters like squab and dumplings seldom disappoint.
Puddings are decidedly Western, calorific and hauled around
the room on a trolley. The wine list is conservative. Service at
the hands of the mainly Italian staff veers from the incredibly
solicitous to downright comic. The art is good if you like that
sort of 'important' sixties stuff, which I tend not to. I have to say
however that Mr Chow has genuine charm, I regard visiting
Mr Chow as something to be anticipated with pleasure. It is
also unlikely to be full of annoying celebrities; the last time I had
Sunday dinner there, the restaurant was packed with a party of
hard-drinking Israelis.

- **DRESS** *Like Harry Handlesman (ceo Manhattan Loft Corporation)*
- **TUBE** *Knightsbridge*
- **HOURS** *Lunch Mon–Sun 12.00–15.00*
          Dinner Mon–Sun 19.00–24.00
- **AVERAGE PRICE** *£30*
- **CREDIT CARDS** *All major cards*
- **MOBILES** *Allowed*
- **CIGARS** *Humidor*

NANDO'S
88 Denmark Hill Road, Camberwell, London SE5
☎ 0171 738 3808

Nando's is a courageous concept in fast food, in that it actually tries and succeeds in injecting a sense of quality, pleasantness and cleanliness into what might politely be called the entry-level restaurant market. It will be sometime yet before Nando's peri-peri flame-grilled chicken makes it into the Michelin Guide, but given that it comes in at only a little more than you might be expected to spend at your local KFC, it is little short of a miracle. Quarter, half or whole chickens are marinated for 24 hours, then flame-grilled to order and basted with your choice of lemon and herb, medium, or hot peri-peri. This is exactly the sort of food that might taste exquisite after a couple of pints down at the pub, but remarkably it is equally palatable stone cold sober (something of a rarity at this end of the market). And out of deference to the kebab addict, one's chicken can be served in pitta. What is more, the whole operation is carried off with commendable wit, for example the list of two vegetarian options is headed with the words: 'We have great respect for vegetarians, all our chickens were vegetarian'. Many branches of Nando's also function as *de facto* meeting places for the local gilded youth, who like to display the latest in trainers, diamond dentistry, baseball caps and night-time sunglass-wearing. And if you like to enjoy a little bit of Nando's chez vous, the famous Portuguese peri-peri sauces can be bought and enjoyed at home.

- **DRESS** *Depends on location, but ranges from informal sportswear to inner city drugs baron*
- **TUBE** *Loughborough Junction*
- **HOURS** *Sun–Thurs 12.00–23.30; Fri–Sat 12.00–24.00*
- **AVERAGE PRICE** *Lunch/Dinner £15*
- **CREDIT CARDS** *No American Express or Diners Club*
- **MOBILES** *Not encouraged*
- **CIGARS** *Allowed*

ALSO AT

63 Westbourne Grove, London W2;
   0171 313 9506 TUBE Bayswater
1–2 Station Bldgs, Uxbridge Road, London W5;
   0181 922 2290 TUBE Ealing Common
59–63 Clapham High St, London SW4;
   0171 622 1475 TUBE Clapham North
204 Earls Court Road, London SW5;
   0171 259 2544 TUBE Earls Court
234–244 Stockwell Road, Brixton, London SW9;
   0171 737 6400 TUBE Brixton
148 Upper Richmond Road, London SW15;
   0181 780 3651 TUBE East Putney
148 Kingsland High Street, London E8;
   0171 923 3555 TUBE Dalston Kingsland
106 Stroud Green Road, London N4;
   0171 263 7447 TUBE Finsbury Park
57–58 Chalk Farm Road, London NW1;
   0171 424 9040 TUBE Chalk Farm
255 Finchley Road, London NW3;
   0171 435 4644 TUBE Finchley Road
300–302 Station Road, London HA1;
   0181 427 5581 TUBE Harrow on the Hill
137–139 Station Road, London HA8;
   0181 952 3400 TUBE Edgware
37–39 High Street, Kingston KT1;
   0181 296 9540 RAIL Kingston
1–1a High St, Hounslow, Middlesex TW3;
   0181 570 5881 TUBE Hounslow East

THE NEAL STREET RESTAURANT
26 Neal Street, London WC2
☎ 0171 836 8368

Antonio Carluccio is the first and still the only Italian media chef
of any consequence in this country. The connections that he has
forged for himself in this country are impeccable, he is brother-in-
law to the great Sir Terence Conran and as a prominent warrant
in the window of this restaurant and food shop proclaims, he
supplies the Prince of Wales with Italian food and truffles. One
of Antonio Carluccio's many titles is that of 'mushroom monarch',
presiding over a fiefdom of funghi – among the starters is a dish
of mixed funghi of the day, among the pasta dishes is pappardelle
with mixed funghi, among the fish dishes is baccala with porcini
sauce and braised calamari with brown cap mushrooms and

beef schiacciata comes with truffle cheese and rucola. In fact, in season, almost anything and everything can come with truffles. The Neal Street restaurant is of course, as its name suggests, a place where one can be served food, but it is probably better known as the holiest site in the cult of Carluccio with his books (including one with a CD on the front) on sale in numerous languages and various images of the man stuck on the wall.

- **DRESS** *Smart Miciologist*
- **TUBE** *Covent Garden*
- **HOURS** *Lunch Mon–Sat 12.00–14.30; (closed Sun)*
  Dinner Mon–Sat 18.00–23.00; (closed Sun)
- **AVERAGE PRICE** *Lunch/Dinner £45–50*
- **CREDIT CARDS** *All major cards*
- **MOBILES** *Not allowed*
- **CIGARS** *Humidor*

NEW CULTURE REVOLUTION
157–159 Notting Hill Gate, London W11
☎ 0171 313 9688

This chain of no-nonsense noodle and dumpling bars is a perfectly respectable addition to the canon of no-frills Asian eateries that seem to be cleaning up at the low-cost, yet style-conscious end of the market. The menu comes complete with a bit of New Age mumbo-jumbo about the emphasis that Chinese food has apparently always placed on the 'proper combination of ingredients to promote good health, long life and energy'. Further gastronomic correctness is flaunted as New Culture Revolution proclaims itself an MSG-free zone. New Culture Revolution is inspired by the dietary ways of northern China where food is wheat-based (noodles, dumplings, etc.), robust (or stodgy depending on your view) and served in big portions. The guo tei noodles, browned and served with sweet-and-sour dipping sauce are certainly filling and value for money, if not the lightest confections ever to hit the palate. Inevitably, the wok makes an appearance with a selection of about half a dozen chow mein dishes. Essentially, what variation there is comes from combining different types and treatments of noodles with chicken, beef, seafood or vegetables. The whole package makes a slick style statement about being low cost, with, for example, tea being served from thermos flasks. The hard-edged furniture and unforgiving lighting do not make it a place to linger; but then if you want to linger over a plate of cheap Chinese dumplings, you will have to be a pretty sad individual. In fact, my tip for a cheap(ish) night would be to pile into the Pharmacy (qv) bar for a few cocktails and soak up the booze across the road at the Notting Hill branch of New Culture Revolution.

- **DRESS** *Casual*
- **TUBE** *Notting Hill Gate*
- **HOURS** *Mon–Sat 12.00–23.00; Sun 13.00–21.30*
- **AVERAGE PRICE** *£10*
- **CREDIT CARDS** *No American Express*
- **MOBILES** *Allowed*
- **CIGARS** *Not allowed*

ALSO AT

442 Edgware Road, London W2;
   0171 402 4841   TUBE Edgware Road
305 King's Road, London SW3;
   0171 352 9281   TUBE Sloane Square
42 Duncan Street, London N1;
   0171 833 9083   TUBE Angel

NICOLE'S
158 New Bond Street, London W1
☎ 0171 499 8408

In-store restaurants have come a long way from the self-service canteens of the *Are You Being Served* years and there can be few better examples of eating on, or in this case below, the shop floor than Nicole's. This pale and elegant basement dining room is the creation of Lady Hare, aka Nicole Farhi, and is every bit as stylish as the shop above. As one might expect, it is a home away from Knightsbridge for lunching ladies, as well as being popular with fashion folk and less stuffy local business types. Nicole's does breakfast, lunch, tea, dinner, bar snacks and just drinks, but don't be fooled into trying to beat the door down for a plate of scrambled eggs at 7 am, this is Bond Street and breakfast in these fragrant purlieus starts at 10 am. The standard of cooking matches the interior for lightness and modernity: grilled chicken breast sandwich with roast vegetables and basil mayonnaise; cornmeal blini with smoked salmon and crème fraîche; warm spinach, fennel and feta salad with balsamic dressing; steamed sea bass with pak choi, lemon grass and fettucine; grilled skewered scallops with pea purée and crispy prosciutto etc. However, the more robust appetite is not excluded: the rib-eye is from Glenbervie and there is braised lamb shank and grilled calf's liver too. Puddings are suitably tempting and are probably engineered to ensnare the seasoned international shopper who says 'I don't normally eat pudding but the maple spice cake with poached pears and zabaglione or the apple and blackberry crumble with Jersey cream sounds so good...'

- **DRESS** *Nicole Farhi*
- **TUBES** *Bond Street; Green Park*
- **HOURS** *Mon–Fri 10.00–22.45; Sat 10.00–18.00; (closed Sun)*
- **AVERAGE PRICE** *Lunch £35; Dinner £45*
- **CREDIT CARDS** *All major cards*
- **MOBILES** *Allowed*
- **CIGARS** *Allowed*

NOBU

19 Old Park Lane, London W1
☎ 0171 447 4747

One of the most fashionable restaurants in London at the close of the twentieth century, this slick operation on the first floor of the trendy Metropolitan hotel has consistently impressed since it opened in 1997. Nobu, or Matsuhisa Nobuyuki to give him his full name, may have trained as a chef in Japan, but he has worked in Peru and lives in California. The cooking, an indefinable hybrid, Latino-Jap-Cal and the rest, is stunning and cannot be compared with anything else. True, the menu embraces sushi, sashimi and tempura, but the Japanese purist would not understand half the dishes that appear on the menu, but then I suspect neither does anyone else, except Nobu himself. I remember once coming in here and being told that Nobu san was in the kitchen, and would like to prepare lunch for me. Six or seven quite remarkable courses followed – it was far from the cheapest lunch I have ever eaten, but it was the sort of thing that one remembers long after the cost has been forgotten. The approach is probably best summed up by the description of Hakusan, on the sake list, 'A popular, semi-dry sake from California's Napa Valley Wine District. Equally enjoyable served warm or chilled'. It is difficult to explain or stereotype the cooking as it flouts convention, so just come here for a be-prepared-to-spend-lavishly experience.

- **DRESS** *Fashionable and expensive black*
- **TUBE** *Hyde Park Corner*
- **HOURS** *Lunch Mon–Fri 12.00–14.15; (closed Sat–Sun)*
       Dinner Mon–Fri 18.00–22.15; Sat 18.00–23.00;
       Sun 18.00–21.45
- **AVERAGE PRICE** *Lunch £40; Dinner £50–60*
- **CREDIT CARDS** *All major cards*
- **MOBILES** *Allowed*
- **CIGARS** *Not allowed*

NOVELLI
LES SAVEURS DE JEAN CHRISTOPHE NOVELLI
37a Curzon Street, London W1
☎ 0171 491 8919

Jean Christophe Novelli is no decorator. His restaurants tend to be daubed with some sort of purple-blue colour, that I suspect must have been going cheap at his local builders' merchants. He cooks better than he paints, but that is not saying much. He actually cooks rather well and although he cannot be everywhere at once (he has places in Cape Town and Normandy too), his style is followed closely by his staff. I have enjoyed eating Novelli's food. Even if the surroundings have been done on the cheap, the food has not. He has pioneered a style of cooking that is best described as polished northern French. He likes to play with his food, piling it into towers, mixing humble and luxurious ingredients or decorating dishes with sprigs of herbs, spirals of caramel etc. You too can attempt it at home with his cookbook, but it is definitely worthwhile eating at his restaurants a few times before you even attempt to braise and stuff a pig's trotter with foie gras and wild mushrooms. Typical dishes include: home-smoked goose neck and gizzard with mixed leaves; cassoulet terrine with white bean and green garlic dressing; monkfish osso bucco; roast sea bream with aubergine risotto; smoked haddock omelette; and hot and cold, dark and light chocolate plate (chocolate fondant with a side order of white chocolate ice-cream). Maison Novelli is where the eponymous empire was founded in the summer of 1996; EC1 is a casual brasserie and bar; Novelli W8 is a busy and cramped local bistro; Les Saveurs is as yet free of Novelli's purple paint and seems to be emerging as his smart West End flagship with ingredients and prices to match.

- **DRESS** *Smart*
- **TUBES** *Hyde Park Corner; Green Park*
- **HOURS** *Lunch Tues–Fri 12.00–14.30; (closed Sat–Mon)*
  Dinner Mon–Thurs 19.00–22.30; Fri–Sat 19.00–23.00;
  (closed Sun)
- **AVERAGE PRICE** *Lunch/Dinner £40*
- **CREDIT CARDS** *All major cards*
- **MOBILES** *Not allowed*
- **CIGARS** *Humidor*

ALSO AT
NOVELLI W8, 122 Palace Gardens Terrace, London W8;
0171 229 4024 TUBE Notting Hill Gate

MAISON NOVELLI, 29 Clerkenwell Green, London EC1;
0171 251 6606 TUBE Farringdon
NOVELLI EC1, 30 Clerkenwell Green, London EC1;
0171 251 6606 TUBE Farringdon

LA NUOVA DELIZIA

63–65 Chelsea Manor Street, London SW3
☎ 0171 376 4111

On a sunny day, la Delizia on Chelsea Manor Street is a good
place to sit outside and watch the world, or at least that bit of it
that lives just off the King's Road, go by. The place has a casual
atmosphere that will not appeal to everyone but I am keen on
it. There are salads and a half dozen or so pastas and risotto
dishes, but pizza is the thing. The list of pizzas is long (two
dozen are offered) and the bases are thin. Among them, the
'4 formaggi' must be one of the best in London – it has the almost
Proustian power to recall a Roquefort pizza I enjoyed once long
ago in Sospel in the hills behind Menton on the Cote d'Azur.
The pizza restaurants of the Cote d'Azur take some beating, but
Delizia would certainly pass muster on the Riviera.

- **DRESS** *Casual*
- **TUBE** *Sloane Square*
- **HOURS** *Mon–Sun 12.00–24.00*
- **AVERAGE PRICE** *£15*
- **CREDIT CARDS** *No Diners Club or American Express*
- **MOBILES** *Allowed*
- **CIGARS** *Allowed*

ALSO AT
246 Old Brompton Road, London SW5;
0171 373 6085 TUBE Earls Court

THE OAK ROOM MARCO PIERRE WHITE

Le Meridien Piccadilly, 21 Piccadilly, London W1
☎ 0171 437 0202

This is the gastronomic equivalent of buying a Rolex, a brand
new Rolls Royce, a Chanel suit and a Prada bag – status symbol
eating at its most impressive. Having said that, and given that
one is eating at one of the holy sites of the London restaurant
scene, the set lunch is not too ruinously priced. It might run
something like this: amuse-gueule, parfait of foie gras and

chicken livers, toasted brioche, tranche of cod with soft herb crust, sabayon of chives, French farmhouse cheeses or soufflé of raspberries (20 minutes), coffee and petits fours. The à la carte menu includes such intoxicating-sounding things as aspic of oysters en gelée de Champagne with watercress and shallot cream. The wine list is the closest thing to heaven on earth if you happen to be a wine drinker and rich...very, very rich. The place is also well-planned and tables are commendably far apart from each other, but then if you are dropping the thick end of ten grand on a bottle of claret, you probably want to drink it in some privacy. On second thought, if you come to the Oak Room, you probably want everyone else to know you can afford to drink claret at several thousand pounds a bottle. Indeed, the Oak Room is a very agreeable place to spend large sums of money. The main dining room is studded with Bugatti bronzes, while the lounge area at the front has some exquisite alabaster pineapple lamps. The menu bears two quotes which might offer insight into Mr White and his work: Brillat-Savarin's 'To know how to eat well, one must first know how to wait' and Salvador Dali's 'At six I wanted to be a chef, at seven Napoleon, and my ambitions have been growing ever since'.

- **DRESS** *Smart*
- **TUBE** *Piccadilly Circus*
- **HOURS** *Lunch Mon–Fri 12.00–14.30; (closed Sat–Sun)*
       Dinner Mon–Sat 19.00–23.15; (closed Sun)
- **AVERAGE PRICE** *Lunch/Dinner £80–90*
- **CREDIT CARDS** *All major cards*
- **MOBILES** *Not allowed*
- **CIGARS** *Humidor; in lounge area only*

L'ODEON

65 Regent Street, London W1
☎ 0171 287 1400

This former British Airways booking office suffers from an entrance that is not on Regent Street, but round the corner, and a vast dining room that is little more than a long corridor, which rather pedestrian design does little to alleviate. The food however is good. L'Odeon fish cake is a tasty lunch dish and the Pommery mustard sauce is delicious. Baked cod with a herb crust on saffron and smoked haddock risotto with caviar sauce is a good dish even if the risotto could be more al dente. There is a nod to North African trendiness with the spicy couscous that accompanies the braised lamb shank and the grilled chicken breast with fondant potato, artichoke and green beans is a comforting inclusion. The wine list makes good reading and drinking; the fine wine insert is particularly instructive and lists such agreeable bottles as Chateau Montrose 1982. Service can get a bit a ragged in the evenings (probably something to do with the unwieldy nature of the room) especially in the bar, which, otherwise is a goodish place for an evening drink.

- **DRESS** *Slick West Ender*
- **TUBES** *Piccadilly Circus; Oxford Circus*
- **HOURS** *Lunch Mon–Sat 12.00–14.30; (closed Sun)*
        Dinner Mon–Sat 17.30–23.30; (closed Sun)
- **AVERAGE PRICE** *Lunch £20–25; Dinner £45*
- **CREDIT CARDS** *All major cards*
- **MOBILES** *Allowed*
- **CIGARS** *Humidor*

OFFSHORE
148 Holland Park Avenue, London W11
☎ 0171 221 6090

Apparently, the best way to sample the cuisine of chef Sylvain Ho Wing Cheong is with the set menu which is a surprise that gives very little away and bears the surprising name 'Picky Picky'. Perhaps when I visited Offshore I ate off the Picky Picky menu, it seemed to consist largely of various permutations of langoustine served in varying degrees of spicines, or perhaps I did not stick around for the rest of the menu. Offshore is a Mauritian-style fish restaurant and the food is tasty: a bit creole, a bit Indian and a bit French. It is possible to have simple things like plain grilled turbot, Dover sole, brill, sea bass etc. served with sauce on the side, but this is not really the point. The reason to visit Offshore is to taste such dishes as calamari in a black bean sauce and sautéed tiger prawns, tamarind and coconut milk sauce. The menu, however, teeters on the twee in its nomenclature, for example lobster, sleeping on its bed of spicy Chinese noodles, but on the whole, with its fresh and airy room, this place is a stylish addition to the relatively limited gastronomic amenities of Holland Park Avenue.

- **DRESS** *Baffling*
- **TUBE** *Holland Park*
- **HOURS** *Lunch Mon–Sun 12.00–15.00*
        Dinner Mon–Sun 18.30–23.00

- **AVERAGE PRICE** *Lunch/Dinner £25–30*
- **CREDIT CARDS** *No Diners Club*
- **MOBILES** *Allowed*
- **CIGARS** *Humidor*

OLIVETO

49 Elizabeth Street, London SW1
☎ 0171 730 0074

Every area should have something like Oliveto – a slick, no-nonsense modern pizzeria. It is an offshoot of the Belgravia Italian Olivo, but stands on its own as a valuable contribution to life in this smart shopping street. I was introduced to Oliveto by Fiona Sleeman whose cashmere sales and bespoke shopping services are a life-saver for those Belgravians whose lives are too full to trail around the shops. Sleeman brings her younger customers here for sustenance after heavy spending sprees. There are generous salads. Pastas such as wild boar ravioli with truffle oil and spaghetti with shavings of bottarga are simple but very good. However pizzas with crispy wafer bases, over a dozen are listed, are mandatory. Pizza Oliveto is topped with tomato buffalo mozzarella, bottarga and basil – the rest are topped with bresaola; San Daniele ham; minced spiced Italian sausages; sautéed mushrooms; chargrilled vegetables; anchovies etc. This being Belgravia, even the pizza-eating classes are rich and chic: on my last visit, I saw not one but two Franck Muller Master Banker wrist-watches on customers' wrists.

- **DRESS** *Eurotrash*
- **TUBE** *Victoria*
- **HOURS** *Lunch Mon–Fri 12.00–15.00; Sat–Sun 12.00–16.00 Dinner Mon–Sun 19.00–23.30*
- **AVERAGE PRICE** *Lunch/Dinner £15–20*
- **CREDIT CARDS** *No Diners Club*
- **MOBILES** *Not allowed*
- **CIGARS** *Not allowed*

OLIVO

21 Eccleston Street, London SW1
☎ 0171 730 2505

Uncomplicated, but marginally more elaborate in both looks and cooking, Olivo is the grown-up sibling of Oliveto(qv). Together they make lower Belgravia an altogether better place to be. The décor is rustic blue and saffron and the tables are covered in paper cloths, however service is professional. Dishes are presented carefully but in a straightforward manner, for example, the green salad with creamy pecorino dressing makes a welcome alternative to the ubiquitous Caesar salad. The gastronomic background here is staunchly Sardinian, a regional bias evident in the wine selection and the inclusion of such delicious dishes as spaghetti alla bottarga – and if I had to recommend but one dish here, it would be this. Carpaccio of swordfish or tuna is a good light starter and the Sardinian influence appears once again with such dishes as spiedino d'agnello con fergola sarda (chargrilled lamb's brochette with Sardinian couscous) and a pudding called sebada (deep-fried pastry filled with cheese and dressed with honey). Cheeses are also Sardinian.

- **DRESS** *Contemporary passport to Pimlico*
- **TUBE** *Victoria*
- **HOURS** *Lunch Mon–Fri 12.00–14.30; (closed Sat–Sun)*
       Dinner Mon–Sun 19.00–23.00
- **AVERAGE PRICE** *Lunch £25; Dinner £35–40*
- **CREDIT CARDS** *No Diners Club*
- **MOBILES** *Not allowed*
- **CIGARS** *Not allowed*

ONE-O-ONE
Sheraton Park Tower, William Street, London SW1
☎ 0171 290 7101

I like the Sheraton Park Tower. This tub-like hotel was, I think, designed by the great Colonel Seifert & Partners, the architect responsible for Centre Point, and opened during the early seventies by Ted Heath. Architecture aside, the Sheraton Park Tower had never particularly distinguished itself until the opening of One-o-One. At first sight, the glasshouse-like space that sprawls out onto the Knightsbridge pavement looks uninviting and inside the sensation is not unlike eating at the side of a motorway with the numerous lanes of traffic whizzing (or crawling depending on the time of day) by. However the food, predominantly fish, prepared by chef Pascal Proyart, is delicious. At times, the presentation suffers from pointless little furbelow that betrays a touch of Michelin envy. However, even though he does not hold a Michelin star, Proyat deserves to be proud of the food he prepares here; it is on the whole extremely good. It is only less than good once he tries to fiddle too much with notions that already work perfectly well, such as the gazpacho, served with crab, which one is expected to tip in along with croûtons. The dish is fine, but a little gimmicky. However when it comes to sea bass – a fish to which a section of the menu is devoted, Proyat demonstrates a sureness of touch that is impressive. A whole sea bass cooked in a crust of Brittany rock salt is a splendid-looking dish that makes a wonderful impact when it arrives at the table and something like, say, fillet of sea bass roasted in olive oil, with a soft crust of tapenade, sandwiched with mozzarella cheese, fresh basil and sauce vierge is a tasty and satisfying dish. Other fish are well represented, for example, there is pan-seared John Dory with forestière potato beurre piment et ail doux; poached turbot with olive oil mash, confit of baby fennel and ratatouille, the latter a delicately-flavoured dish. Care has gone into the selection of wines offered, which, while displaying the customary hotel mark-ups manage to offer something for most palates and pockets (given that this is not a cheap restaurant). Clarets, for example, are concisely chosen if inevitably a little patchy as regards a full range of Chateaux and vintages. Service under the aegis of Andrew Morgan is brilliant, although, as in common with some hotel restaurants, the staff uniforms are extremely silly.

- **DRESS** *Vaguely suity*
- **TUBES** *Knightsbridge; Hyde Park Corner*
- **HOURS** *Lunch Mon–Sat 12.00–14.30; Sun 12.30–14.30 Dinner Mon–Sun 19.00–22.30*
- **AVERAGE PRICE** *Lunch £35–45; Dinner £45–55*
- **CREDIT CARDS** *All major cards*
- **MOBILES** *Allowed*
- **CIGARS** *Humidor*

L'ORANGER
St James's Street, London SW1
☎ 0171 839 3774

Fine dining in relaxed surroundings seem to work for this outpost of the A–Z restaurant group. The star chef may have been lost to Petrus (qv) but the place trucks on happily and such dishes as the salted cod and potato tartelette with shallots and tomato is genuinely worth ordering. Roasted monkfish tail rolled in black pepper crushed with spinach and antiboise (from Antibes – olive oil and tomato) is almost tasty and the idea of 'pomme dauphin' (a sort of rosti cake) topped with scallops, lobster sauce and shallots was only slightly marred by the adhesive tendencies of the scallop slices arranged around the top.

- **DRESS** *Vaguely smart*
- **TUBE** *Green Park*
- **HOURS** *Lunch Mon–Fri 12.00–14.30; (closed Sat–Sun)
      Dinner Mon–Sat 18.00–23.00; (closed Sun)*
- **AVERAGE PRICE** *Lunch £30; Dinner £50*
- **CREDIT CARDS** *All major cards*
- **MOBILES** *Not allowed*
- **CIGARS** *Humidor; in bar only*

THE ORANGERY

Kensington Palace, Kensington Gardens, London W8
☎ 0171 376 0239

On July 10th 1704, Queen Anne approved Sir John Vanbrugh's
design for a greenhouse. Queen Anne was not the sort of
woman to make do with the eighteenth century equivalent of
what Homebase had to offer. At 170 feet long, with Corinthian
columns, marvellous wood carvings and long sash windows,
cool and bright in summer, this is one the most agreeable spaces
in London. Food is superior picnic stuff, for example, croissant
filled with ham and cheese, fillet of smoked trout with horseradish
and leaf salad, oak-smoked venison salad with juniper chutney,
terrine of wild mushrooms served with leaf salad and breads
and so on. From about three o'clock, it becomes a lovely tea
room with great old-fashioned cakes, clotted cream and even
cucumber sandwiches.

- **DRESS** *Summer in the park*
- **TUBES** *Bayswater; High Street Kensington*
- **HOURS** *Mon–Sun 10.00–18.00*
- **AVERAGE PRICE** *Lunch £8–10; Tea £6.50*
- **CREDIT CARDS** *Visa; Mastercard*
- **MOBILES** *Discouraged*
- **CIGARS** *Not allowed*

THE ORIENTAL RESTAURANT

The Dorchester, Park Lane, London W1
☎ 0171 629 8888

This is possibly the most expensive Chinese restaurant in London
and almost certainly the best. The last time I ate Chinese food
as good was at the Man Wah restaurant on the top floor of
the Mandarin Hotel in Hong Kong and the only thing that the
Oriental at the Dorchester cannot compete with is the view.

The winning combination here is excellent food, highly polished service, under the direction of the charming Benson, and pleasant surroundings. The private rooms are attractive: one is Indian, one Chinese and one Thai in style. However, food is resolutely Chinese, and I find it inspires me to want to find out more about the regional cooking of China. All the food is likely to be good and things like the lobster, the squid and the abalone are first rate. Instead of coffee, have a cup of the pungent po-nee tea and watch the leaves being washed first – most relaxing. The trick here, provided you have financial nerves of steel – or perhaps titanium – is to state your preferences and let Benson order for you. There are however set menus with wine recommendations.

- **DRESS** *Smart; jacket required*
- **TUBES** *Hyde Park Corner; Marble Arch*
- **HOURS** *Lunch Mon–Fri 12.00–14.30; (closed Sat–Sun)*
  Dinner Mon–Sat 19.00–23.00; (closed Sun)
- **AVERAGE PRICE** *Lunch £45–50; Dinner £65–100*
- **CREDIT CARDS** *All major cards*
- **MOBILES** *Not allowed*
- **CIGARS** *Humidor*

ORRERY

55 Marylebone High Street, London W1
☎ 0171 616 8000

This is something of a sentimental journey for Sir Terence Conran, as one of his first restaurants was called Orrery. But that is where all similarities end – Orrery I was a King's Road coffee bar, with a then plain Mr Conran serving behind the bar. Orrery II is an extremely smart restaurant attached to the Marylebone High Street Conran shop. Orrery slots neatly into the upper brackets (price/food quality/linen quality etc.) of Conran's operations. It is, I suppose, a Pont de la Tour (qv) style operation for those who live in the fragrant purlieus of Hampstead or St John's Wood and cannot be bothered to trek all the way to Butler's Wharf. Food here is serious and predicated on simple things done extremely well: potted Cornish crab; roast rump of lamb with dauphinoise potatoes, flageolets; roast sea bass, celeriac, truffles and red wine jus etc. The wine list has been compiled for expensive North London palates. The little bar is well worth visiting, if only to see Sir Terence, well at least his Tastevin certificate, and to eat a lunch of lighter dishes off the main menu.

- **DRESS** *North London on a night out*
- **TUBES** *Baker Street; Regent's Park*
- **HOURS** *Lunch Mon–Sat 12.00–15.00; (closed Sun)*
  Dinner Mon–Sat 19.00–23.00; Sun 19.00–22.30
- **AVERAGE PRICE** *Lunch £35; Dinner £60*
- **CREDIT CARDS** *All major cards*
- **MOBILES** *Not encouraged*
- **CIGARS** *Humidor*

ORSINO

119 Portland Road, London W11
☎ 0171 221 3299

Orsino should be a good thing. It has a pleasant wood-floored room, wooden shutters and a menu of just-about-rustic-enough Italian food. The sort of things that appear on the menu might include: dandelion, green cauliflower and roast onion salad with black olives and green beans; radicchio, pancetta and ricotta ravioli with tomato and tarragon; roast butternut squash, chestnut and orange; veal chop with sage and lemon. Pizzas are delicious and crispy if a little on the small side. Much thought has gone into the preparation of the wine list. The only problem is that service can be arrogant to the point of being offensive. For instance, order a plate of the admittedly rather good pizza bread (think of carta di musica sprinkled with rosemary) and instead of 'yes of course' you are likely to hear 'OK...but it might take a while', uttered in a way that infers you are at best a pest, and then repeated to make you feel at worst a moron. It is such behaviour that leeches any pleasure from a visit and makes one exit thinking one might have spent a quarter of the money and experienced four times more friendliness at Pizza Express. A pity, because the food itself is actually rather tasty.

- **DRESS** *Relaxed affluent*
- **TUBE** *Holland Park*
- **HOURS** *Mon–Sat 12.00–23.30; (closed Sun)*
- **AVERAGE PRICE** *Lunch/Dinner £35*
- **CREDIT CARDS** *No Diners Club*
- **MOBILES** *Not encouraged*
- **CIGARS** *Prohibited*

OSTERIA ANTICA BOLOGNA

23 Northcote Road, London SW11

☎ 0171 978 4771

Back in the early nineties, this cosy wood-lined Italian restaurant was a key gastronomic destination. And while it no longer exerts the cross-city pulling power it used to, this place is still a superior Battersea address. Inexpensive, hearty dishes, flickering candle-light and wine served in ceramic pitchers give the place a weird time-warped feel that places it in beatnik days – it is decidedly not of the late 20th/early 21st centuries. The section of the menu entitled Assaggi dell'Osteria encourages an almost tapas-like style of eating with interesting dishes, many of which purport to come from Ancient Rome. These include sardam farsilem sic facere (sardines stuffed with walnuts, pine nuts, cumin, mint and honey, rolled in grape leaves and grilled); epityrum (herbed ricotta with green olive, cumin, coriander and fennel pesto with fennel, broad beans, chicory and garlic crostino); and ofellas apicinas (torta of sausage, snails, chicken balls, leeks, turnips, plums and egg and grape leaves). Pasta dishes are good, for instance, garganelli with roast pumpkin, fresh mint and smoked provola cheese or abruzzese egg ribbon pasta with hare and wild mushroom ragu. Main courses range from Sicilian-style goat cooked with tomato and almond pesto to Veneto boned roast duck stuffed with livers bread, turkey, amaretti, egg and parmesan.

- **DRESS** *Beatnik*
- **RAIL** *Clapham Junction*
- **HOURS** *Lunch Mon–Fri 12.00–15.00*
  Dinner Mon–Fri 18.00–23.30
  Sat 12.00–23.00; Sun 11.30–22.30
- **AVERAGE PRICE** *Lunch £13; Dinner £20*
- **CREDIT CARDS** *All major cards*
- **MOBILES** *Allowed*
- **CIGARS** *Prohibited*

OSTERIA BASILICO

29 Kensington Park Road, London W11

☎ 0171 727 9372

I would imagine that Osteria Basilico tries to be a little bit of what people living in Notting Hill might think of as a Tuscan farmhouse or a small holding. There is a choice of starters from the buffet or a selection from the menu that includes bruschetta with tomato and rocket; seafood salad; carpaccio with pesto, rocket and parmesan shavings; deep-fried prawns and calamari and so on. Pasta dishes are hearty. Pizzas are good, crispy and can be taken away. There is a commendably concise selection of simple fish and meat dishes, for example, oven-baked rack of lamb served with potatoes and rosemary sauce. Osteria Basilico is not the biggest of restaurants and as the evening draws on, it can get extremely crowded.

- **DRESS** *Notting Hill casual*
- **TUBE** *Ladbroke Grove*
- **HOURS** *Lunch Mon–Fri 12.30–15.00; Sat 12.30–16.00;*
    Sun 12.30–15.15
    Dinner Mon–Sat 18.30–23.00; Sun 18.30–22.30
- **AVERAGE PRICE** *Lunch/Dinner £22*
- **CREDIT CARDS** *No Diners Club*
- **MOBILES** *Allowed*
- **CIGARS** *Preferably not*

OXO TOWER

Barge House Street, London SE1
☎ 0171 803 3888

Many people claim to have been disappointed by the food here. I am not one of them, I have only ever eaten well at the Oxo Tower. I much prefer it to its sister restaurant Fifth Floor at Harvey Nichols. Dishes manage to be modern without being too 'nancy' and most avoid being too oddly flavoured for the sake of it. Sometimes the cooking rises well above the competent and trendy. In fact, the juxtaposition of rich and piquant and the varying textures of squid, risotto nero and sea bass evinced in a dish of roast tranche of sea bass with risotto nero and sauce vierge was exemplary. Pan-fried fillet of John Dory with braised little gem lettuce, peas and bacon did not compare as well. However, tarte d'Agen with prune and Armagnac ice-cream was wonderful. Service could be a little quicker, but when they arrive, staff are knowledgeable, correct and courteous. Dinner here cannot be described as a bargain, but then 'in part' one is paying for the view, which is spectacular. If you have rich visitors from abroad who want to sample a bit of modern London, complete with designer drinks trolleys and groovy architecture, then this is the place. The brasserie is less swanky, the tables are closer together and the food less elaborate with quite a bit of searing, pan-frying, and chargrilling. Although less expensive than the main restaurant, one is still paying a hefty premium for the view, so I would tend to advise going for the 'reet proper grand' option and enjoying a bit of space and comfort.

- **DRESS** *Vaguely smart casual; Eddie Bell wears a Bvlgari watch*
- **TUBES** *Blackfriars; Waterloo*
- **HOURS** *Lunch Mon–Fri 12.00–15.00; Sun 12.00–15.30;*
  (closed Sat)
  Dinner Mon–Sat 18.00–23.00; Sun 18.30–22.30
- **AVERAGE PRICE** *Lunch £45; Dinner £65*
- **CREDIT CARDS** *All major cards*
- **MOBILES** *Allowed*
- **CIGARS** *Humidor*

LE PALAIS DU JARDIN
136 Long Acre, London WC2
☎ 0171 379 5353

This large Covent Garden brasserie seems to run happily enough.
The almost self-effacing frontage with a lone blackboard, more
likely than not proclaiming advantageous prices for lobster, belies
a vast interior that stretches back a great distance, the bar area
giving way to a dining hall. It looks shiny and slick, if slightly
anonymous … but then how does one make a 350 seat
restaurant intimate? The brasserie-style is carried through to the
menu: yes, you guessed it, a Niçoise-style salad, a goats' cheese
dish, roast breast of duck, grilled fillet steak and a selection of
fruits de mer. The whole effect seems to be brought off with
reasonable success and the general manager is a likeable man.

- **DRESS** *Smart casual*
- **TUBE** *Covent Garden*
- **HOURS** *Lunch Mon–Sun 12.00–15.00*
  Dinner Mon–Sun 17.30–24.00
- **AVERAGE PRICE** *Lunch/Dinner £35–40*
- **CREDIT CARDS** *All major cards*
- **MOBILES** *Allowed*
- **CIGARS** *Humidor*

PALMS
3–5 Campden Hill Road, London W8
☎ 0171 938 1830

This is an adequate pasta restaurant that is better than many
chain offerings in the field. Stick to pasta, such as the spicy penne
arrabiata or the spaghettini a la rustica with its thin, glass-like
pasta and coarsely-chopped tomatoes and you will do well.
However, stray from the pasta dishes and all is not as consistent
as it could be. Dishes such as a starter of crab cakes or the main

course of salmon fish cakes should really be renamed 'potato cakes with a hint of crab and salmon' respectively and the starter of Caesar salad is fine in a lack-lustre, portion-controlled sort of way. However, spinach and parmesan tart is a good starter and the tiramisu, served in a ramekin and dusted with chocolate to display the Palms logo is a good 'rich' creamy pudding, if not necessarily what I would term a tiramisu. The look of Palms is pleasant in a dated eighties sort of way and a mural allegedly depicting Mediterranean life dominates the Covent Garden branch.

- **DRESS** *Casual*
- **TUBE** *High Street Kensington*
- **HOURS** *Mon–Sun 12.00–23.00*
- **AVERAGE PRICE** *Lunch/Dinner £17*
- **CREDIT CARDS** *No American Express*
- **MOBILES** *Allowed*
- **CIGARS** *Not allowed*

ALSO AT
39 King Street, London WC2;
    0171 240 2939   TUBE Covent Garden

PASHA
1 Gloucester Road, London SW7
☎ 0171 589 7969

Best described as couscous for the Cartier-wearing classes, this is the third of the trilogy of restaurants founded and then sold by Mogens Tholstrup, the Great Dane and most famous son of Denmark since Hamlet. However, for some reason, he and his Moroccan restaurant incurred the wrath of journalist, author, critic, orator and fashion leader AA Gill who famously slammed the place and the Dane in a savage review. I have to admit to a soft spot for Mogens, the only thing he has ever done wrong in my view is to swap his Breitling for a Rolex Daytona. I also happen to think that for what it is, ie. Daphne's (qv) in a djibbah, Pasha is perfectly good. The set lunch is good value. Start with the mezze (for two) and follow with something like chicken skewers with okra, chickpea and tomatoes or lamb prune and almond tagine. On the whole, I have tended to prefer the food here to what is served at arch rival Momo (qv). At night the menu is more expansive and might include: sweet almond, pigeon and cinnamon pastilla; spiced raw tuna with tabbouleh; roast cod with fava beans, chard, mint, lemon and olive oil; spiced whole lobster tagine. Eating here in the evening is not as cheap as lunch, but then you do have the added extra of sitting in on the set of the soap opera that passes for everyday life in fashionable Kensington. The house cocktail, called Pasha, is a soothing brain marinater of lime-infused vodka, fresh lime juice, and mint syrup infused with lime. Wines are mainly French with a few Spanish and Lebanese bottles chucked in for authenticity's sake. If you think you will be getting up and down during dinner to do a lot of air-kissing of new arrivals, ask for table 20, it is next to the door and best for monitoring arrivals.

- **DRESS** *As if you are going on to the K–Bar after dinner*
- **TUBE** *Gloucester Road*
- **HOURS** *Lunch Mon–Sat 12.00–15.00; (closed Sun)*
        Dinner Mon–Sat 19.00–23.30; Sun 19.00–22.30
- **AVERAGE PRICE** *Lunch £15; Dinner £30*
- **CREDIT CARDS** *All major cards*
- **MOBILES** *Tolerated*
- **CIGARS** *Humidor*

PASTA DI MILANO

373 Kensington High Street, London W8
☎ 0171 610 5552

This no-bookings-taken operation is the pasta-eating answer to Pizza Express and not to be confused with the less than wonderful Café Milan (qv). And while it is not the sort of place for ground-breaking excursions into the hinterland of Italian gastronomy, Pasta di Milano is a useful enough place for say, a post-cinema plate of pasta. The vaguely-updated mozzarella and tomato salad appears here as buffalo mozzarella with sun-dried tomatoes. Pastas are divided between 'Tradizionale', for example, linguine al pesto, penne alla carbonara spaghetti al ragu (Spag bol to the rest of us), and 'Moderno', for example, tagliatelle corazza (asparagus, prawns, chopped tomatoes), penne alla barese (tomato, aubergine, parma ham, chillies), risotto di mare. There are salads too. I was, however, less than impressed with the allegedly 'traditional Italian garlic bread'. Wines are slightly better than at Pizza Express, with Planeta Merlot and the ace Italian sparkler Bellavista featuring at the upper end.

- **DRESS** *Casual*
- **TUBES** *High Street Kensington; Earls Court; Olympia*
- **HOURS** *Mon–Sat 11.30–24.00; Sun 11.30–23.30*
- **AVERAGE PRICE** *Lunch/Dinner £12*
- **CREDIT CARDS** *All major cards*
- **MOBILES** *Allowed*
- **CIGARS** *Allowed*

ALSO AT

15 Greek Street, London W1;
    0171 434 2545 TUBE Tottenham Court Road
94 Upper Richmond Road, London SW15;
    0181 780 2224 TUBE East Putney
12 Crouch End Hill, London N8;
    0181 347 6090 RAIL Hornsey; Finsbury Park

PATISSERIE VALERIE

44 Old Compton Street, London W1
☎ 0171 437 3466

Valerie's, as it was once considered hip to call it, was a key
hang-out in late eighties Soho. It had actually started life in 1926
on Frith Street but, bombed by the Luftwaffe, it relocated to its
present Old Compton Street site. It was bought by the brothers
Scalzo in 1987 and has since expanded to various sites across
London, of which the Marylebone operation (originally a
chocolatier called Sagne) complete with 1920's mural depicting
Lake Geneva, is the prettiest. Patisserie Valerie is a good enough
place for a toasted or club sandwich or a salad. They do make
an effort with their patisserie: windows are typically decorated
with quite wonderfully preposterous white chocolate wedding
cakes, a towering croque en bouche or an imposing Babel-like
construction of profiteroles.

- **DRESS** *Casual*
- **TUBE** *Leicester Square*
- **HOURS** *Mon–Sat 7.30–19.00; Sun 8.00–19.00*
- **AVERAGE PRICE** *£10*
- **CREDIT CARDS** *No Diners Club*
- **MOBILES** *Allowed*
- **CIGARS** *Allowed*

ALSO AT

8 Russell Street, London WC2;
    0171 240 0064 TUBE Covent Garden
Royal Institute of British Architects, 66 Portland Place, London W1;
    0171 631 0467 TUBES Great Portland Street;
    Regent's Park; Oxford Circus
105 Marylebone High Street, London W1;
    0171 935 6240 TUBES Bond Street; Baker Street
215 Brompton Road, London SW3;
    0171 823 9971 TUBE Knightsbridge

PETRUS

33 St James's, London SW1
☎ 0171 930 4272

Opened under the aegis of Gordon Ramsay (qv), this swanky
St James's restaurant is named after the fabulously expensive
Pomerol wine. The room is spacious and expensively, if
anonymously, decorated. Staff are well drilled – Said is the
wonderful barman who adds a spark of humour to an otherwise
serious, yet not disagreeable, operation. Food is of a high
standard. A typical meal might start with marinated foie gras
de canard and truffle with pickled artichoke and mixed salad
leaves or sautéed sea scallops served with a velouté of chestnuts.
Mains might be something like halibut braised with cos lettuce,
asparagus, Sauternes sauce and grapefruit or roasted loin of
venison, potato rosti with a fricassee of peas and girolles.
This is the sort of place where the food is delivered and then
a well-meaning member of staff will stand over you and give
you the entire cv of every ingredient on the plate. Get up from
your table and when you return your napkin will be folded in a
geometrically correct fashion and laid across your place. This
place is clearly gunning for high Michelin status and given all the
accessorising behaviour it will probably achieve it. However, if
you serve an amuse-bouche of gazpacho – very tasty by the way
– in a chilled little cup, why place the low temperature cup on a
saucer that seemed dishwasher warm? The staff are very kind
and certainly know what they are doing – more than can be said
of my visit to La Tante Claire (qv). But while I can just about take
this religious atmosphere when the cooking is as exquisite as at
say Gordon Ramsay (and there the atmosphere is easier), here
to my mind the food, while very good, does not warrant being
treated like a sacred religious object. Nevertheless, this is a
professional operation and the wines are stunning, extremely
well-cellared and bought with care. This is where knowing the
biography of each rare bottle really counts (you do not want to buy
a bottle of '61 Petrus that has been bought and sold everywhere
from Bordeaux to Hong Kong and back). Hats off to the besotted
oenophile who put this delightful little cellar together.

- **DRESS** *As if for Church*
- **TUBE** *Green Park*
- **HOURS** *Lunch Mon–Fri 12.00–14.45; (closed Sat–Sun)*
  Dinner Mon–Fri 18.45–23.00; Sat 18.45–23.00;
  (closed Sun)
- **AVERAGE PRICE** *Lunch/Dinner £50*

- **CREDIT CARDS** *All major cards*
- **MOBILES** *Can be left at the front desk*
- **CIGARS** *Humidor; in the bar area only*

PHARMACY
150 Notting Hill Gate, London W11
☎ 0171 221 2442

If you ever wanted to know what it is like to eat in a Damien Hirst
artwork, just book a table at Pharmacy and you will find out.
Pharmacy takes the concept of the themed restaurant to its most
extreme and has apparently been mistaken for a chemist. The
Royal Pharmaceutical Society got a bit worked up about this
and for a while the letters outside were rearranged into various
anagrams, for example, 'ARMY CHAP', in a way that recalls
Fawlty Towers. Now it seems that the issue has been resolved
as the place is now signed as the Pharmacy Restaurant and
Bar. The ground floor bar, decorated with cabinets of medicinal
bottles and boxes is too groovy by far. It offers cocktails like
the 'Pharmaceutical Stimulant' (vodka, coffee liqueurs and
espresso); 'Anaesthetic Compound' (vodka, Chartreuse and
Krupnik, shaken) and the evocatively named 'Russian Qualuude'
(Chartreuse, Galliano and vodka, flambéed). To soak up the
effects of such beverages, the bar has a toast menu including
baked beans on toast with ventreche bacon, Welsh rarebit, and
chargrilled sardines on toast. The first floor dining room is light,
bright, and slightly less pharmaceutically oriented. It is the place
for simple(ish), but deadly serious, food along the lines of foie
gras cooked en sel with shaved fennel, chargrilled asparagus
with poached egg and truffle vinaigrette, roast Scottish lobster
'en cocotte' with coral jus and spit-roast Landes duck with apple
juice and seasonal greens. Wittiest pudding by far is the distinctly
tea-flavoured Earl Grey crème brulée – an inspired touch.

- **DRESS** *Modern to Notting Hill Bohemian*
- **TUBE** *Notting Hill Gate*
- **HOURS** *Lunch Mon–Sun 12.00–14.45*
          Dinner Mon–Sun 18.45–22.45
- **AVERAGE PRICE** *Lunch £30; Dinner £45–50*
- **CREDIT CARDS** *All major cards*
- **MOBILES** *Allowed, with discretion*
- **CIGARS** *Allowed, with discretion*

PIED A TERRE

34 Charlotte Street, London W1
☎ 0171 636 1178

This is actually a very good restaurant. It manages to combine the seriousness of Michelin-starred cooking with a pleasant atmosphere which is mercifully short on the kind of hushed religiosity that characterises the goings-on at such places as Petrus (qv). Eating here is not cheap, and there are proabably some insecure people who might feel slightly short-changed if they do not get the full quota of napkin-folding and fawning flunkeys. However, one is attentively and pleasantly served and the food is very good. The little assiette of amuse-gueules that I was served was both clever and tasty with a tiny caramelised poached egg standing out as a feat of ingenuity. Main dishes come heavily arranged on plates encircled with 'reductions-of-this' or 'vinaigrettes-of-that' or sauces of the other, but there is a point and homogeneity about the things on the plate – little is superfluous. Roasted sea bass with red pepper sauce and braised fennel is simple and exquisite; boudin of guinea fowl with asparagus French bean salad and cep vinaigrette comes in a little tower and looks too pretty to defile with knife and fork. The chef's seriousness is compensated for by his wife's pretty bubbliness as front of house. What is more, I have to salute a restaurant that is happy to serve a Dr Tanhnisch Riesling by the glass as an aperitif; more people should appreciate the fine steely Rieslings of the Mosel and its tributaries, the Saar and Ruwer.

- **TUBE** *Goodge Street*
- **DRESS** *Suits*
- **HOURS** *Lunch Mon–Fri 12.15–14.15; (closed Sat–Sun)*
        Dinner Mon–Sat 19.00–22.30; (closed Sun)
- **AVERAGE PRICE** *Lunch/Dinner £60*
- **CREDIT CARDS** *All major cards*
- **MOBILES** *Allowed but preferably left at the bar*
- **CIGARS** *Humidor*

PIZZA EXPRESS

Pizza Express is one of those national institutions that really can be said to have made a difference to life in England at the end of the twentieth century. This is the restaurant as amenity, in that as far as cost is concerned it is a viable alternative to eating in – just right if you have been to the movies, have children, have nothing in the fridge or any of the other excuses for not cooking yourself.

The pizzas may not be very best you will ever eat, but they are good and a long way ahead of the offerings of the other large chains. There is also something agreeable about walking into clean, well-designed premises almost anywhere in London and being able to order your favourite pizza (at Pizza Express, most people establish a favourite and stick to it.) What is more, there is a good chance that it will be cooked the way you like it – consistency from one end of London to the other, and even across the nation, is one of this chain's strengths. My favourite is the Fiorentina with a soft egg.

LOCATIONS AT

30 Coptic Street, London WC1;
   0171 636 3232 TUBE Holborn; Tottenham Court Road
9–12 Bow Street, London WC2;
   0171 240 3443 TUBE Covent Garden
80–81 St Martins Lane, London WC2;
   0171 836 8001 TUBE Leicester Square
125 Alban Gate, London Wall, London EC2;
   0171 600 8880 TUBE Moorgate
7–9 St Bride Street, London EC4;
   0171 583 5126 TUBE Farringdon
21–22 Barrett Street, St Christopher's Place, London W1;
   0171 629 1001 TUBE Bond Street
23 Bruton Place, London W1;
   0171 495 1411 TUBE Green Park
7–9 Charlotte Street, London W1;
   0171 580 1110 TUBES Tottenham Court Road; Goodge Street
10 Dean Street, Soho, London W1;
   0171 437 9595 TUBE Piccadilly
20 Greek Street, London W1;
   0171 734 7430 TUBE Piccadilly Circus
6 Upper James Street, Golden Square, London W1;
   0171 437 4550 TUBE Piccadilly
29 Wardour Street, London W1;
   0171 437 7215 TUBE Piccadilly
133 Baker Street, London W1;
   0171 486 0888 TUBE Baker Street
26 Porchester Road, Bayswater, London W2;
   0171 229 7784 TUBE Bayswater
252 Chiswick High Road, London W4;
   0181 747 0193 TUBE Turnham Green
23 Bond Street, Ealing, London W5;
   0181 567 7690 TUBE Ealing Broadway; South Ealing
53 Earls Court Road, London W8;
   0171 937 0761 TUBE High Street Kensington

137 Notting Hill Gate, London W11;
0171 229 6000 TUBE Notting Hill Gate

7 Rockley Road, Shepherds Bush, London W14;
0181 749 8582 TUBE Shepherds Bush

46 Moreton Street, Pimlico, London SW1;
0171 592 9488 TUBE Pimlico

154 Victoria Street, London SW1;
0171 828 1477 TUBE Victoria

The Pheasantry, King's Road, London SW3;
0171 351 5031 TUBE Sloane Square

43 Abbeville Road, Clapham, London SW4;
0181 673 8878 TUBE Clapham Common; Clapham South

895–896 Fulham Road, London SW6;
0171 731 3117 TUBE Fulham Broadway

363 Fulham Road, London SW10;
0171 352 5300 TUBE Fulham Broadway

46–54 Battersea Bridge Road, Battersea, London SW11;
0171 924 2774 RAIL Clapham Junction

230–236 Lavender Hill, London SW11;
0171 223 5677 RAIL Clapham Junction

305 Upper Richmond Road West, East Sheen, London SW14;
0181 878 6833 RAIL Mortlake

144 Upper Richmond Road, Putney, London SW15;
0181 789 1948 TUBE Putney

198 Trinity Road, Wandsworth, London SW17;
0181 672 0200 RAIL Wandsworth Town

539–541 Old York Road, Wandsworth, London SW18;
0181 877 9812 RAIL Wandsworth Town

34–36 Streatham High Road, London SW18;
0181 769 0202 RAIL Streatham

84 High Street, Wimbledon, London SW19;
0181 946 6027 TUBE Wimbledon

45–47 Old Church Road, Chingford, London E4;
0181 529 7866 TUBE Walthamstow

Salway Road, Stratford East, London E15;
0181 534 1700 TUBE Stratford

76 High Road, South Woodford, London E18;
0181 924 4488 TUBE South Woodford

The Cardaman Building, 31 Shad Thames, London SE1;
0171 403 8484 TUBE London Bridge

London Bridge, 4 Borough High Street, London SE1;
0171 407 2995 TUBE Borough

64–66 Tranquil Vale, Blackheath, London SE3;
0181 318 2595 RAIL Blackheath

70 Westow Hill, Crystal Palace, London SE19;
   0181 670 1786 RAIL Gipsy Hill
94 The Village, Dulwich, London SE21;
   0181 693 9333 RAIL West Dulwich
335 Upper Street, Islington, London N1;
   0171 226 9542 TUBE Angel
30 High Street, Highgate, London N6;
   0181 341 3434 TUBE Highgate
290 Muswell Hill Broadway, London N10;
   0181 883 5845 TUBE East Finchley
820 High Road, Finchley, London N12;
   0181 445 7714 TUBE Woodside Park
94–98 Chaseside, Southgate, London N14;
   0181 886 3300 TUBE Southgate
1264 Whetstone High Road, London N20;
   0181 446 8800 TUBE Totteridge & Whetstone
701–703 Green Lanes, Winchmore Hill, London N21;
   0181 364 2992 TUBE Southgate then bus 125
187 Kentish Town Road, London NW1;
   0171 267 0101 TUBE Kentish Town
83–87 Parkway, Camden, London NW1;
   0171 267 2600 TUBE Camden Town
227 Finchley Road, Swiss Cottage, London NW3;
   0171 794 5100 TUBE Swiss Cottage
70 Heath Road, Hampstead, London NW3;
   0171 433 1600 TUBE Hampstead
194a Haverstock Hill, Belsize Park, London NW3;
   0171 794 6777 TUBE Belsize Park
319 West End Lane, London NW6;
   0171 431 8229 TUBE West Hampstead
92–94 The Broadway, Mill Hill, London NW7;
   0181 959 3898 RAIL Mill Hill Broadway
39 Abbey Road, London NW8;
   0171 624 5577 TUBE St John's Wood
94 Golders Green Road, London NW11;
   0181 455 9556 TUBE Golders Green

PIZZA METRO
64 Battersea Rise, London SW11
☎ 0171 228 3812

Pizza Metro is quite brilliant. This small, frenetic restaurant is one of the few good reasons I can think of for crossing the river. What is more, I am told it is also a haunt of Mediterranean Eurotrash who come here when they feel homesick for good pizza. The staff are crazy in that unique Italian way that seems to appeal to a certain kind of English person, and embarrasses others: lots of bellowing of customers' names and so on … and this is if you just walk through the door. I have never been to Pizza Metro when somebody has been brave enough to announce to the staff that they are celebrating their birthday, but I can imagine the entire restaurant erupting into shouts of congratulation and jubilation. The pizzas are quite excellent in that papery-thin, Neapolitan way of which I am immensely fond. There are starters, for example, the Neapolitan aubergine, parmesan and tomato-layered bake, and there are main courses like linguine alla puttanesca, but the pizzas are the thing. For groups, pizzas arrive in lengths (starting at 1/2 metre) and are placed on a little trestle in the middle of the table. From margherita (tomato, mozzarella and basil) to ripieno (folded pizza stuffed with ricotta, ham, tomato, mozarella and mushrooms), the pizzas are unlikely to disappoint.

- **DRESS** *Off-duty Eurotrash*
- **RAIL** *Clapham Junction*
- **HOURS** *Lunch Sat–Sun 12.00–15.00; (closed Mon–Fri)*
      Dinner Tues–Sun 19.30–23.30; (closed Mon)
- **AVERAGE PRICE** *£20*
- **CREDIT CARDS** *No Diners Club*
- **MOBILES** *Allowed*
- **CIGARS** *Allowed*

POISSONNERIE DE L'AVENUE
82 Sloane Avenue, London SW3
☎ 0171 589 2457

This old-fashioned restaurant is a treasure. It is frequented by the sort of woman *d'un certain age* who believes Raine Spencer to be a fearless leader of fashion; but then that only heightens its charm. This is a gracious restaurant that deals with fish in its own, straightforward and traditional manner. Coquille de poissons et crustaces gratinées and moules au vin blanc et échalotes à la crème are typical starters. Tartare of fresh mackerel with capers, onions and cayenne pepper is a brisk and invigorating way to begin a meal here. Main courses include such immortals as Finnan haddock Monte Carlo and fillets de sole Veronique but there are also plain grills including Dover sole, sea bass and turbot. Extra orders of frites arrive the instant they are ordered. Puddings are crème brulée, crêpes au Grand Marnier and their ilk. Prices, while not low, offer reasonable value and if you fancy a bit of fresh fish for supper, but want to stay home, the Poissonnerie also boasts a smart little fishmonger.

- **DRESS** *Smartish*
- **TUBE** *South Kensington*
- **HOURS** *Lunch Mon–Sat 12.00–14.30; (closed Sun)*
  Dinner Mon–Sat 19.00–23.30; (closed Sun)
- **AVERAGE PRICE** *Lunch/Dinner £38–40*
- **CREDIT CARDS** *All major cards*
- **MOBILES** *Allowed*
- **CIGARS** *Humidor*

POMEGRANATES
94 Grosvenor Road, London SW1
☎ 0171 828 6560

Patrick Gwynn-Jones, the bon vivant patron of this Pimlico basement, is a great man. He is the apotheosis of the restauranteur of the Ancien Régime: a man who derived a living from an appreciation of the good things in life. If Pomegranates looks like a slice of vintage seventies, then appearances do not deceive. A headline from the Evening Standard over a review of this restaurant said it all with the words 'at the cutting edge of nostalgia'. The steak tartare is exemplary, the gravadlax is a classic and the Thai crab cakes are memorably good. That Gwynn-Jones is a connoissueur of wines and spirits can be spotted by the inclusion of such hors d'oeuvres as melon with pineau des Charentes, duck liver pâté with Calvados and cheese pâté with port and Armagnac. Move on to breast of wild duck with apple and Calvados and wind up with home-made honey and Cognac ice-cream. As well as an alcoholic theme, there is also a strong multicultural current running through the menu: curried goat with fried plantain, for example, or Turkish bureks with Sudanese pepper sauce. But what is so enchanting about the place is the feel: Pomegranates is a place where you can really relax and escape from the modern world.

- **DRESS** *Early seventies Savile Row*
- **TUBE** *Pimlico*
- **HOURS** *Lunch Mon–Fri 12.30–14.00; (closed Sat–Sun)*
      Dinner Mon–Sat 19.00–23.15; (closed Sun)
- **AVERAGE PRICE** *£30–40*
- **CREDIT CARDS** *All major cards*
- **MOBILES** *Allowed, but reception is poor*
- **CIGARS** *Humidor*

LE PONT DE LA TOUR

Butlers Wharf, Shad Thames, London SE1
☎ 0171 403 8403

The view of many, including I suspect Sir Terence himself, that this
is the showpiece of the Butlers Wharf gastrodrome, was given
government endorsement when Mr and Mrs Blair took Mr and
Mrs Clinton here for supper. (I actually prefer the Butlers Wharf
Chop House, but then what do I know?). The views are of course
spectacular, and the food tends towards the simple, good and
expensive. About the most complicated your food is going to
get is something like tranche of calf's liver with cumin-spiced
celeriac and grilled bacon, or roast rabbit wrapped in herbs and
pancetta with girolles and mustard vinaigrette. Otherwise, it is
a case of whole roast buttered lobster with herbs and fillet steak
au poivre. If you have visitors who have never heard of Terence
Conran – they probably come from Norfolk or Mars – then Pont
de la Tour is a good starting point. There is a good selection of
fruits de mer from the crustacea bar at the front of the restaurant
and as well as the crustacea altar, there is that other Conran
signature – the see-and-be-seen kitchen. Add to that a good
selection of cigars and a more moderately priced Bar and Grill
for simpler dishes (salads, lobster mayonnaise, plain grills and
so forth), and you have a microcosm of the Conran world.

- **DRESS** *City/New Labour suits*
- **TUBES** *Tower Hill; London Bridge*
- **HOURS** *Lunch Fri–Sun 12.00–15.00; (closed Mon–Thurs)*
      Dinner Mon–Sun 18.00–23.00
- **AVERAGE PRICE** *Lunch £50; Dinner £70*
- **CREDIT CARDS** *All major cards*
- **MOBILES** *Not encouraged*
- **CIGARS** *Humidor*

LA PORTE DES INDES
32 Bryanston Street, London W1
☎ 0171 224 0055

Lunch is not a particularly thrilling time to drop in at this vast double-decker, Franco-Indian curry hall, with its screens, domed glass ceiling, 40 ft high wall-mounted waterfall and an assortment of curious decorative knick-knacks. The evening is a more amusing time as the vast place fills up and acquires some atmosphere: the Mogul waterfall tinkles away and parties are led by traditionally-clad waitresses up the marble stairs from the Jungle Bar. Indeed the Jungle Bar is a remarkable place. At about 10 pm, its floor is carpeted with a thick layer of peanut shells that is almost enough to have me believing spent peanut shells are the new seagrass. The atmosphere is more decorous than that of your average curry house and this must be due to the intense seriousness with which chef Mehernosh Mody approaches his cooking. He spent several months in Pondichery, mastering the unique brand of French-Creole cooking practised there. Among his specialities are a dish called crab Malabar (a warm salad of crabmeat and corn spiked with mustard seeds and turmeric and fresh curry leaves) and the delicious crevettes assadh (prawns, mangoes, green chillies, ginger and poppy seed in coconut curry). Rices are lively affairs, with for example, lime rice and riz au coco aka riz sauvage. Even the breads have a French feel, for example, pain creole (pan-fried lacy rice flour pancakes – a speciality from Ponichery, a French settlement in southern India that the French did not actually quit until 1954, seven years after independence. The menu shows a charming postcard from *Les Colonies Francaises. Etablissements de l'Inde.*) The excellent and refreshing Cobra beer is served in delightfully decorated glasses.

- **DRESS** *Business suits*
- **TUBE** *Marble Arch*
- **HOURS** *Lunch Mon–Fri 12.00–14.30; Sun 12.00–15.00; (closed Sat) Dinner Mon–Sat 19.00–23.30; Sun 18.00–22.30*
- **AVERAGE PRICE** *Lunch £20; Dinner £30–35*
- **CREDIT CARDS** *All major cards*
- **MOBILES** *Allowed*
- **CIGARS** *Humidor*

PREMIER

3rd Floor, Selfridges, 400 Oxford Street, London W1
☎ 0171 318 3155

Premier is the Conran-designed showcase restaurant of almost
a dozen food and drink opportunities strewn around Gordon
Selfridge's handsome, over-scaled, reinvented retail temple.
Vittorio Radice, former top dog at Habitat, has made over
Selfridge's as the millenial department store par excellence.
Premier occupies what is possibly the best slot in the entire
building: in the middle, at the front, on the third floor at around
the top level of the heavily-ornamented Ionic columns. Occasional
stained glass panes filter light in an agreeable way and when the
clock strikes, you really know about it – the noise reverberates
around the restaurant, making one feel as if one is taking part in
the titles of *News At Ten*. Do not adjust your hearing aid – this is
a perfectly natural result of putting a restaurant next to a large
public time-piece. The food is rather better and more fashion-
aware than your regular department store offering, without being
too stridently innovative. Typical starters are pan-fried sea scallops
with baby fennel, artichoke and tomato with lemon grass jus,
linguine with chanterelle mushrooms and rosemary cream sauce
and seared foie gras with grapes, apple and Armagnac.
Mains run from the simple, grilled or pan-fried Dover sole, to the
elaborate, roast wild duck supreme with honey and macadamia
nuts in its own juice. When it comes to puddings, choose
between things like iced Champagne and red berry parfait with
macerated berries or chilled caramelised passion fruit cream with
strawberries and passion fruit syrup. There are also three types
of afternoon tea: 'cream', 'premier' and 'sparkling afternoon' –
the last benefits from the judicious inclusion of a glass of
Champagne.

- **DRESS** *As you would for a shopping trip*
- **TUBE** *Bond Street*
- **HOURS** *Lunch Mon–Sat 11.30–15.00; Sun 12.00–16.00
        Tea Mon–Tues 15.00–18.00; Wed–Fri 15.00–19.00;
        Sat 15.00–18.00*
- **AVERAGE PRICE** *Lunch £23–25; Tea £11.50*
- **CREDIT CARDS** *All major cards*
- **MOBILES** *Allowed*
- **CIGARS** *In bar only*

PRISM RESTAURANT AND BAR
147 Leadenhall Street, London EC3
☎ 0171 256 3888

Brought to you by the people who brought you Harvey Nix's
restaurants, Prism occupies the sort of cavernous space that
might happily serve as a railway station or a place for a nice
long Stalinist harangue. However this being the City, it is
more likely that this was the show-piece banking hall of some
financial institution or other. The main dining room is situated
in the large ground floor space and there is a contrastingly
claustrophobic subterranean bar. The food, like the place, seems
to go for safe, if unexciting, anonymous modernity. Peppered
seared salmon and new potato terrine was the sort of dish
that might have come out of a supermarket deli counter.
Morroccan-spiced chicken livers, lemon parsley couscous and
chilli sauce was better; while peppered haddock with brandade
cake and mustard seed sauce, was good and might have been
delicious had the brandade cake not turned out to be a potato
cake with the occasional shard of fish. Monkfish wrapped in
pancetta with potato hash and red wine sauce compensated for
its crudity of flavours with good presentation and a heartiness not
often seen in fish dishes. The wine list is good and boasts such
entertainingly absurd bottles as 'ABC Wild Boy, Chardonnay,
Santa Barbara'. Service was excellent and this is a good place
to go in the City if you want a contemporary, yet unchallenging
gastro-experience.

- **DRESS** *City suits – in the evenings men take their jackets off and hang them on the backs of their chairs (ugh!)*
- **TUBES** *Bank; Monument*
- **HOURS** *Lunch Mon–Fri 11.30–15.30; (closed Sat–Sun) Dinner Mon–Fri 18.00–22.00; (closed Sat–Sun)*
- **AVERAGE PRICE** *Lunch £35–40; Dinner £40–50*
- **CREDIT CARDS** *All major cards*
- **MOBILES** *With discretion*
- **CIGARS** *Humidor*

PUKKABAR AND CURRY HALL
42 Sydenham Road, London SE26
☎ 0181 778 4629

Pukkabar sits at the back of its bar, now called the Two Halfs.
Pukkabar is the devastatingly simple offspring of the imagination
of Trevor Gulliver, the man responsible for St John (qv). Put simply,

it amalgamates those two traditional British pastimes of drinking large amounts of beer in the pub and then going for a curry, placing them under one roof. The gilded youth of Sydenham adore the concept, slobbing out in the leather armchairs to down their lager and then piling into the canteen-like surroundings of the curry hall with its open kitchen at the rear. Set meals are listed under Pukkalunch, Pukkasuppa and Pukkabrunch. Starters show imagination and wit, for example, tandoori quail, chicken tikka masala pancake, deep-fried spicy lamb burger, tandoori cheese and vegetable kebab and so on. Naan breads come plain, peshawari or stuffed with cheese, lamb or potato. Curries, while not the best I have ever tasted, are perfectly nice and well priced: the Goan prawn and coconut curry was tasty and the aromatic lamb curry with yoghurt met with approval. Wines are a pleasant surprise, with bottles such as Lawson's Dry Hills Gewürztraminer 1997 NZ selected with an eye to pleasing the curry-loving oenophile. What was truly impressive was that even late on a Friday night, the place was packed but service remained efficient and pleasant.

- **DRESS** *As for a fight*
- **RAIL** *Sydenham*
- **HOURS** *Lunch Sun 12.00–15.30; (closed Mon–Sat)*
      Dinner Mon–Sat 18.00–23.30; Sun 19.00–22.30
- **AVERAGE PRICE** *Lunch/Dinner £15*
- **CREDIT CARDS** *All major cards*
- **MOBILES** *Allowed*
- **CIGARS** *Not allowed*

PUTNEY BRIDGE RIVER RESTAURANT & BAR
2 Lower Richmond Road, Embankment, London SW15
☎ 0181 780 1811

I have yet to get the hang of Putney, as I think has Trevor Gulliver. Gulliver was the man who, invigorated by the success of his City restaurant St John (qv), presided over the first incarnation of Putney Bridge a couple of years ago. The building, a few holds barred RIBA award-winning confection of wood, steel, glass and concrete, was mercilessly hyped as the first purpose-built restaurant to appear in London for over 40 years and much was made of the art: contemporary and modern. It was to be a democratic food station, a sort of microcosmic gastrodrome: vaguely formal, yet uncomplicated – fine dining on the first floor and a relaxed bar with informal snacking on the ground floor. However, not everyone can fill the footprints of Sir Terence

Conran: it takes more than a riparian location, a few million quid and some neologistic architecture, as Gulliver found out. He had to bale out of Putney Bridge and is now practising his gastronomic experiments in Sydenham, with the Pukkabar (qv). Meanwhile, back in SW15, things have gone decidedly upmarket at Putney Bridge. There is a new chef called Anthony Demetre, who was at L'Odeon from 1995 until the autumn of last year, when he turned up at Putney Bridge. The food is much fancier and more prepared than it used to be and if Monsieur Demetre is not aiming for a Michelin star, then my name is AA Gill. The food is good. A typical dish might be something like 'daurade with saffron risotto and spring onions, light chicken jus flavoured with orange and rosemary'. There are times when Demetre really gets it right as with a deceptively simple dish of asparagus and morels – a triumph in terms of texture and flavour. He also tries hard with his puddings: crème brulée is interestingly presented as a dollop of the crème bit, with a pane of the brulée bit balanced on top; and the intriguing, not unsuccessful, idea of basil and mascarpone ice-cream. All this effort seems to be appreciated by the 'quality' of this bourgeois bit of south London. It seems that by establishing itself as the local grand restaurant, complete with the pageantry of well-drilled staff and a likeably-lugubrious deputy wine waiter who might have been the understudy for Lurch in the Addams Family, Putney Bridge attracts the local grandees.

- **DRESS** *Vaguely*
- **TUBE** *Putney Bridge*
- **HOURS** *Lunch Mon–Sat 12.00–14.30; Sun 12.30–15.00*
        Dinner Mon–Sat 19.00–23.00; (closed Sun)
- **AVERAGE PRICE** *Lunch £25; Dinner £45*
- **CREDIT CARDS** *All major cards*
- **MOBILES** *Allowed*
- **CIGARS** *Allowed*

QUAGLINO'S
16 Bury Street, London SW1
☎ 0171 930 6767

It is difficult to think back to St Valentine's day 1993 when Terence Conran's Quaglino's, revamped as a London riposte to such Parisian places as La Coupole, opened for business. Quag's had been the dinner and dancing joint of choice of the deco years and beyond, but by the sixties it was losing its gloss and subsequently closed. Back in the early nineties, it seemed vast and people questioned the wisdom of opening such an abnormally large restaurant at the nadir of a terrible recession. Well, as he almost always is, Sir Terence was right. The place was packed and of course the trend for Brobdingnagian eateries became a mid-nineties obsession. Predictably, it came in for a critical backlash with people moaning that the place was being taken over by the bridge-and-tunnel crowd (why shouldn't they be allowed to eat too?) Then there was the time that Joel Kissin hounded a man who had not tipped adequately. After that, Quag's was left to get on with it, which, on the whole, it has done admirably. I still think it is a stunning-looking, cavernous room and on the whole the brasserie-style menu delivers a good standard of relatively simple food. If there are glitches, bear in mind that something like 7000 people are said to eat here each week. Quaglino's salad is a tasty take on a Caesar salad; the crustacea altar, now a Conran signature, is always an option. The shoulder of pork has been on the menu for ages and has attracted favourable comments. Thai fish cakes make an appearance here with sweet chilli dressing; sevruga, oscietra and beluga, served with crème fraîche and melba toast can be ordered in 30 or 50 gram portions; and grills and rotisserie dishes are served with tasty frites. The cocktail list is divided into long drinks, Quaglino's martinis, classic cocktails, Champagne cocktails and Absolut Breezes. The grande dame mother of an industrialist friend would be pleased to see her favourite 'Stinger' highlighted in red on the list of Classics. But be warned, the menu comes with its own health warning and it is nothing to do with the cigarette and cigar girls who sashay around the place – 'We do not recommend the consumption of spirits with oysters or clams', it says in bold type.

- **DRESS** *Smart*
- **TUBE** *Green Park*
- **HOURS** *Lunch Mon–Sun 12.00–15.00*
  Dinner Mon–Thurs 17.30–23.30; Fri–Sat 17.30–00.30;
  Sun 17.30–22.30
- **AVERAGE PRICE** *Lunch/Dinner £35*
- **CREDIT CARDS** *All major cards*
- **MOBILES** *No reception*
- **CIGARS** *Humidor*

THE QUALITY CHOP HOUSE

92–94 Farringdon Road, London EC1

☎ 0171 837 5093

The Quality Chop House used to be an unreconstructed greasy spoon. I once visited it about about a dozen years ago; it was dreadful but it had potential: old benches and windows etched with such slogans as the immortal 'Progressive Working Class Caterer'. Then it was taken over by the talented Charles Fontaine and, ever since, it has been a Farringdon landmark. Although it is still possible to order eggs, bacon and chips, the emphasis is heavily on fish and seafood: jellied eels; grilled kippers with poached egg; roast cod with garlic and plum tomato; scallop, clam and saffron potato stew; chilled lobster mayonnaise; sevruga and blinis. Wines are well chosen and there cannot be many working class caterers that run to Puligny Montrachet, 1er Cru Les Combettes and Krug. Since he opened, Fontaine has expanded next door and installed another acid-etched window that reads 'London's noted salmon fish cake.'

- **DRESS** *Progressive working class*
- **TUBE** *Farringdon*
- **HOURS** *Lunch Mon–Fri 12.00–15.00; Sun 12.00–16.00;*
  (closed Sat)
  Dinner Mon–Fri 18.30–23.30; Sat 18.30–23.30;
  Sun 19.00–23.30
- **AVERAGE PRICE** *Lunch/Dinner £25*
- **CREDIT CARDS** *No American Express or Diners Club*
- **MOBILES** *Not encouraged*
- **CIGARS** *Prohibited*

QUO VADIS

26–29 Dean Street, London W1

☎ 0171 437 9585

Remade by Marco Pierre White with an abundance of Damien Hirst artwork, this Soho landmark serves rather interesting, distinguished food. For instance, the tronconette de homard with white port sauce and salad of herbs, was a refined lobster dish; a risotto of oysters with watercress purée was soupy, but tasty, with top-flight mollusc flesh. Although not cheap, for the money, the service is very well drilled, and the staff knowledgeable, helpful and apologetic whenever appropriate. The food is very serious. Typical dishes include: pithivier of snails and wild mushrooms, barolo jus; roast barbarie duckling with a Banyuls wine, cinammon sauce, spiced cherries; roast suckling pig with black pudding and choucroute, Dijon mustard, marjolaine jus; and pot-au-feu of beef and confit duck leg with root vegetables and served with remoulade sauce. Upstairs there is a dark, intimate bar with plenty of Mr Hirst's work on display and I have to say it is a rather nice space – a bit like turning the Pitt Rivers Museum at Oxford into a bar. However, apparently the place is up for a revamp and the wallpaper bill alone runs into many tens of thousands of pounds. The wine list is as serious as Marcel Proust's *Remembrance of Things Past*, and almost as long. It also bears the warning: 'We respectfully inform our guests that all wines over 30 years old are the responsibility of the guest, should the tasting quality of the wine be in any way compromised.'

- **DRESS** *Suits, unless you are Damien Hirst in which case you wear what you like*
- **TUBES** *Tottenham Court Road; Leicester Square; Piccadilly Circus*
- **HOURS** *Lunch Mon–Fri 12.00–14.30; (closed Sat–Sun)*
  Dinner Mon–Sat 18.00–23.30; Sun 18.00–22.30
- **AVERAGE PRICE** *Lunch/Dinner £35–40*
- **CREDIT CARDS** *All major cards*
- **MOBILES** *Allowed*
- **CIGARS** *Humidor*

RAGS

1a Chesterfield Street, London W1
☎ 0171 629 2592

Founded by Johnny Gold, this Mayfair members club was where Ringo Starr celebrated his wedding to Barbara Bach and where I used to go drinking with a motley crew in the early nineties. Since then, this handsome Georgian house has been refurbished beyond recognition, and although I miss its previous raffishness and its pool table, it has to be said, facilities and food have improved beyond measure. What is more, three apartments on the floors above the restaurant and bar can be rented at scandalously reasonable rates by members – indeed, the money saved on a night in a suite at the Dorchester will more than pay for membership. The dining room is decorated in an overwhelming shade of red that brings to mind a Parisian brothel of the Belle Epoque, but the views over the gardens of the Saudi Embassy are tranquil in the extreme. The executive chef is the same man who cooks at the Belvedere (qv), so expect to eat well. Typical dishes include langoustine wrapped in basil and filo pastry, with seasonal leaves and mango dressing; oak-smoked salmon with potted shrimps (a personal favourite); seared scallops with with warm potato salad, parmesan tuile and light truffle dressing; roast fillet of veal on creamed ceps with a lemon and rosemary sauce; grilled sole; and best end of lamb with a leek soufflé, foie gras and mint cappuccino.

- **DRESS** As you want but Gold usually wears Doug Hayward suits
- **TUBES** Green Park; Hyde Park Corner
- **HOURS** Mon–Fri 12.00–1.00 am; Sat 18.00–1.00 am; (closed Sun)
- **AVERAGE PRICE** Lunch/Dinner £35
- **CREDIT CARDS** All cards
- **MOBILES** Not in the evening
- **CIGARS** Humidor

RAIN

303 Portobello Road, London W10
☎ 0181 968 2001

Billed as New Asian cuisine, Rain offers rather good food in charming, if slightly home-made, surroundings. Staff are delightful and dishes range from chargrilled prawns with coriander cakes through to Hunanese roast rack of lamb with aromatic spices, vietnamese-glazed pumpkin, scallion and sesame breadcake, to agedashi tofu steak with shiitake and oyster mushroom sauce and spring onion cake. A starter of sesame-encrusted scallops on a bed of leaves with miso dressing was perfectly ok, however, a Thai green curry of prawns would be worth returning for. The Vietnamese shaking beef is a wonderfully named dish that does not disappoint on arrival. Puddings include the rather un-Asian white chocolate cake. Guzzle copious quantities of Kirin lager.

- **DRESS** New Age Notting Hill
- **TUBE** Ladbroke Grove
- **HOURS** Lunch Tues–Fri 12.30–14.30; (closed Mon) Brunch Sat–Sun 11.30–16.00 Dinner Mon–Sat 19.00–23.00; (closed Sun)
- **AVERAGE PRICE** Lunch £15–20; Dinner £20–25
- **CREDIT CARDS** All major cards
- **MOBILES** Allowed
- **CIGARS** Allowed

RHODES IN THE SQUARE

Dolphin Square, Chester Street, London SW1
☎ 0171 798 6767

Apparently Mr Rhodes wants his lobster omelette thermidor to become a classic. I agree with him. This potent, concentrated little pan of the best bits of thermidor served in something similar to the consistency of a cheese fondue may not be everyone's idea of an omelette, but it is a marvellous idea. It is what Rhodes does best: a rich, flavoursome dish that is far from self-effacing. The menu is littered with this type of food. Take, for example, this brace of starters: a rich pigeon faggot on a potato cake with mustard cabbage; beef fillet, bacon, chicken liver and red wine ragu with buttered pasta. Equally as inspired as the lobster omelette thermidor was a main course of spring onion risotto and poached egg pie with a fresh herb beurre blanc, the egg hiding the risotto waiting for the first touch of the fork. The bread and butter pudding, a dish more modish chefs might serve individually, is a hearty slab of something quite supernaturally good. The lighter dishes just do not compare anything like as well; they sit oddly on the menu and recall the English section of an old-fashioned Chinese restaurant – present only as a sop to customers whose tastes do not match those of the chef's. The room, situated in Dolphin Square's fitness club is big, blue and windowless but well lit. It glistens with much highly polished metal and recalls either an ocean liner or the set of a 1970s TV spectacular: one half expects to see the black and white minstrels or Danny La Rue come high kicking down the stairs. The service is faultless, well-drilled, and a credit to Mr Rhodes and his fashion-defying hairdo. Wines are not cheap.

- **DRESS** *Smart*
- **TUBE** *Pimlico*
- **HOURS** *Lunch Sun–Fri 12.00–14.30; (closed Sat)*
  Dinner Mon–Sat 19.00–22.00
- **AVERAGE PRICE** *Lunch £20–30; Dinner £40–50*
- **CREDIT CARDS** *All major cards*
- **MOBILES** *Not allowed*
- **CIGARS** *Allowed*

RICHARD CORRIGAN AT LINDSAY HOUSE

21 Romilly Street, London W1
☎ 0171 439 0450

This pale, handsome and slightly rackety eighteenth century
house is Richard Corrigan's latest roost. Corrigan is something
of a veteran of the London restaurant scene. His cooking has
been variously described as gutsy contemporary British and
earthy modern Irish. Such gastro-labels are so silly as to be
almost meaningless. I am sure we will be seeing the emergence
of such diverse food styles as Neo-Norfolk or Crude Cornish and
I look forward to eating at a robust modern Welsh restaurant.
The food at Lindsay House runs along these sort of lines: grilled
red mullet; lasagne of sardines with salad and rouille; salad of
skate with aubergine, capers and parsley salad; sea bass with
clam vinaigrette, chorizo & coriander salad; stuffed salad of
rabbit, shellfish sabayon and artichoke and English veal cutlet,
shallot purée and roast garlic. Puddings are simple without being
boring – caramelised apple cake with Calvados syrup, Neal's
Yard cheeses etc. The wine list is reasonably priced for the West
End and a close reading will reveal some wonderfully eccentric
descriptions. One bottle is described as 'rich, anchovy-oily,
tobacco-scented wine', while a Crozes Hermitage gives off
'aromas of warm tar and woodsmoke'.

- **DRESS** *Smart*
- **TUBE** *Leicester Square*
- **HOURS** *Lunch Mon–Fri 12.00–14.30; (closed Sat–Sun)*
        Dinner Mon–Sat 18.00–23.00; (closed Sun)
- **AVERAGE PRICE** *Lunch £33; Dinner £38*
- **CREDIT CARDS** *All major cards*
- **MOBILES** *Not allowed*
- **CIGARS** *Not allowed*

RICHOUX

Richoux Coffee Lounge, 28a Kensington Church Street, London W8
☎ 0171 938 2880

Richoux is one of the London institutions that has been trundling
on for most of the century. These days, such polite tea rooms/
coffee houses/lightish restaurants/cake shops find themselves
under the ownership of Laurence Isaacson's Groupe Chez
Gerard. They are not bad places to visit, in a vaguely Palm
Court, sub Fortnums sort of way. Do not decide to test the menu
to its limits, instead stick to things like kedgeree or scrambled

eggs with smoked salmon on toasted brioche (although I like my eggs more loosely scrambled than is the Richoux way). 'The late breakfast grill' (best back bacon rashers, Cumberland sausage, fried eggs, grilled mushrooms, fried onion, roast tomato and toast), a plateful that is forever Britain, costs about a tenner. And the buck rarebit (with poached egg and anchovy) is the sort of thing that I find extremely comforting in an old-fashioned way. Much is made of the patisserie and the ice-cream sundaes, the latter known by such names as cappuccino delight, chocoholic's dream, Richoux rumba and so on. However, the genteel and the twee side Richoux, has its alter ego: the trendy coffee bar and panini shop of Richoux Coffee Co, bang next to the flagship Richoux on Piccadilly. If Richoux is a little old lady in a tweed suit, then Richoux Coffee Co is a foxy chick in a pussy pelmet and something by Prada … with good muffins, sandwiches and coffees from Hawaii to Yemen.

- **DRESS** *Casual*
- **TUBE** *High Street Kensington*
- **HOURS** *Mon–Sat 8.00–23.00; (closed Sun)*
- **AVERAGE PRICE** *Lunch/Dinner £18*
- **CREDIT CARDS** *All major cards*
- **MOBILES** *Allowed*
- **CIGARS** *Humidor*

ALSO AT
172 Piccadilly, London W1;
  0171 493 2204 TUBES Piccadilly Circus; Green Park
41a, South Audley Street, London W1;
  0171 629 5228 TUBE Bond Street
Richoux Coffee Co., 171 Piccadilly, London W1;
  0171 629 4991 TUBE Piccadilly Circus
86 Brompton Road, London SW3;
  0171 584 8300 TUBE Knightsbridge
3 Circus Road, London NW8;
  0171 483 4001 TUBE St John's Wood

THE RITZ
150 Piccadilly, London W1
☎ 0171 493 8181

Under the aegis of Giles Shepard, the Ritz has reasserted itself as one of the great hotels of London. I know Shepard is all right because we share a shirtmaker and, although I seldom admit the superiority of another to me in matters of dress, his stickpins and the watch-chain that loops across his waistcoat, are I think the finest in St James's. What is more, at his fabulous country retreat, guests are given angora blankets in which to swathe themselves and ward off the grim British weather. Shepard is constantly refining the Ritz and hardly ever misses a thing. The room is one of the most beautiful in London and as a grand summer lunch spot, there are few places to beat it. Along with the Connaught, I would probably rate it as my favourite London hotel dining room. Classics like oak-smoked wild Scottish salmon, royal beluga caviar, lobster thermidor, Dover sole bonne femme and noisettes of Southdown lamb provide the backbone of the menu. However, there are frequent occasions when guest chefs fly in to cook here for a week or two to give added interest.

- **DRESS** *Smart; jacket and tie required*
- **TUBE** *Green Park*
- **HOURS** *Breakfast Mon–Sat 7.00–10.30; Sun 8.00–11.00*
  Lunch Mon–Sun 12.30–14.30
  Dinner Mon–Sat 19.00–23.00; Sun 18.30–22.30
- **AVERAGE PRICE** *Lunch £45; Dinner £60*
- **CREDIT CARDS** *All major cards*
- **MOBILES** *Not allowed*
- **CIGARS** *Humidor*

RIVA
169 Church Road Barnes, London SW13
☎ 0181 748 0434

To my mind this is the best restaurant in London. I first discovered it when I was Fay Maschler's editor and was reading a proof of her pages the night before it appeared in the paper. She sounded so impressed that I went and ate there that night, assuming that once such a review became public property, I would be unable to get a table. That was in 1990, now Andrea Riva has become a friend, we have taken holidays together, he is godfather to my son and I let him beat me at backgammon. The man's devotion to his metier is, I think, unrivalled in the restaurant profession. Although he has had many offers to open Riva's in the West End and abroad, he prefers instead to do what he likes best, the way he likes to do it, in south west London. And if people like it, they can jolly well make the effort to travel to Barnes – and travel they do. Pop stars, film legends, sporting impressarios, and titans of the business world, as well as slavish foodies, have made Riva a place of pilgrimage. I remember once in the early nineties when I was a guest at a house party in a remote part of Spain near the Portuguese border, that even there my hosts talked reverentially of the reputation of Riva … though they had yet to visit the place themselves. However, cashmere-clad Riva's eponymous restaurant is not to everyone's taste: paper tablecloths and smoked glass ashtrays deter those in search of an altogether more formal restaurant experience. The food is deceptively clever and in the best part of a decade that Riva has been around, this understated umber-coloured Barnes dining room has supplied the inspiration for dishes that have appeared with fanfares in many highly-acclaimed West End restaurants. Riva was the first place that I ever ate baccala mantecato. Later I began to notice it on every other London menu, ditto risotto nero. Dishes range from the hearty, iron-rich fegato e polenta unta (calf's liver with garlic polenta and wild mushrooms) to the delicate sturgeon with Swiss Chard and saffron potatoes. Cooking of the northern Italian lakes is much in evidence here with such dishes as fillets of perch with tuna mayonaise and fillets of sun-dried shad on grilled polenta. Puddings are especially noteworthy – Riva was the conduit through which such traditional Italian dishes such as panna cotta became popular in London.

- **DRESS** *Casual*
- **TUBE** *Hammersmith*
- **HOURS** *Lunch Mon–Fri, Sun 12.00–14.30; (closed Sat)*
    Dinner Mon–Sat 19.00–23.00; Sun 19.00–21.30
- **AVERAGE PRICE** *Lunch/Dinner £35*
- **CREDIT CARDS** *All major cards*
- **MOBILES** *Not allowed*
- **CIGARS** *With discretion*

THE RIVER CAFÉ
Thames Wharf, Rainville Road, London W6
☎ 0171 381 8824

When reading what I have to say about Italian restaurants, it helps to bear in mind the fanatical devotion I have for Riva (qv). So forgive me if I cannot get quite as worked up about the River Café as its many devotees. Ruthie and Rosie do good telly and theirs are the cookbooks that set in motion the tidal wave of gastro-porn that has engulfed every Rajastahni coffee table from Hammersmith to Hampstead. This is the place where the chattering classes discovered that Italian food was more than big pepper mills, checked tablecloths and cries of bella signora. It is an expensive restaurant, so I would only go if someone else is paying, although I did have a brief spell of popping in for dinner when a friend (a keen amateur motor racer and vintage car nut) was wooing the then manageress (they married and live in splendour south of the river with a baby called Natasha). Baked fish is a good thing here and I recall that pasta dishes, Tuscan bread soup, Tuscan bean stew and probably Tuscan anything else is well worth ordering, as are seasonal offerings of game. This was also the place where cavolo nero was launched upon an unsuspecting capital and subsequently re-exported to Italy. As far as I can remember, there was an informality about the service that I found annoying, considering the price. Nevertheless this is an important part of London's culinary rebirth, that still continues to influence the way that a great many people eat in London and beyond – the New Yorker declared it the finest Italian restaurant in Europe. On a pleasant day, the light-filled room and the riparian setting are a delight. It also helps to be a member of New Labour's classless aristocracy when it comes to getting a table.

- **DRESS** *New Labour*
- **TUBE** *Hammersmith*
- **HOURS** *Lunch Mon–Sun 12.30–15.00*
  Dinner Mon–Thurs 19.00–23.00; Fri–Sat 19.00–23.20
- **AVERAGE PRICE** *Lunch £45; Dinner £55*
- **CREDIT CARDS** *All major cards*
- **MOBILES** *With consideration for others*
- **CIGARS** *Prohibited*

RIVER RESTAURANT
The Savoy Hotel, Strand, London WC2
☎ 0171 836 4343

Tucked away at the back of the Savoy, this large restaurant with its river views and Anton Edelmann's cooking must be among the most underrated establishments in London. 'Let's meet at the River Restaurant and make a night of it' is not a cry that one hears too frequently in fashionable circles, which is a pity as the place is fun, in a grand hotel dining room sort of way, and the food superb. The atmosphere veers towards dignified when the place is quiet and a suburban wantonness, when Friday comes and the place fills up with the dinner and dance (yes, honestly) crowd, family birthdays, wedding anniversary celebrations and so on. The band on a Friday night is a kitsch classic. Like its front of hotel counterpart, the Savoy Grill (qv), The River Room is fond of the trolley, in that things like wild Scottish smoked salmon and the roast of the day are carved at your table. While not pushing back the envelope of gastronomic fashion, the River Room is the place to go for mildly imaginative things done extremely well. For starters, expect things like lobster salad in curry dresssing with toasted pine nuts and mustard leaves; smoked baby eel with horseradish sauce and mustard leaves; tian of crabmeat and marinated scallops in coconut milk. As far as mains go, elegant simplicity, albeit served in good portions, is the idea. Mix-grill of Atlantic fish with smoked paprika aioli is an excellent piscine choice, while grilled calf's kidney with herb crust on parsnip mash and roasted vegetables or braised suckling pig with marinated cabbage and dumplings are good examples of carnivorous offerings. However, there are occasional wild cards, for example, asparagus, tofu and wild mushroom strudel with dahl, striking an incongruous vegetarian note. Spicy pain perdu with banana ice-cream is an excellent pudding, hotly followed by the chocolate and ginger truffle torte. Wines are as good as those in a grand hotel should be. It is difficult to find anything bad to say about the River Room, so I won't. I would only caution that you do not go expecting it to be cheap.

- **DRESS** *Smart*
- **TUBES** *Embankment; Charing Cross; Covent Garden*
- **HOURS** *Lunch Mon–Sun 12.30–14.30*
      Dinner Mon–Sat 18.00–23.00; Sun 19.00–22.30
- **AVERAGE PRICE** *Lunch/Dinner £50*
- **CREDIT CARDS** *All major cards*
- **MOBILES** *Not allowed*
- **CIGARS** *Humidor*

THE ROOM

Halcyon Hotel, 129 Holland Park Avenue, London W11
☎ 0171 221 5411

This west London hotel dining room is a consistently pleasant, if pricey, place to come and eat. Although it is on the basement or lower ground floor, it is a light, pleasantly informal space. In the summer, the little terrace at the back is a delightful place to lunch under large sunshades. Food is vaguely Mediterranean and sufficiently modern to keep abreast of culinary trends without offending conservative palates: typical starters are pressed red mullet and saffron terrine with chive oil; artichoke hollandaise with poached egg, while the grilled baby Dover sole with lobster sauce was of almost adolescent proportions. Mains might include sea bass with an oyster beignet and grilled cod fillet with olive tapenade and potato purée. In winter, expect hearty stuff like braised knuckle of veal with Madeira sauce. The bar is a useful little hideaway and a good place to settle into some reviving martinis.

- **DRESS** *Smart; rich rockstar*
- **TUBE** *Holland Park*
- **HOURS** *Breakfast Mon–Fri 7.00–10.30; (closed Sat–Sun)*
  Lunch Mon–Sun 12.00–14.30
  Dinner Sun–Thurs 19.00–22.30; Fri–Sat 19.00–23.00
- **AVERAGE PRICE** *£35–40*
- **CREDIT CARDS** *All major cards*
- **MOBILES** *Not allowed*
- **CIGARS** *Humidor*

ROYAL CHINA

13 Queensway, London W2
☎ 0171 221 2535

The Queensway branch of Royal China is indeed a remarkable building: it looks like a discothèque that has been carefully preserved from the Saturday Night Fever days. This look is also replicated at Baker Street. The décor alone is enough to recommend it for at least one visit and thereafter people tend to return, especially for the dim sum. The London Chinese restaurant staple of sea bass is well done at the Baker Street branch, while sweet and sour fish is spicy, and sufficiently delicious, to convert those who do not even like the idea of sweet and sour food. Among the many vegetable and beancurd dishes, the Shaolin Monks vegetable pot is outstanding. Apparently it is a Sunday tradition on Baker Street to take in a vaguely arthouse movie at the Screen on Baker Street and then pile into Royal China for dim sum.

- **DRESS** *Smart/casual*
- **TUBE** *Queensway*
- **HOURS** *Mon–Thurs 12.00–23.00; Fri–Sat 12.00–23.30;*
  Sun 11.00–22.00
- **AVERAGE PRICE** *Lunch/Dinner £25–30*
- **CREDIT CARDS** *No Diners Club*
- **MOBILES** *Allowed*
- **CIGARS** *Allowed*

ALSO AT
40 Baker Street, London W1;
0171 487 4688 TUBE Baker Street

SAFFRON

306b Fulham Road, London SW10
☎ 0171 565 8183

Saffron is the sort of Indian restaurant that deserves to be packed.
The food is consistently well-above-average standard and the
prices low. Perhaps the proximity of this long narrow restaurant
to Brompton cemetery puts people off; then again it might be the
music: a weird Ravi Shankar meets Stockhausen hybrid noise
that pumps from the speakers. However, the food and indeed
the informal yet knowledgeable and caring service more than
compensate. For example, a Punjabi fish tikka, demonstrated
an exciting range of quite haunting and intriguing flavours,
while the little cauldron of black dal that was recommended as
an accompaniment proved more than satisfactory. The menu also
offers intriguing dishes such as khand khargosh, a rabbit-based
dish that is apparently a Royal delicacy from Jaipur – traditionally
cooked in hot ash underground and adapted today by cooking
in live embers above ground'. It is presumably this dish's regal
antecendence that accounts for the strip of silver laid over the top
as a garnish. The place is used by gourmets all over west London
for its take-aways and one fan of the place just rings up and asks
for a take-away, leaving the owner to decide what he should eat.
The beer of choice is Lal Toofan.

- **DRESS** *Hardly matters*
- **TUBE** *Fulham Broadway*
- **HOURS** *Lunch Sun–Fri 12.00–15.00; Sat (when there is a
          football match)*
          Dinner Mon–Sun 18.00–24.00
- **AVERAGE PRICE** *£15–20*
- **CREDIT CARDS** *No Diners Club*
- **MOBILES** *Allowed*
- **CIGARS** *Allowed*

ST JOHN

26 St John Street, London EC1
☎ 0171 251 0848

St John leapt to national prominence when it put a raw carrot
and a hard-boiled egg on the menu and found this daring combo
mentioned in most newspapers. Although a trifle attention-
grabbing, this dish gives an idea of chef Fergus Henderson's
approach to food. The surroundings, a former smokehouse on
the fringes of Smithfield market, share the cooking's unadorned

rigour. A stylised drawing of a pig taken from an old reference book and now copyrighted as the logo of St John coupled with the cheery little motto, 'Nose To Tail Eating', give an accurate idea of the hearty type of food on offer here. If you like crispy pig's tail and red mustard; sweetbread terrine; pig tongue and green sauce; roast bone marrow and parsley salad, then you will *lurv* St John. There are some piscine dishes, uncomplicated things like langoustines and mayonnaise. Puddings delight fans of Mrs Beeton with their traditional overtones: Bakewell tart, raspberries and Jersey cream, and even Eccles cake served with Lancashire cheese. I would have thought that this is one of the best places in London to go if you fancy suckling pig – simply gather together a group of like-minded friends and order a week in advance. Roaring City boys adore the carnivorous atmosphere. Experimental new Labourites think it slightly edgy. Not the place to bring your vegetarian friends.

- **DRESS** *City suits*
- **TUBE** *Farringdon*
- **HOURS** *Lunch Mon–Fri 12.00–15.00; (closed Sat–Sun)*
      Dinner Mon–Sat 18.00–23.00; (closed Sun)
- **AVERAGE PRICE** *£30*
- **CREDIT CARDS** *All major cards*
- **MOBILES** *Not allowed*
- **CIGARS** *Humidor*

SAN LORENZO
22 Beauchamp Place, London SW3
☎ 0171 584 1074

Poor old San Lorenzo got a frightful drubbing from the celebrated AA Gill, in fact it was supposed to be one of his cruellest of '98. Even staunch supporters admit that prices are high and that food can at times be unremarkable. Nevertheless, San Lorenzo is one of the most famous restaurants in the world and inevitably one goes there for other than purely gastronomic reasons. While celebrity is no excuse for slipping standards, the place does have a unique charm that keeps on attracting world famous stars year after year. If you are passably famous, don't care about money, are not looking for the most dynamic, palate-stimulating Italian food and just want to feel comfortable and welcomed in an informal environment, then San Lorenzo is the place. The Wimbledon branch is packed during the tennis tournament and is popular at weekends with weekday regulars from Beauchamp

Place looking for somewhere to come with the family. The last time I was there, I seem to remember eating a particularly good pizza.

- **DRESS** *As you would for a Hello! photoshoot*
- **TUBE** *Knightsbridge*
- **HOURS** *Lunch Mon–Sat 12.30–15.00; (closed Sun)*
       Dinner Mon–Sat 19.30–23.30; (closed Sun)
- **AVERAGE PRICE** *£35–50*
- **CREDIT CARDS** *Not accepted*
- **MOBILES** *Allowed in cloakroom*
- **CIGARS** *Allowed*

ALSO AT

San Lorenzo Fuoriporta, Worple Road Mews, London SW19;
   0181 946 8463   TUBE *Wimbledon*

SARTORIA

20 Savile Row, London W1
☎ 0171 534 7000

This is probably the closest that Sir Terence Conran has ever got to a themed restaurant. Appropriate touches include Rex Harrison's pattern hanging on a back wall; a needle and thread embroidered on to the antimacassars; vaguely Fornasetti-style ashtrays that look like coiled tape measures and bastes (half-made suits) from six of the Row's finest tailors, framed and stuck on the wall. The food is a peculiar type of smart urban Italian that pretends to be regional or rustic, but that one only ever tends to eat in London. The flavours are well-defined and exciting without being too much for the palates of local high-end lunchers, for example, sea bass with organic zucchini, runner beans and anchovies. The wine list has key super Tuscans: tignanello, ornellaia, solaia and sassicaia and serious drinkers will welcome a list of almost two dozen grappas. Sir Terence does contemporary luxury very well and this is everything a smart, sleek, modern West End restaurant should be, but expect to pay for it.

- **DRESS** *Savile Row suits*
- **TUBES** *Piccadilly Circus; Oxford Circus*
- **HOURS** *Lunch Mon–Sat 12.00–15.00; (closed Sun)*
       Dinner Mon–Sat 18.30–23.30; Sun 18.00–22.30
- **AVERAGE PRICE** *Lunch £35; Dinner £40*
- **CREDIT CARDS** *All major cards*
- **MOBILES** *Allowed*
- **CIGARS** *Humidor*

LES SAVEURS DE JEAN CHRISTOPHE NOVELLI

See NOVELLI page 160

THE SAVOY GRILL ROOM

The Savoy Hotel, Savoy Hill, Strand, London WC2
☎ 0171 836 4343

There are times when only the full-on pageantry of the Savoy Grill will suffice: its old-style Italian service, its old-style American and industrialist customers and trolleys wheeling between the tables. The room has that smell of roasting flesh and gravy that in some weird Proustian way I associate with the dining room at my grandmother's house. She would insist that the leg or joint would be installed in the oven some time shortly after breakfast had been cleared away, and certainly before she went off to church. Then after several hours of exposure to high temperatures, this charred hunk of flesh would be extricated from its incineration and served with great aplomb. Given her predeliction for meat that was one step away from charcoal, I am not sure my grandmother would have approved of the food at the Savoy Grill – it is, well, rather good. She would however have been very flattered by the attention of Angelo Maresca the Maitre d' hotel. Service at the Savoy Grill is not always faultless unless, of course, you are a captain of industry who has invested a sizeable chunk of his shareholder's money in eating here. I have experienced less than helpful staff at the Savoy. What is worse, an important friend of mine (who was lunching someone even more important), experienced the embarrassment of having his booking lost, being ignored, and having to leaf through the ledger himself to find that the booking had been made under his Christian name. At a place which has such a reputation and charges such prices, these things should not happen. However, one evening of good food, fine wine and excellent service restores faith in the Grill and its position as a national icon. Time has not quite stood still at the Grill – there is, for example, a pasta dish of penne with roast organic tomatoes – it just moves slowly. On the whole, it is best not to mess with culinary neologisms and tuck into oysters, smoked salmon, dressed crab 'Savoy Grill', omelette Arnold Bennett, steak, sole, duck – and there will always be roast saddle of lamb on the trolley.

- **DRESS** *Chief Exec*
- **TUBES** *Charing Cross; Embankment*

- **HOURS** *Lunch Mon–Fri 12.30–14.30; (closed Sat–Sun)*
  Dinner Mon–Fri 18.00–23.15; Sat 18.00–23.15;
  (closed Sun)
- **AVERAGE PRICE** *Lunch/Dinner £50–80*
- **CREDIT CARDS** *All major cards*
- **MOBILES** *Not allowed*
- **CIGARS** *Humidor*

SCOTTS RESTAURANT
Oyster Terrace and Bar, 20 Mount Street, London W1
☎ 0171 629 5248

Scotts has been a part of the smart London scene for a century
and a half. Apparently, it was at Scotts that Ian Fleming asked for
his Martini to be shaken rather than stirred and it even received
the dubious accolade of being attacked by the IRA during the
seventies as a bastion of the British Establishment. It has survived
its 150 years by adapting to the times. When its original location
near to Leicester Square became less than salubrious, it moved to
civilised Mount Street and then in the mid-nineties the place was
taken over by Laurence Isaacson's Groupe Chez Gerard and
relaunched as a contemporary fish restaurant. At the time, I was
sceptical. I was rather fond of the Scotts that had been owned by
Nicky Kerman – it was a slightly down-at-heel raffish place,
where the staff had known the customers for decades. When
Isaacson made it over, I asked him if I could have four of the old
chairs – red leather things from the fifties as a memento as I felt
Scotts would not be to my taste in the future. Happily, I have been
proved wrong, Scotts is a great place to go. Surroundings and
food are contemporary and while it is possible to eat traditionally
with oysters, sole and so on, there are more adventurous dishes
too, for example, grilled monkfish with crispy potatoes, herb and
Madeira sauce; roast halibut fillet wth oysters and Champagne;
poached haddock with a crab and dill sauce and whole roast
John Dory with apple and garlic. There are a few meat dishes.
Puddings, typified by things like sticky date pudding and
banoffee cheesecake are unashamedly tempting and come with a
helpful list of ports and sweet wines available by the glass and
bottle to help you on your way. The basement bar, reached by a
spiral staircase wrapped around a pillar of bubbling water, is
where one should start and finish an evening visit.

- **DRESS** *Smart*
- **TUBES** *Green Park; Bond Street*

- **HOURS** *Lunch Mon–Sun 12.00–15.00*
  Dinner Mon–Sat 18.00–23.00; Sun 18.00–22.00
- **AVERAGE PRICE** *Lunch/Dinner £32–45*
- **CREDIT CARDS** *All major cards*
- **MOBILES** *Allowed*
- **CIGARS** *Humidor*

J SHEEKEY

28–32 St Martin's Court, London WC2
☎ 0171 240 2565

J Sheekey is the first new restaurant in almost a decade to be launched, or more accurately relaunched, by Messrs. Corbin and King, the Barclay brothers of the London restaurant scene. It is quite impossible to imagine London without The Ivy and Le Caprice and with fish restaurant J Sheekey, they are going for the hat-trick. The restaurant comprises a series of cosy rooms, hung with black and white photographs of classic actors and is a welcoming space. The chairs and banquettes are covered with a grained claret-coloured hide that recalls Louis Vuitton's epi leather. There is even the judicious decorative neologism of walls of baked resin that has resulted in a pleasing creamy craquelure finish. Chef Tim Hughes's food, while not a replication of group executive chef Mark Hix's menus at The Ivy and Le Caprice, bears the hallmarks of fondness for proper food done well. Dishes include jellied eels; soused herrings; grilled cuttlefish with creamed polenta; oak-smoked Irish salmon with scrambled eggs, smoked fillet of cod with poached egg and colcannon; roasted sea bass with red wine and ceps; treacle tart with clotted cream; double chocolate pudding soufflé and of course the legendary fish cakes – one of the most important contributions to the London culinary canon of the last 20 years. As an unabashed fan of Messrs. King and Corbin, I am pleased to see the place is on its way to becoming a classic West End haunt.

- **DRESS** *Fashionably smart*
- **TUBE** *Leicester Square*
- **HOURS** *Lunch Mon–Sat 12.00–15.00; Sun 12.00–15.30*
  Dinner Mon–Sun 17.30–24.00
- **AVERAGE PRICE** *Lunch £25–30; Dinner £40*
- **CREDIT CARDS** *All major cards*
- **MOBILES** *Allowed*
- **CIGARS** *Allowed in the bar*

SHOELESS JOE'S
555 King's Road, London SW6
☎ 0171 610 9346

Shoeless Joe's in Fulham was Christopher Gilmour's second
foray into the restaurant business, following the opening of
Christopher's (qv). Initially it suffered from no one being entirely
sure what kind of restaurant it was supposed to be. On the one
hand, one might have thought it a smart restaurant, retaining as it
did the services of Liz Mortimer (now at the Metropolitan Hotel).
Then again, I once went down there and met a man who had
come all the way from the Canary Islands to help Shoeless Joe's
'specialise in burgers'. Shoeless in Fulham has since settled
down to being a hooray sports bar, with plenty of telly screens.
However, the new Shoeless Joe's at Temple is an altogether
different operation. Part-night club, part-restaurant I have dubbed
the place 'Shoeless Joe's Home of the Stars' since I turned up
there once on a Tuesday night to see David Soul, numerous
models and television types hanging out. The food, superintended
by consultant chef John Burton Race, chef patron of the Michelin-
starred L'Ortolan, is considerably more to my taste than the
offerings in Fulham. Typical starters include ballotine of ham hock
and foie gras served with a home-made piccalilli; tempura of
tuna with a coriander sour cream dressing and salad of seared
scallops served with marinated new potatoes and balsamic
dressing. Mains are particularly strong on fish with, for example,
chargrilled turbot with roasted vegetables and a sauce Choron
and cod served with sautéed gem lettuce in a sauce gribiche.
There are also about half a dozen hearty meat dishes and even a
couple of vegetarian options. Puddings are highfalutin' versions
of established favourites, for instance, apple pie and ice-cream
is presented as 'baked apple tart with a vanilla seed ice-cream
and a calvados butter' and banana cheesecake is billed as
'banana cheese tart'.

- **DRESS** *Sporty spice*
- **TUBE** *Fulham Broadway*
- **HOURS** *Sun–Wed 12.00–24.00; Thurs–Sat 12.00–1.00 am*
- **AVERAGE PRICE** *Lunch/Dinner £15–20*
- **CREDIT CARDS** *All major cards*
- **MOBILES** *Allowed*
- **CIGARS** *Not allowed*

ALSO AT
Temple Place, Embankment WC2;
   0171 240 7865 TUBE Temple

SIMPSON'S-IN-THE-STRAND
100 Strand, London WC2
☎ 0171 836 9112

This leviathan of a restaurant has been a feature of life on the
Strand since the 1820s, when it started as a coffee house,
chess parlour and cigar divan. These days it is a destination for
trenchermen and tourists who throng a building that has changed
little since the end of the nineteenth century when the place was
last remodelled. Apparently Dickens used to come here for a
game or two of chess and some of the staff look as though they
were recruited from a Dickens novel. The trolley of roast sirloin
of beef is wheeled up and down the sombre panelled dining
hall, a room thick with the aromas of over 100 years of the
roast beef of Old England. Simpsons is not the place to come
for anything even remotely forward-looking in the way of food.
The 'Bill of Fare', as the menu calls itself, is nothing if not
reactionary: oysters; potted shrimps; grilled sole; roast Aylesbury
duck with sage and onion stuffing and apple sauce; pan-fried
calf's liver with purée of King Edwards, bacon and onion gravy.
Puddings recall the school days of Jimmy Edwards: bread and
butter; spotted dick and treacle sponge. Although times have
moved on, these puddings if anything seemed to have regressed
– nevertheless, they have a curious, almost Proustian interest.
Neither food nor service is particularly refined and nor is it
cheap, yet from time to time it is worth popping into this
gastronomic time machine to savour the flavours of things past.

- **DRESS** *Touristic or suited*
- **TUBES** *Charing Cross; Embankment; Covent Garden; Temple*
- **HOURS** *Breakfast Mon–Fri 7.00–11.00; (closed Sat–Sun)*
  Lunch Mon–Sun 12.00–14.30
  Dinner Mon–Sat 17.30–23.00; Sun 18.00–21.00
- **AVERAGE PRICE** *Breakfast £13; Lunch/Dinner £35–40*
- **CREDIT CARDS** *All major cards*
- **MOBILES** *Not allowed*
- **CIGARS** *Humidor*

SOFRA
36 Tavistock Street, London WC2
☎ 0171 240 3773

Prompt, rapid service, fresh food and the extravagant pledge
'Dear Guests, If you are not entirely happy with your choice,
we shall replace it without hesitation. We guarantee that you

will leave your table completely satisfied,' bode well for this seemingly ever-expanding chain of restaurants. And if your expectations run to classic Middle Eastern dishes, you will not be disappointed. The Sofra 'healthy lunch or dinner' of 11 hot and cold mezze dishes is an excellent starting point and extremely well priced. Otherwise, there are plenty of grilled dishes and numerous guvechs (Middle Eastern casseroles simmered slowly in a covered pot and served with rice). Sofra offers brilliant value and peddles its message of health and vitality with a commendable vigour.

- **DRESS** *Casual*
- **TUBE** *Covent Garden*
- **HOURS** *Mon–Sun 12.00–24.00*
- **AVERAGE PRICE** *Lunch/Dinner £12*
- **CREDIT CARDS** *All major cards*
- **MOBILES** *Allowed*
- **CIGARS** *Prohibited*

ALSO AT

18 Shepherd Street, London W1;
  0171 493 3320 TUBE Green Park
1 St Christopher's Place, London W1;
  0171 224 4080 TUBE Bond Street

SOTHEBY'S CAFÉ

Sotheby's, 34–35 New Bond Street, London W1
☎ 0171 293 5077

This is the *locus classicus* of the lunching and shopping lady who thinks herself a cut or two above her clothing-addicted sisters on Sloane Street. The café in the lobby of the famous auction house is a logical extension of the in-store dining boom that gripped shops in the mid to late nineties. The signature dish here is the lobster club sandwich – a little bit of everyday luxury to punctuate a day spent browsing through sale catalogues and looking in the windows of local art and antique dealers. Cooking here is simple, sensible and chic. Start with something like Italian air-dried beef, celeriac, bitter leaves and grain mustard dressing or rillettes of salmon, cornichons and melba toast. Pasta might be something like conchiglie with pancetta, gorgonzola and thyme. Expect a salad along the lines of wild rocket, poached eggs, Jerusalem artichokes, garlic croûtons and truffle oil. A pudding of pear and almond strudel with vanilla cream brings on delightful twinges of Mittel Europa. Breakfast and tea menus also make it popular with Americans taking a rest between shops, while the wine list packs in a great deal of interest in a short space. Sotheby's own-label Champagne, truffles and teas can be bought and make extremely polite little gifts.

- **DRESS** *Ladies who lunch*
- **TUBES** *Oxford Circus; Bond Street*
- **HOURS** *Mon–Fri 9.30–16.45; (closed Sat–Sun)*
- **AVERAGE PRICE** *Breakfast £5–7; Lunch £25; Tea £5–10*
- **CREDIT CARDS** *All major cards*
- **MOBILES** *Not encouraged*
- **CIGARS** *Prohibited*

SPIGA

84–86 Wardour Street, London W1
☎ 0171 734 3444

These pizza-peddling offshoots of the Giorgio (Zafferano) Locatelli's empire are welcome additions to the quality end of the London pizza market. I have eaten great crispy-bottomed pizzas in both of these modern-looking establishments and I hope that Locatelli might be persuaded to open up another branch somewhere near where I live. In addition to pizza margherita and napoletana, typical of the sort of things one might expect are pizza caprino (goats' cheese, tomato sauce, rocket salad and Parma ham) and pizza ortolana (tomato sauce, mozzarella cheese, peppers, aubergines, radicchio, zucchini and fresh tomatoes). There are simple grills and a short but good selection of pasta dishes, but pizzas are the stars. Spiga also caters to Soho's trendy subterranean K-Bar.

- **DRESS** *Casual*
- **TUBES** *Tottenham Court Road; Oxford Circus*
- **HOURS** *Lunch Sun–Tues 12.00–15.00; Wed–Sat 12.00–15.00 Dinner Sun–Tues 18.00–23.00; Wed–Sat 18.00–24.00*
- **AVERAGE PRICE** *Lunch/Dinner £25*
- **CREDIT CARDS** *No Diner's Club*
- **MOBILES** *Allowed*
- **CIGARS** *Allowed*

ALSO AT
SPIGHETTA, 43 Blandford Street, London W1;
    0171 486 7340 TUBES Marble Arch; Baker Street; Bond Street

THE STAR OF INDIA
154 Old Brompton Road, South Kensington, London SW5
☎ 0171 373 2901

This consistently enjoyable Indian restaurant in the depths of
affluent Sloane land delivers far more in the way in the way of
camp, but well executed Pompeiian décor and good Indian food,
than the burghers of the nearby Boltons and Drayton Gardens
have any right to expect. The menu is nothing like as long and
rambling as that of some Indian restaurants – which inspires
confidence. Worth trying are dishes like kebab-e-samundri
(salmon marinated in dill, mustard, lemon and honey, lightly
smoked in a sealed pot and then removed and cooked in the
tandoor) and karvari prawn curry (king prawns poached in a
large stone ground coastal blend of regional spices). There are
also about half a dozen tandoor dishes, the most ambitious of
which is probably malai adraki panje (baby lamb chops steeped
in a cream cheese and ginger-flavoured marinade, glazed in the
tandoor and garnished with pickled ginger juliennes). Vegetable
dishes demonstrate imagination, for instance, kaju posho thoran
(cashewnut and beans tempered and braised with mustard seeds
and coconut).

- **DRESS** *Casual*
- **TUBES** *Gloucester Road; South Kensington; Earls Court*
- **HOURS** *Lunch Mon–Sun 12.00–15.00*
  Dinner Mon–Sat 18.00–24.00; Sun 19.00–23.30
- **AVERAGE PRICE** *£25*
- **CREDIT CARDS** *All major cards*
- **MOBILES** *Allowed*
- **CIGARS** *Allowed*

STEFANO CAVALLINI RESTAURANT AT THE HALKIN
5–6 Halkin Street, London SW1
☎ 0171 333 1234

This sleek restaurant in a smart Belgravia hotel offers an antidote
to the rustic Italian food that we hear so much about; it tends to
be a polenta-free zone. It has even won a Michelin star, without
compromising its innate Italianness. There are alleged to be 400
Italian wines on the list, I confess to not having counted them.
And although staff members are Italian, there is none of that
brandishing of pepper mills or bella signora stuff – service is
all very precise and Armani-clad. Food is billed as 'La Cucina

Essenziale' – whatever that means. It is light, elegant and flavoursome stuff, and was typified on one visit by an amuse-bouche of langoustine deluged in truffle shavings and served with a bit of what seemed like scrambled egg – delicious. The sort of starters one can expect include: salad of teal, lentils and colonnato lard or steamed foie gras served with savoy cabbage and red beetroot vinaigrette. When it comes to rice and pasta dishes, expect such uncompromising combinations as rabbit ravioli with mushrooms and lobster and risotto with tufted duck, mint and cep mushrooms. Fowl is also treated interestingly, for example, partridge with pomegranate sauce, turnip confit; pumpkin purée; mallard with red wine sauce, artichokes a la romana, crispy potatoes and celeriac purée. Though far from cheap, Cavallini is good for a different Italian restaurant experience.

- DRESS *Armani sleek*
- TUBE *Hyde Park Corner*
- HOURS *Lunch Mon–Fri 12.30–14.30; (closed Sat–Sun) Dinner Mon–Fri 19.30–23.00; Sat 19.30–23.00; Sun 19.00–23.00*
- AVERAGE PRICE *Lunch £30–35; Dinner £55*
- CREDIT CARDS *All major cards*
- MOBILES *Allowed*
- CIGARS *Humidor; but cigars in lounge only*

STEPHEN BULL
5–7 Blandford Street, London W1
☎ 0171 486 9696

I first went to a Stephen Bull on Blandford Street at the very dawn of the nineties, or perhaps at the fag end of the eighties, with my wife. My chief recollection of the evening a decade later is of an intense but cordial discussion with a man I took to be Bull himself about a dish with some cream in it. My wife wanted the dish *sans* cream. However the man I took to be Mr Bull, insisted that the dish needed the cream, what is more that it would be unbalanced without the cream and I received the strong impression that the absence of cream in this dish might sound the death knell for civilisation as we were enjoying it at that moment – in short, the cream was staying. The subtext of which I took to be, that if I wanted to stay too I had better belt up. Bull tends not to compromise and has therefore stuck around for a decade or so. To be honest I cannot remember whether we did stay for dinner all those years ago; but I hope that we did, because on the evidence of a recent visit to Stephen Bull on Upper St Martin's Lane, Bull knows what he is doing. His three restaurants stack up in the following way: Blandford Street (smart and formal), Smithfield (relaxed and cheaper), Upper St Martin's Lane (newest and most gastronomically adventurous). The look, like the food, is modern and as Bull puts it a trifle pretentiously, 'All my restaurants are meant to be stylishly modern, both because I like understated linear elegance and because my food is very much in the same idiom'. In recent months Bull and his chefs have been putting effort and thought into a good selection of vegetarian dishes. The result is offerings like the excellent vegetable platter (parsley and potato gnocchi, tortellini of wild mushrooms, baked parsnip cheesecake and hazelnut salad) and the beetroot, onion, and walnut tart with endive, lemon and walnut oil. Outside the vegetarian zone, roast pheasant with Jerusalem artichoke and potato gratin, foie gras velouté and caramelised apple came in for praise. Dishes range from the robustly recondite, for example, warm rabbit, Cumbrian ham, snails and ceps bordelais; to the ubiquitous seared rare tuna, pleasingly presented here with aubergine, lemon and mint salad, lavash wafer. Among the puddings, quince and pear assiette is king, but poached clementines, ginger ice-cream and orange and honey madeleines is a good pretender to the throne. The wine list is cleverly balanced between France and the New World, with some favourites like the Leeuwin Estate Riesling. Accompanying me on my visit was the noted architect Alfred Munchenbeck III, who was complimentary about both the wickerwork wall and the tan leather seating.

- **DRESS** *Modern*
- **TUBES** *Bond Street; Baker Street*
- **HOURS** *Lunch Mon–Fri 12.15–14.30; (closed Sat–Sun)*
      Dinner Mon–Sat 18.30–22.30; (closed Sun)
- **AVERAGE PRICE** *Lunch £35; Dinner £40*
- **CREDIT CARDS** *All major cards*
- **MOBILES** *Allowed*
- **CIGARS** *Prohibited*

ALSO AT
12 Upper St Martin's Lane, London WC2;
    0171 379 7811 TUBE Leicester Square
71 St John Street, London EC1;
    0171 490 1750 TUBE Farringdon

THE SQUARE

6–10 Bruton Street, London W1
☎ 0171 495 7100

Chef Philip Howard had something of an *annus mirabilis* in
1998: a second Michelin star and a string of other awards
cemented the Square's position near the top of London's fine
dining tree. The Square is the sort of place you go if you feel that
Le Gavroche is a little bit old, and that you want a change, once
in a while, from Harry's Bar. Serious and expensive are the two
adjectives I would use to describe the place ... rather too serious
for my tastes. Nevertheless there are many who regard The
Square as one of the holiest gastronomic sites in London. And
even though it may not be where I would choose to drop a
couple of hundred quid for dinner, I am compelled to salute the
dedication of owner Nigel Platts-Martin (the man who set up
Marco Pierre White south of the river all those years ago). I find
Platts-Martin slightly annoying (by the same token, I am sure there
are many who find me infuriating), but he cares deeply about
grand yet modern French food. Typical dishes include roast
foie gras with caramelised endive and must grapes; sauté of
langoustines and scallops with morels, thyme and garlic; roast
pigeon from Bresse with 'pommes rossini'; loin of monkfish with
pearl barley, button onions and red wine; and lemon and lime
soufflé with coconut ice-cream. The setting is one of subdued
modern grandeur with expensive fabrics on the tables and chairs
and bold abstract art on the walls.

- **DRESS** *Smart and serious*
- **TUBES** *Green Park; Bond Street*
- **HOURS** *Lunch Mon–Fri 12.00–15.00; (closed Sat–Sun)*
  Dinner Mon–Sat 18.30–22.45; Sun 18.30–22.00
- **AVERAGE PRICE** *Lunch £30–35; Dinner £55*
- **CREDIT CARDS** *All major cards*
- **MOBILES** *Allowed with discretion*
- **CIGARS** *Humidor; cigars in the bar only*

THE SUGAR CLUB

21 Warwick Street, London W1
☎ 0171 437 7776

The Sugar Club was one of the gastronomic phenomena of the
latter half of the 1990s. From its modest premises on All Saints
Road, first it became one of those gastronomic best kept secrets
one hears so much about, then it became a talking point, next a

book and it is now a substantial restaurant on the fringes of allegedly-fashionable Soho. The Sugar Club became famous for its curious, almost postmodern menu: for example, spicy kangaroo salad with coriander, mint, peanuts and lime-chilli dressing; roast corn-fed chicken breast on cumin roast parsnips and pumpkin with Swiss chard and smoked paprika-feta pesto; roast Australian reef fish on potato purée with ruby chard mizuna, red cabbage, galangal and truffle salad; or roast Trelough duck breast on wok-fried green beans and butter beans with tomato-chilli jam. Puddings are by comparison very low-key affairs, for example, sticky black rice and coconut pudding with mango-toasted coconut and pandan syrup; terrine of Poire William and hazelnut, kumquat ripple and prune ice-cream and white chocolate cheesecake with pecan crust and blueberry coulis. It is almost all delicious and so singular is the style of cuisine that it defies any trite definition. Service is chummily Antipodean while also managing to be competent and polite.

- **DRESS** *Soho slick*
- **TUBES** *Piccadilly Circus; Oxford Circus*
- **HOURS** *Lunch Mon–Sat 12.00–15.00; Sun 12.30–14.30*
        Dinner Mon–Sat 18.00–23.00; Sun 18.00–22.30
- **AVERAGE PRICE** *Lunch/Dinner £40*
- **CREDIT CARDS** *All major cards*
- **MOBILES** *With discretion*
- **CIGARS** *Prohibited*

SWEETINGS

39 Queen Victoria Street, London EC4
☎ 0171 248 3062

No bookings, no coffee, no dinner, no credit cards and next-to-no-meat, but plenty of fish. Forget the ravens at the Tower and the chimes of Big Ben; Sweetings is perhaps the most enduring symbol of unchanged Englishness in a fast-changing land. This City fish restaurant is decidedly not the kind of place celebrated in Tony Blair's brave new Britain, of forward-looking, exciting, innovative, groovy, on-message, training shoe-clad technocrats. The Sweetings stamped tankards, the décor, and the tastes of the majority of the customers would seem to date from the nineteenth century. Tankards by the way are the vessel of choice for consumption of Black Velvet (Guinness and Champagne). The 'Bill of Fare' (no kidding) lists soups from tomato to crab. Hors d'oeuvres include all my favourites: prawn cocktail, smoked cod roe, potted shrimps, fried whitebait and smoked Scotch salmon.

The list of fish specialities is similarly reassuring and includes: grilled Dover sole; turbot grilled (with mustard sauce), poached or fried; smoked haddock with poached eggs (a splendid dish) and fried plaice fillets. Home-made sweets have the ring of authenticity that comes with baked jam roll, steamed syrup pudding, apple pie and spotted dick. However, aficionados tend to order off the savouries section of the menu – Welsh rarebit, roes on toast etc – and show their expertise by cross-hatching the Welsh rarebit before drizzling on the Worcestershire sauce. I do not mean to infer that Sweetings is completely rigid in the face of change, in fact just to show its flexibility, the menu changes twice a year: once when oysters go off the menu and again when they come back on.

- **DRESS** *City suits*
- **TUBE** *Mansion House*
- **HOURS** *Lunch Mon–Fri 11.30–15.00; (closed Sat–Sun)*
- **AVERAGE PRICE** *£25*
- **CREDIT CARDS** *Not accepted*
- **MOBILES** *Allowed*
- **CIGARS** *Allowed*

TAMARIND
20 Queen Street, London W1
☎ 0171 629 3561

Mayfair's definitive modern Indian restaurant is well-established as the place for a chic kebab or fashion-conscious curry. Much has been made of the wave of 'designer' Indians, but this Emily Todhunter-designed central London basement is incredibly tough to beat. Under the heading 'appetisers' is the subj chaat, a salad of fruit and veg that is an intriguing sub continental reinvention of a Waldorf salad. Dishes from the tandoor, especially the jingha khyber (king prawns marinated in ginger, yoghurt, sunflower and caraway seeds) and machchi sofiyani (monkfish marinated in saffron and yoghurt) should form at least part of your tamarind experience. Similar care is evident in the side dishes (saag paneer is exemplary) and the vegetable biryani is a valiant rice dish. Apple sorbet for pudding is deliciously astringent. Over-attentive and at times inept service merely gets in the way.

- **DRESS** *Smart*
- **TUBE** *Green Park*
- **HOURS** *Mon–Fri 12.00–23.30; Sat 18.00–23.30; Sun 12.00–22.30*

- **AVERAGE PRICE** *Lunch/Dinner £45*
- **CREDIT CARDS** *All major cards*
- **MOBILES** *Allowed*
- **CIGARS** *Allowed*

LA TANTE CLAIRE
The Berkeley Hotel, Wilton Place, London SW1
☎ 0171 823 2003

Pierre Koffman is highly regarded by chefs, who tend to respect him for staying off the telly (thus allowing them to go and forge careers in broadcasting for themselves) and diners. His new David Collins-designed berth at the Berkeley Hotel is smart in the extreme, and the food, although expensive (the à la carte menu carries the footnote 'minimum charge £50.00 per person', but it is very easy to spend much, much more) is tasty and not excessively complicated. A starter of tartare of mackerel wrapped in smoked salmon and topped with a generous amount of caviar was the essence of simple and tasty luxury. Turbot, something I do not get to eat enough of, is also good and of course this being a Koffman joint, there is a pig's trotter, farcie de morelles (my favourite fungus). Alternatively there is 'poulette de Bresse rotie simplement'. On my visit the exquisitely wintry touch of warm chestnuts wrapped in French newspaper came with the coffee. Admittedly I visited only a week after opening, nevertheless I have to say that service though charming, was memorably incompetent, but according to one member of staff a considerable improvement on the first day! I dare say it has improved, but for the money and the location in a Savoy Group property, one might have expected more.

- **DRESS** *Smart*
- **TUBES** *Knightsbridge; Hyde Park Corner*
- **HOURS** *Lunch Mon–Fri 12.30–13.45; (closed Sat–Sun)*
        Dinner Mon–Sat 19.00–23.00; (closed Sun)
- **AVERAGE PRICE** *Lunch/Dinner £70–80*
- **CREDIT CARDS** *All major cards*
- **MOBILES** *Not allowed*
- **CIGARS** *Humidor; smoking with consideration*

TEATRO

93–107 Shaftesbury Avenue, London W1
☎ 0171 494 3040

Teatro was devised by former footballer Lee Chapman and TV starlet Leslie Ash (the blonde one in *Men Behaving Badly*). It is a pleasant contrast to the ghastliness of Shaftesbury Avenue. The corner site may look unassuming from the outside, but then this anonymous exterior is probably some sort of defence against the hordes of tourists tramping up and down like lobotomised lemmings. Inside and up the stairs, there is a club room and a late bar for members as well as a fairly minimalist-looking dining room for members of both Teatro and the public. While the Keith Hobbs designed surroundings may be deliberately simple, Stuart Gillies's food is often the direct opposite – take for example this chicken dish: poached then seared breast of corn-fed chicken, puy lentils, salsify, bacon and sauce foie gras. Gillies' simpler dishes are more to my taste (it may sound boring but the Niçoise here is exemplary). Perhaps the most humorous thing on the menu is the foie gras du jour – an amusing conceit and oblique commentary on the way conspicuous consumption is headed. Puddings are properly flavoured and deftly presented. The wine list is carefully put together if a little patchy when it comes to fine claret. Indeed the whole operation is put together with more care, thought and attention to detail than one might have thought possible from a couple with such busy social and professional schedules as Ash and Chapman.

- **DRESS** *Trendy*
- **TUBE** *Leicester Square*
- **HOURS** *Lunch Mon–Fri 12.00–15.00; (closed Sat–Sun)*
     Dinner Mon–Sat 18.00–22.45; (closed Sun)
- **AVERAGE PRICE** *Lunch/Dinner £35*
- **CREDIT CARDS** *All major cards*
- **MOBILES** *Not allowed*
- **CIGARS** *Humidor*

TECA

54 Brooks Mews, London W1
☎ 0171 495 4774

This is a relatively recent addition to the charms of Brooks Mews. In fact Mews is something of a misnomer: although it is sandwiched between Claridges and Grosvenor Street, in parts it is almost as broad as Piccadilly and yet at night it has a curiously deserted air about it. Teca is in a corner site that used to house a bookmaker, although all signs of its former existence have vanished under a minimalist makeover. The owner is a Swiss banker and the cooks have graduated from the Halkin – training which shows in the quality and presentation of the food. If this style of Italian food can be said to have a genus, it is probably sleek urban, a change from the pastiche rustic that has dominated Italian menus throughout most of the last decade. Salads such as skate with squid ink vinaigrette or rabbit and celery are almost too imaginative for Mayfair, while seemingly unsurprising dishes such as pennette with clams and red pepper sauce are a genuine revelation in terms of subtlety of flavour. Almost every aspect of the dishes is well thought out including the idea of a tart for two, for instance marinated peach, which is carved at the table, adding a little ceremony to the whole occasion. The owner is also a cigar nut – a welcome trait – and his humidor has some interesting bits and pieces including hard-to-find Trinidads and Cuban curiosities like Juan Lopez. Service needs to sort itself out and there is the slight feeling that the standard of food and wine might be wasted on a clientele of Ferrari-driving Eurotrash and bemused-looking American guests from Claridges.

- **DRESS** *Eurotrash or rich American hotel guest*
- **TUBE** *Bond Street*
- **HOURS** *Lunch Mon–Fri 12.00–14.30; Sat 12.00–15.00;*
    (closed Sun)
    Dinner Mon–Sat 19.30–22.30; (closed Sun)
- **AVERAGE PRICE** *Lunch/Dinner £30*
- **CREDIT CARDS** *No Diners Club*
- **MOBILES** *Allowed with discretion*
- **CIGARS** *Humidor*

THE TERRACE, LE MERIDIEN PICCADILLY
21 Piccadilly, London W1
☎ 0171 734 8000

The Terrace occupies second place, after the Oak Room, in the pecking order of eateries at the Meridien; however in many hotels food of this quality would be taking pole position. When less than full, this place takes on all the charm of a large, albeit expensively furnished greenhouse plonked in the middle of a desert. However under the aegis of Yves Saboua, who took over at the beginning of the summer of '99 as restaurant manager, the atmosphere should improve markedly. I have followed Yves since he was wine waiter for Joel Antunes and he blossomed while running Monte's. I have since bumped into him at polo matches, where he was keeping the company of the mysterious Mexican financier Jimmy Sanchez, and even encountered Yves in Havana. I hope that he injects this space with all the joie de vivre he brought to his earlier job. The food at the Terrace is in some way connected with the French Chef Michel Rostang, and even though it is some sort of franchised operation, it is remarkably good. The croustillant de parmesan et de crabe en millefeuille, tomates confites et aubergine is a delicious and beguiling dish, and I have to say that the lobster and lightly curried crushed wheat risotto is the sort of dish that makes one want to return quickly. In fact I have a soft spot for the lobster dishes served here, the gratin of macaroni and lobster deserves a wide audience – it is a wonderfully luxurious and comforting dish. If the crustacea does not grab you, then maybe the brochette of quails or the roasted sweetbreads will. The list of puddings includes a section called 'The Chocolate Corner', of which the star is 'Chocolate Cream "Michel Rostang" with Honey Warm Madeleine.'

- **DRESS** *Jimmy Sanchez buys his suits Vincci*
- **TUBE** *Piccadilly Circus*
- **HOURS** *Lunch Mon–Sun 12.00–14.30*
  Dinner Mon–Sat 18.00–23.00; Sun 18.00–22.30
- **AVERAGE PRICE** *Lunch/Dinner £40*
- **CREDIT CARDS** *All major cards*
- **MOBILES** *Allowed*
- **CIGARS** *Humidor*

TEXAS EMBASSY CANTINA
1 Cockspur Street, Trafalgar Square, London SW1
☎ 0171 925 0077

Apparently Tex Mex 'cuisine' was not invented merely with the object of sating the appetites of lager louts. Instead it is supposed to have a long and glorious heritage, which dates from shortly after the Battle of the Alamo and the return match at San Jacinto, when peace broke out between Mexico and Texas. Thereafter people on both sides of the border discovered each other's foods, (tortillas, jalapenos, beans, rice, beef, chicken and fresh vegetables) thus laying the foundations of countless themed restaurants, of which the the Texas Embassy Cantina is an impressive example. This is classic office party territory, but carried off with some concern for quality. The menu boasts the full roster of nachos, enchilada, tamale, guacamole, burrito, chimichanga, fajitas. And the appearance reflects the dual nationality of Tex-Mex cuisine. The ground floor of this vast restaurant is intended to represent the Mexican side of the border, and looks as if someone has been asked to create a film set depicting a Mexican village. Texas is upstairs and is represented decoratively by such touches as the rodeo bunting a bull's head from the Texas Rangers Museum, tables made from the wood of old barns and a saddle donated by the Sheriff of Dallas. Beers are served in chilled glass tankards with a slice of lime. There is an abundance of cocktails, many of which seem to rely heavily on liberal amounts of Jose Cuervo Gold Tequila. There are five different types of margarita and also one drink called Texas Swirl, 'a frozen twist of our house margarita and sangria.' Adventurous oenophiles might want to try the Texan and Mexican wines on offer.

- **DRESS** *Yeehaw*
- **TUBES** *Piccadilly Circus; Charing Cross*
- **HOURS** *Mon–Wed 12.00–23.00; Thurs–Sat 12.00–24.00; Sun 12.00–22.30*
- **AVERAGE PRICE** *Lunch £10; Dinner £15*
- **CREDIT CARDS** *All major cards*
- **MOBILES** *Allowed*
- **CIGARS** *Allowed*

TEXAS LONE STAR
154 Gloucester Road, London SW7
☎ 0171 370 5625

On July 4 1980, the corner of Gloucester Road and Harrington Gardens became the site of a Tex–Mex Restaurant and life for the unsuspecting burghers (forgive the bun … sorry, pun) of South Kensington was never to be the same again. The Texas Lone Star's place in posterity is assured. It was an early example of the power that chilli con carne, chilled beers, frozen margaritas and yeehaw-style décor could have over young people. At the time, the place was a revelation with exotic items such as Dos Equis beer and chilli con carne that benefitted from the apparently authentic touch of chocolate powder in the sauce. These days Tex Mex is old stetson, but this is a good place to visit for those nostalgic for the gastronomic innocence of the eighties, for those who like ice cold beer and frozen margaritas or those with noisy children in possession of large appetites. The chef does not like customers to leave hungry. Portions are huge and offer excellent value. While the menu may lack the gastronomic complexity of some of London's more high-end eateries, the quesadilla and his vegetarian chimichanga have a loyal following. The Texas 'Big Boy' sirloin is described thus: '12oz of "Big Boy" eating, pure Texas-size sirloin, served with french fries or potato au gratin and a crisp side salad. We only serve this prime sirloin rare or medium rare'. Otherwise the rib dinners are the thing. There is a small wine list, plenty of beer and margaritas are served either frozen or 'on the rox'. Mugs of fruit margaritas are available and flavours include strawberry, melon, peach and mango.

- **DRESS** *Wear something you will not mind spattering with BBQ sauce or pico de gallo Mexican Relish; if in doubt Texas Lone Star T-shirts are available for purchase*
- **TUBE** *Gloucester Road*
- **HOURS** *Mon–Sat 12.00–23.00; Sun 12.00–22.30*
- **AVERAGE PRICE** *£12*
- **CREDIT CARDS** *No Diners Club*
- **MOBILES** *Allowed*
- **CIGARS** *Prohibited*

ALSO AT
50–54 Turnham Green Terrace, London W4;
0181 747 0001 TUBE Turnham Green

TIGER LIL'S
270 Upper Street, London N1
☎ 0171 226 1118

The idea is to wok it for just over a tenner. Simply select your raw ingredients from the buffet and then gasp as the wok-operators turn them into something rather tasty, and probably quite highly seasoned, before your very eyes. Formal it ain't, but it certainly offers value and amusement provided that either this sort of thing amuses you or you quaff enough of the excellent draught Czech beer.

- **DRESS** *Irrelevant*
- **TUBE** *Highbury & Islington*
- **HOURS** *Lunch Mon–Fri 12.00–15.00 Dinner Mon–Thurs 18.00–23.30; Fri 18.00–24.00; Sat 12.00–24.00; Sun 12.00–23.00*
- **AVERAGE PRICE** *Lunch/Dinner £10–16*
- **CREDIT CARDS** *No American Express or Diners Club*
- **MOBILES** *Allowed*
- **CIGARS** *Prohibited*

ALSO AT
16a Clapham Common, London SW4;
0171 720 5433 TUBE Clapham Common
500 King's Road, London SW10;
0171 376 5003 TUBES Fulham Broadway; Sloane Square

THE TITANIC

81 Brewer Street, London W1
☎ 0171 437 1912

Titanic is basically a huge bar and nightclub thinly disguised as a large restaurant in the West End – imagine Quaglino's with mirror balls, crossed with the Met Bar on steroids and you have got the picture. There is food of course; but fat cats and gastro-bores hoping to get the type of Michelin-influenced restaurant pageantry, and highfalutin', high-cost cuisine that prevails at Marco Pierre White's Oak Room, the Damien Hirst-decorated Quo Vadis or the delightful subterranean Mirabelle will be disappointed. Titanic is the sort of place where you get bang bang chicken, or steak haché à la McDonald's for £9.50. And the emphasis on late night hedonism is stressed with the inclusion of a breakfast menu, served from 11.30 pm–2.30 am, that lists scrambled eggs with smoked salmon and steak and eggs; a reasonably priced full traditional English breakfast will set you back £7.50. Titanic is a generation thing – visit it at lunch if you are over 25 and/or allergic to loud noise. Try it after dark if you want the full-on, rock and roll experience, dimmed lighting, sparkling mirror balls, ferocious din, and the kind of atmosphere I imagine used to prevail at such sprawling pleasure palaces as Studio 54 in its heyday.

- **DRESS** *For a big night out 'up West'*
- **TUBE** *Piccadilly Circus*
- **HOURS** *Breakfast Mon–Sat 24.00–2.30 am; (closed Sun)*
        Lunch Mon–Fri 12.00–14.30; (closed Sat–Sun)
        Dinner Mon–Sat 17.30–23.30; Sun 17.30–22.00
- **AVERAGE PRICE** *Lunch/Dinner £30–40*
- **CREDIT CARDS** *All major cards*
- **MOBILES** *No reception*
- **CIGARS** *Humidor*

TURNER'S

87–89 Walton Street, London SW3
☎ 0171 584 6711

Brian Turner is the prototypical telly chef – a man who defined the role of the media cook in our society today. Also a very busy consultant and a prominent restaurant industry figure, it is remarkable that he manages to be in his restaurant more often than not. His cooking is French with Chelsea overtones. Typical dishes include crab sausage in a cream sauce of green peas, saddle of rabbit stuffed with white beans and spicy sausage, brill with sesame seed crust and sweet peppers, seared skate wing with asparagus and a shrimp butter sauce and roast young pigeon on a bed of red cabbage with a shallot and red wine sauce. The best of puddings is a deceptively light upside-down banana tart with ice-cream and the sorbets change daily. At a guess, I would say that this restaurant looks like the drawing and dining rooms of many of the conservative locals (think pre-Sloane Ranger handbook), and affluent out-of-town (think Virginia Water) customers – walls somewhere between yellow and ochre with extremely deeply upholstered banquettes into which one sinks almost without trace. Turner's may not be in the very vanguard of foodie faddishness, it may not be the cheapest of restaurants and the kitchen may not perform with uniform perfection every time; but then it does not set itself up as a culinary paragon where the commis is publicly flogged if the veg. is not the shape it should be. What Turner's is, is a stayer with a loyal following and a damn good wine list.

- **DRESS** *Virginia Water comes to town*
- **TUBE** *South Kensington*
- **HOURS** *Lunch Mon–Sat 12.30–14.30; (closed Sun)*
  Dinner Mon–Sat 19.30–23.15; (closed Sun)
- **AVERAGE PRICE** *Lunch £20–25; Dinner £55*
- **CREDIT CARDS** *All major cards*
- **MOBILES** *Allowed*
- **CIGARS** *Humidor*

VAMA
438 King's Road, London SW10
☎ 0171 351 4118

'Indian Cookery has a system, an architecture of its own,' runs the blurb on a flyer that you can pick up at at this King's Road restaurant, although quite what form this culinary architecture takes is left to your imagination. The food is billed as 'untamed Northwest frontier cuisine'. However if this leads you to believe that it is all highly seasoned and excessively fiery, think again. A dish such as naryal wali machli (fresh salmon sautéed with herbs and spices and simmered in coconut milk) is a delicate delight. Starters are almost worth ordering in abundance and enjoying as a repast on their own. Typical first courses include for example, aloo katlangi (scooped-out Royal potatoes, stuffed with a combination of fresh homemade cheese, grated potatoes, and finely chopped fresh coriander, skewered and grilled in the clay oven) and tandoori jhinga (Royal tiger prawns cured in a marinade of cream, yoghurt, garlic, ginger, fennel and something called kashmiri deghi mirch, then roasted on charcoal). The stuffed kulcha breads are positively addictive. With its modern rustic décor and strong regional culinary bias, Vama is a welcome place for residents of and visitors to the World's End end of the King's Road.

- **DRESS** *Casual*
- **TUBE** *Sloane Square*
- **HOURS** *Lunch Mon–Sun 12.00–14.30*
  Dinner Mon–Sat 18.00–23.30; Sun 18.30–22.30
- **AVERAGE PRICE** *Lunch £15; Dinner £28*
- **CREDIT CARDS** *Visa; Mastercard*
- **MOBILES** *Discouraged*
- **CIGARS** *Humidor*

VENDÔME

20 Dover Street, London W1
☎ 0171 629 5417

The first thing that I noticed about the owner of Vendôme was his cufflinks, vast Krugerrand–sized gold oval, deeply engraved with some armorial beastie: they are quite the most wonderful and impressive pieces of heraldic bric-a-brac I have seen in a long time. However such cufflinks and the life that goes with them are no doubt expensive to maintain, which would probably account for the reasonably high prices in this restaurant. The décor is wonderfully exuberant and excessive with walls a shade of what Marbella's top decorator Jean Pierre Martel, who I took along for lunch one grey day, assured me was Schiaparelli pink. This restaurant and bar was decorated by David Collins and displays his customary swagger and flair. Food is fine: Caesar salad, crab cakes, fish and chips, liver and bacon with bubble and squeak, sirloin steak, salad of lobster and asparagus. The flesh of braised lamb shank (pesto mash, confit tomato and basil sauce) seemed to fall from the bone in a fashion that so impressed Martel, that all talk of pink walls had to wait until he had finished.

- **DRESS** *Gold signet rings and crested gold cufflinks*
- **TUBE** *Green Park*
- **HOURS** *Mon–Fri 12.00–23.00; (closed Sat–Sun)*
- **AVERAGE PRICE** *Lunch/Dinner £35*
- **CREDIT CARDS** *All major cards*
- **MOBILES** *Allowed*
- **CIGARS** *Humidor*

VONG

Berkeley Hotel, Wilton Place, London SW1

☎ 0171 235 1010

The basement of the Berkeley Hotel used to house the Perroquet, a bar and buffet, the charm of which resided in its usual emptiness. The same cannot be said for Vong, the London outpost of Jean Georges Vongerichten's smart Franco-Thai restaurant empire. Vong in London opened at the end of 1995 and had a seismic impact on London restaurants at that time – it was one of the earliest of the really chic Oriental eateries. These days the atmosphere is more bustling and brasserie-like than it used to be, but the standards of cooking are still enjoyably high. If you fancy a decent rabbit curry, this is the place to come. The rice crackers and peanut dip plonked on the table much as other places offer a bit of bread, are delicious – the lobster Daikon roll with rosemary ginger dip deserves classic status as a great London starter. And if that is not enough lobster – try the lobster with Thai herbs. The menu is highly imaginative – grilled Angus sirloin, with bean sprout fritter and soy onions, sitting alongside roasted monkfish with spiced almond sauce and baby leeks or aromatic lamb shank with purple mash and sautéed choy. Even roast chicken comes enlivened with spiced yoghurt and dried fruit chutney and chocolate cake and ice-cream emerges as warm valrhona chocolate cake with lemon grass ice-cream. It is such attention to detail that no doubt accounts for Vong's enduring popularity. I preferred Vong when it was more sedate, but then that might be me getting old … the flavours are still as sharp, fresh and exciting as ever.

- **DRESS** *Expensive casual*
- **TUBE** *Hyde Park Corner*
- **HOURS** *Lunch Mon–Fri 12.00–14.30; Sat–Sun 11.30–14.00*
  Dinner Mon–Sat 18.00–23.30; Sun 18.00–22.00
- **AVERAGE PRICE** *Lunch/Dinner £50*
- **CREDIT CARDS** *All major cards*
- **MOBILES** *No reception*
- **CIGARS** *Humidor; in bar area only*

WAGAMAMA

10a Lexington Street, London W1
☎ 0171 292 0990

Wagamama is not so much a restaurant as 'a non-destinational food station', which is really a right-on way of saying that they don't take bookings. The noodle bar is to the late nineties what the coffee bar was during the late fifties and early sixties – a vaguely hip yet unthreatening and inexpensive place to hang out. The menu is plastered with all sorts of bien pensant 'quality is our first priority' platitudes about 'positive eating for positive living' and so on. What this translates as is plates of noodles topped with stir-fried seafood or vegetables or bowls of soupy noodle-based dishes. Most dishes are tasty and the menu is long enough to accommodate a few curry dishes and things like salmon korroke (three salmon and potato cakes in a sweet tamarind sauce served with green leaves and garnished with seaweed and shredded crabstick). Yet this is not so much popping in for a quick and filling plate of noodles or dumplings, but rather an edible induction into a way of life, in this case the way of the noodle. There is a commendably democratic, almost identikit trendiness about the operation. However the canteen-like dining facilities, benches and tables (often shared) do not make this a place for long intimate suppers. What is more, orders are radioed to the appropriate kitchen station and prepared immediately; this results in dishes that are ordered together, but arrive at different times. Smoking is of course prohibited. However, Japanese beers, some wines and a few sakes do apparently make a valid contribution to positive eating and positive living and are thus tolerated. Actively endorsed is the raw juice, an 'all-round high-nutrient and high energy drink' composed of carrot, cucumber, tomato and apple, which was so foul that it had me shrieking for the Diet Coke. Yet, raw juice aside, the Wagamama experience is a pleasant one; there is a kindness about the operation that leads one to believe it is all being done for one's own good.

- **DRESS** Nicole Fahri grey
- **TUBE** Piccadilly
- **HOURS** Mon–Sat 12.00–23.00; Sun 12.00–22.00
- **AVERAGE PRICE** Lunch/Dinner £10
- **CREDIT CARDS** No Diners Club
- **MOBILES** Allowed
- **CIGARS** Prohibited

ALSO AT

4a Streatham Street, London WC1;
    0171 323 9223   TUBE Tottenham Court Road
101a Wigmore Street, London W1;
    0171 409 0111   TUBE Bond Street
9–11 Jamestown Road, London NW1
    0171 428 0800   TUBE Camden Town

WILTONS
55 Jermyn Street, London SW1
☎ 0171 629 9955

This rapaciously priced fish restaurant is wonderful fun …
provided someone else is paying. I think I first visited Wiltons with
that prince among cigar smokers Nicholas Freeman. He once
owned part of the place and his visage is still to be seen in a
portrait that hangs above the stairs on the way to the loo.
Apparently it is now owned entirely by a scion of the Hambro
dynasty and although you don't need to own your own bank to
eat here, it sure as hell helps. There must have been a time when
all restaurants in England were either like this or Sweetings (qv).
Wiltons is considered the place to eat grouse in season, but
the fishes are the thing, with the emphasis on the quality of
ingredients rather than anything particularly clever being done
with them. Order oysters, or lobster cocktail, then something like
grilled sole (with lashings of tartare sauce), a slab of turbot or the
lobster thermidor. Puds are good but it seems a shame not to have
a savoury. Wines are as one would expect – smart, French and
expensive. Service has been described by a rather smart friend
of mine, as having all the charm of a nursing home in the home
counties. I feel this is a little harsh on the Eastern European
waitresses; they do their best and can be made to smile if you put
your mind to it. If you are short of conversation, just sit back in your
booth and eavesdrop on some slightly spivvy merchant banker
recalling his time at Eton … there is usually one on the next table.

- **DRESS** *Jacket and tie*
- **TUBE** *Green Park*
- **HOURS** *Lunch Mon–Fri, Sun 12.30–14.30; (closed Sat)*
        Dinner Mon–Fri 18.30–22.30; Sun 18.30–22.00;
        (closed Sat)
- **AVERAGE PRICE** *Lunch/Dinner £55*
- **CREDIT CARDS** *All major cards*
- **MOBILES** *Not allowed*
- **CIGARS** *Humidor*

WINDOWS ROOF RESTAURANT

Hilton Park Lane, London W1
☎ 0171 493 8000

I must be one of the few people who have a real fondness for this sixties tower hotel and the rooftop bar and restaurant gets me thinking back to *Towering Inferno*. This should be a great restaurant, after all it has one of the best views in the country – at lunch, see into the Queen's back garden, in the evening gaze out over the carpet of lights spread out a couple of dozen storeys below. The food too is incredibly serious and good – far better than most of the customers here deserve. Jacques Rolancy is the chef de cuisine – his style is to capture the intense and intoxicating flavours of traditional cuisine bourgeoise within dishes of surprising lightness. I reckon he pulls it off. A pumpkin soup topped with an airy cappuccino froth was outstanding. Simple yet perfectly textured, it was a soup that in its excellence might change the way we tend to view all soups, a dish of such honest elegance that I raved about it for days … you might say that I liked it. Scallops marinated in Alba oil and lemon juice and interleaved with chunky slices of truffle atop a celeriac mash, seemed to evaporate in the mouth. Pan-fried fillet of sea bass and chicory scented with walnut and ginger was good if not remarkable. And fillet of venison in a parsley and truffle crust with potato was apparently a revelation in terms of lightness. The cheese trolley is one on which time should be spent. The staff are knowledgeable about the menu and there is a desire to guide one to the more interesting things on it – Monsieur Rolancy has drilled his team well. I think the trouble is that people come here just for the view, because they happen to find themselves staying in the Hilton or because they feel that the venue might impress their date. The atmosphere is unworthy of the good food: there is a pianist whose repertoire includes the theme tune from *Titanic* and apparently an entire band at weekends. The décor does not know whether to be offensive or just ludicrous and the waiters' outfits would not disgrace a Star Trek convention.

- **DRESS** *Captain Kirk*
- **TUBE** *Hyde Park Corner*
- **HOURS** *Lunch Mon–Fri 12.30–14.30; (closed Sat–Sun)*
  Dinner Mon–Thurs 19.00–22.30; Fri–Sat 19.00–23.30;
  (closed Sun)
- **AVERAGE PRICE** *Lunch £55; Dinner £65*
- **CREDIT CARDS** *All major cards*
- **MOBILES** *Not allowed*
- **CIGARS** *Humidor*

WIZ

123a Clarendon Road, London W11

☎ 0171 229 1500

Wiz is another one of Wozza's (qv) wizard wheezes. I view the menu here as a gastronomic amusement arcade. AWT (Anthony Warrall Thompson) has taken the tapas/mezze principal and then split it up into various geographical zones, with about half a dozen dishes listed under national headings. The Americas have, for example, cornmeal-crusted softshell crab, papaya salsa; France has, among others, pork rillettes with prunes and cornichons; Italy is best represented by pumpkin ravioli, sage butter and mustard fruits; the catch-all 'Mediterranean – general' includes couscous and chermoula; the highlight of Spain and Portugal is the outstanding 'world beating acorn-fed Iberico cured black leg ham'; and the Spice trail lists everything from dahl, sour cream, spring onions, to Thai green chicken curry and the United Kingdom bills potted Arbroath smokie and some nice tangy cod's roe with horseradish cream and watercress salad. You can either choose the country you like and stick with it or, as it is put in the introduction to the menu, 'surf the world'. It is a nice enough idea. My associate and I surfed the world fairly energetically and found most things well done.

- **DRESS** *Casual*
- **TUBE** *Holland Park*
- **HOURS** *Lunch Mon–Fri 12.00–15.30; Sat–Sun 11.30–16.00*
  Dinner Mon–Wed 18.30–23.00; Thurs–Sat 18.30–24.00;
  (closed Sun)
- **AVERAGE PRICE** *Lunch/Dinner £25–30*
- **CREDIT CARDS** *No Diners Club*
- **MOBILES** *Allowed*
- **CIGARS** *With consideration*

WODKA

12 St Alban's Grove, London W8

☎ 0171 937 6513

As the name and spelling suggest, this is a Polish place with a good line in vodkas. Wodka, housed in a former dairy, has been a part of Kensington life for many years, yet it still manages to look contemporary enough. It and its proprietor John Woriniecki have established together a sufficient following to have warranted expansion, first into neighbouring premises and now into another area of town with a sibling restaurant, Baltic, due to appear on the Blackfriar's road in the spring of 1999. A few Wodka classics are: pierogi filled with cheese potato and spring onion; herring fillet salad with apple, onion and sour cream; leniwe (cheese and herb dumplings with sun-dried tomatoes and olives); blinis with a variety of piscine toppings; kulebiak (salmon and pastry with mushroom and spinach) and kaczka (roast duck with roasted beetroot and sour cherries). Vodkas are the thing to drink, with Krupnik, a honey-infused vodka served warm being a fine way to bring proceedings to a close.

- **DRESS** Kensington casual
- **TUBE** High Street Kensington
- **HOURS** Lunch Mon–Fri 12.30–14.30; (closed Sat–Sun)
        Dinner Mon–Sun 19.00–23.15
- **AVERAGE PRICE** Lunch/Dinner £25
- **CREDIT CARDS** All major cards
- **MOBILES** Allowed
- **CIGARS** Humidor

WOK WOK
140 Fulham Road, London SW10
☎ 0171 370 5355

That competitively-priced hybrid Asian cuisine was destined to become smart London convenience food was made clear to me when the pleasantly themed American burger bar on the street corner opposite the cinema formerly known as the Fulham ABC closed. The site became a Wok Wok in May 1997. That Fulham Man and his pearly girlfriend have embraced the street food – or at least what they think of as the street food – of Vietnam, Thailand, Malaysia and that part of the world is a cultural shift indeed. The menu is brief but to the point and has the sort of appetising things with which we have become familiar over the last few years: Thai beef salad, Thai fish cakes, bowls of noodles, wok-fried this and that. Popular dishes include nasi goreng and the seafood coconut broth. While perfectly creditable, this is more of a place for a snack while shopping or a pre/post cinema supper than somewhere to sit and linger; an activity that the plain no-nonsense interior might discourage; nevertheless, the further flung cantons of London could do with a few more Wok Woks. My, haven't we come a long way from the Wimpy bar?

- **DRESS** Casual
- **TUBE** South Kensington
- **HOURS** Mon–Thurs 12.00–23.30; Fri–Sat 12.00–24.00;
        Sun 12.00–22.30

- **AVERAGE PRICE** *£15*
- **CREDIT CARDS** *All major cards*
- **MOBILES** *Allowed*
- **CIGARS** *Prohibited*

ALSO AT

10 Frith Street, London W1;
    0171 437 7080 TUBE Leicester Square
7 High Street Kensington, London W8;
    0171 938 1221 TUBE High Street Kensington
51–53 Northcote Road, London SW11;
    0171 978 7181 TUBE Clapham Common
67 Upper Street, London N1;
    0171 288 0333 TUBE Angel

YAZ

7 Hammersmith Road, London W14
☎ 0171 603 9148

Across the road from Olympia, Yaz offers an insight into
the world of Persian cuisine – something that even in our
gastronomically polyglot era is not mentioned too frequently.
It is hard to know why we don't hear more about the cooking
of this part of the world, as Yaz is a good place to spend time
and with hours that stretch from noon to five am, it is also a
spectacular amenity. Large rectangular breads are cooked to
order in the beehive-shaped oven at the front in the window,
and portions are generous. Even a refreshing starter like a
portion of Persian cheese, served with a variety of seasonal
herbs, comes with an immense pile of mint, tarragon and what
have you. A dish of kufteh shevid-baghala (steam-cooked prime
minced lamb meat mixed with broad beans and fresh dill and
served with Persian bread) comprises two large mounds that one
would need for the kind of appetite generated by a day spent
digging. Specials change according to the day and are often
some of the best dishes. For example, Monday might be the day
for khoresh-e fesenjan (chicken stew cooked with walnuts and
pomegranate juice and served with saffron rice) while Thursday
could give you the opportunity to order fresh diced fillet of wild
salmon marinated and charcoal grilled. Puddings are interesting,
especially the Bastani, best described as a Persian ice-cream with
a pleasing flavour of pistachios and aftershave.

- **DRESS** *Casual*
- **TUBE** *Olympia*
- **HOURS** *Mon–Sun 12.00–5.00 am*

- **AVERAGE PRICE** *Lunch/Dinner £15*
- **CREDIT CARDS** *All major cards*
- **MOBILES** *Allowed*
- **CIGARS** *Allowed*

YO! SUSHI

52 Poland Street, London W1
☎ 0171 287 0443

Sushi made simple. While this is not the first place that the connoisseur of the very finest in Japanese food might want to visit, Yo! Sushi is a grand starting point for the sushi neophyte, the casual grazer or the technologically curious. The sushi careering around on the bartop conveyor belt and the almost space age/MTV ambience that prevails at the Poland Street branch certainly makes this a lively, if less than relaxing, eating experience. The sort of facilities that identify Yo! Sushi are push button attendant call and the opportunity to identify dishes on a Microsoft 150 item menu. Maki rolls – seaweed and rice balls of salmon or tuna are as popular as are Yo! Rolls, a jumbo-multi-filling version of Maki. Of nigiri – the one with the slabs of fish on the top, with the rice pressed by machine into rectangles – salmon is the cheapest and most popular, but more interesting are oyster, eel and sweet shrimp nigiri. Aficionados advise arrival at the beginning of the lunchtime service so as to get the sushi as it is prepared and before it spends too long on the belt. Arrive too late, says one regular, and run the risk of shrivelled sushi or flaccid futomaki. However, ultraviolet lights indicate to the staff when dishes have been around too long, and the word from the Finchley branch is that at peak times nothing tends to hang around for more than about an hour and a half. What is more, for sushi to your door – in certain postal districts – it is possible to fax your order through and experience the snappily-named Yo! To Go. Yo! Events brings a portable conveyor belt to your venue.

- **DRESS** *As you would for an MTV cyber space speed garage electro house weekend*
- **TUBE** *Oxford Circus*
- **HOURS** *Mon–Sun 12.00–24.00*
- **AVERAGE PRICE** *Lunch/Dinner £13*
- **CREDIT CARDS** *All major cards*
- **MOBILES** *Allowed*
- **CIGARS** *Prohibited*

ALSO AT
SELFRIDGES, 400 Oxford Street, London W1;
    0171 318 3885 TUBE Bond Street
FIFTH FLOOR HARVEY NICHOLS, Brompton Road, London SW1;
    0171 235 5000 TUBE Knightsbridge
Unit 8b, O2 Centre, 255 Finchley, London NW3;
    0171 431 4499 TUBE Finchley Road

ZAFFERANO
15 Lowndes Street, London SW1
☎ 0171 235 5800

If Riva (qv) were full or closed and someone asked me where else
they might go to eat good and imaginative Italian food, I would
direct them to Zafferano. Chef Giorgio Locatelli has acquired
a remarkable reputation and, happily for those who come to
eat here, it is thoroughly deserved. Enzo is the charming face of
front of house, whose easy manner and seemingly imperturbable
smoothness slips down easily with the rich multinational
Belgravians who treat this as their local. The food is assured and
it is for this, rather than the décor or the opportunity to see pop
stars, that people come. In season, truffles are shaved reasonably
generously over scrambled eggs and plain pasta, but at the
risk of sounding blasé truffles can be had anywhere at a price,
but not Locatelli's cooking. French bean salad with Jerusalem
artichokes and parmesan deceives with its simplicity and emerges
as a light elegant starter, while a main of sliced roasted sea bass
with artichoke and Vernaccia wine is perfectly executed. The
pan-fried, stuffed sardines have become something of a classic
dish. Otherwise the menu is broad in its scope encompassing
such accessible dishes as beef carpaccio with truffle oil and
parmesan shavings; a good range of pastas, including tagliolini
with courgette and bottarga; and baroque touches like lamb
sweetbreads in sweet and sour sauce. If you can, ask Enzo to
help choose the wine.

- **DRESS** *Multi-cultural Belgravia*
- **TUBE** *Knightsbridge*
- **HOURS** *Lunch Mon–Sat 12.00–14.30; (closed Sun)*
      Dinner Mon–Sat 19.00–23.00; (closed Sun)
- **AVERAGE PRICE** *Lunch £30–35; Dinner £40–50*
- **CREDIT CARDS** *All major cards*
- **MOBILES** *Not allowed or leave them at reception*
- **CIGARS** *Allowed*

ZAIKA

257–259 Fulham Road, London SW3
☎ 0171 351 7823

This is a posh, or at least a gastronomically-aware Indian restaurant on a site that has seen more restaurants in recent years than most. Chef Vineet Bhatia, used to have an eponymous place in Hammersmith, got some good reviews and was snapped up by Claudio Pulze, a short Italian, Breitling-wearing gastro-impresario who is a great talent-spotter when it comes to cooks. Zaika is apparently not the place to come and ask for a scorching vindaloo and a few vats of Carlbsberg. It likes to think of itself as a cut above and certainly a grim-faced woman on reception would give the curry louts short shrift. What is more, if the traditional curry house crowd got past her they would probably not know what to do with the amuse-gueule, a saffron drink, that I was served on a recent visit. The food is good. A dish like the Dhungar Malchi Tikka (a smoked salmon kebab that is a sub continental take on gravadlax), where the salmon flesh is served in medallions, is so good that it liberates the cooking from its genre. Side dishes like the Paneer Mirch Bhuja (Indian cheese tossed with peppers in spiced masala) are inventive and delicious as are the breads. The only thing that disappointed was the crab masala, not a fault of the dish, rather my choosing it, it was a bit too like a chowder in consistency for my taste. The key to enjoying the food here is to not expect a searingly seasoned dish, but rather to be able to enjoy, appreciate and identify individual flavours within each dish. The surroundings have not changed much since the place's previous incarnation as Chavot, however decorative interest is usually supplied by one's fellow diners – one rather grand man seemed to be wearing a bespoke suit and floral, yes floral, rugger shirt … perhaps he had been at the mind-expanding drugs. Anyway – a trip to Zaika is a wonderful palate-expanding opportunity.

- **DRESS** *Suits and floral rugger shirts*
- **TUBE** *South Kensington*
- **HOURS** *Lunch Mon–Fri 12.00–14.45; (closed Sat–Sun)*
  Dinner Mon–Sat 18.00–22.45; (closed Sun)
- **AVERAGE PRICE** *Lunch/Dinner £20–25*
- **CREDIT CARDS** *No Diners Club*
- **MOBILES** *Allowed*
- **CIGARS** *Allowed*

ZEN

ZEN CHELSEA
Chelsea Cloisters, 5 Sloane Avenue, London SW3
☎ 0171 589 1781

When it first opened in the early 1980s, Zen had a profound
impact on the way Chinese food was treated. The supremely
eighties epithet 'designer' might characterise the approach that
Zen pioneered. The food at Zen is always dependably good and
the service willing and attentive. The starter of scallops with the
well-judged astringent chilli sauce is an invigorating way to start
a Zen meal, however a dumpling dish of shrimp and pork tended
to be a little obscured by the soy-based sauce. The Zen Zen
chicken is sweet and sour and lingers in the memory for its
remarkable yellow colour.

- **DRESS** *Casual*
- **TUBE** *South Kensington*
- **HOURS** *Lunch Mon–Sun 12.00–15.00*
  Dinner Mon–Sat 18.00–23.30; Sun 18.00–22.00
- **AVERAGE PRICE** *Lunch/Dinner £30–35*
- **CREDIT CARDS** *All major cards*
- **MOBILES** *Allowed*
- **CIGARS** *Allowed*

ALSO AT
ZEN CENTRAL, 20–22 Queen Street, London W1;
   0171 629 8089 TUBE Green Park
ZEN GARDEN, 15 Berkeley Street, London W1;
   0171 493 1381 TUBE Green Park
ZEN SPICE MARKET, 215 Sutherland Avenue, London W9;
   0171 266 1888 TUBE Meadow Vale
ZEN W3, 83 Hampstead High Street, London NW3;
   0171 794 7863 TUBE Hampstead
ZEN ORIENTAL, Heathrow Hilton, Heathrow Airport Terminal, TW6;
   0181 759 7755 TUBE Heathrow Terminal 4

ZINC BAR AND GRILL
21 Heddon Street, London W1
☎ 0171 255 8899

This is diffusion rather than destination Conran. Pared down,
even to a degree in price, Zinc offers a Conran interpretation of
a contemporary pub/café/bar. The interior, dominated by the
eponymous Zinc Bar, is a bit bare and tends to be noisy once
the place fills up. Food is unambitious but of a good standard.

Soups, salads, sandwiches and other smart snacks make this a place for a light or casual lunch. Should more sustaining dishes be required, head for liver and bacon, fish and chips, sausages and colcannon. There are a couple of vegetarian dishes, for example, risotto of mushrooms and courgettes or pasta, tomato rocquette and parmesan and a section of appropriately priced dishes for the under-12s. The weekend brunch (kedgeree, eggs Benedict) which runs from noon till six pm, is well priced. Should the place ever be rolled out across London as a chain, it deserves to do well.

- **DRESS** *Hedonistic West End office worker*
- **TUBES** *Oxford Circus; Piccadilly Circus*
- **HOURS** *Mon–Sat 12.00–24.00; (closed Sun)*
- **AVERAGE PRICE** *Lunch/Dinner £20*
- **CREDIT CARDS** *All major cards*
- **MOBILES** *Allowed*
- **CIGARS** *Humidor*